THE REFORMATION.

THE REFORMATION

A RELIGIOUS AND HISTORICAL SKETCH.

By REV. J. A. BABINGTON, M.A.

KENNIKAT PRESS
Port Washington, N. Y./London

THE REFORMATION

First published in 1901
Reissued in 1971 by Kennikat Press
Library of Congress Catalog Card No: 71-118513
ISBN 0-8046-1135-1

Manufactured by Taylor Publishing Company   Dallas, Texas

PREFACE.

———

When an unknown author comes before the public with a book on one of the most important periods of history, an apology is needed. It is doubly needed when he is conscious of the manifold imperfections and short-comings of his work. I can only plead that the history and theology of the Reformation have constantly occupied my thoughts and engrossed much of my leisure time for more than twenty-five years, that I have attempted to treat it comprehensively, that I have endeavoured to look at it from every point of view, and that it has been my constant effort to write of it, not as a member of any particular Church, but as one who can sympathize deeply with all the Evangelical Churches, and who can recognize and admire the distinctive merits of each of them.

Though the Reformation was before all else a religious movement, and though for this reason its moral, theological, and ecclesiastical aspects claim the special attention of the student, yet I have attempted, so far as my limits would allow, to point out that it indirectly produced political, national, and international results of the highest importance.

As this book does not claim to be more than a sketch, I have not thought it necessary to load my pages with explanatory or controversial notes, nor to give a list of the works in English, Latin, German, French, Dutch, Danish, and Italian which I have studied or consulted. I cannot pretend to have exhausted the vast literature of the subject, but I trust that I have not suffered anything of real importance to escape my notice.

In some countries, such as Italy, Spain, Poland, Austria, Bavaria, and Ireland, the Reformation only penetrated skin deep, or had only a partial influence, or gained only a partial success. To trace the progress of the Evangelical doctrines in these countries would have contributed little to the real knowledge of the Reformation, and I have, therefore, thought it advisable to pass them over in the following sketch.

It is, perhaps, needless to add that this book is not intended for professed students of history or theology, who will find in it nothing which they did not know already, but for thoughtful members of the Protestant Churches who are interested in religious questions, who are anxious to understand the Reformation better, and who wish to know what the aims, the principles, and the methods of the Reformers were. If the following pages enable any of them to realize that they have achieved together a great spiritual emancipation, that they possess in common an inalienable heritage of religious truth, and that the invisible bonds of Christian fellowship which unite them are incomparably mightier than the visible differences which still divide them, I shall have fulfilled a wish which I have long cherished.

JOHN ALBERT BABINGTON.

TONBRIDGE,
1901.

CONTENTS.

CHAPTER I.

INTRODUCTION.

CHAPTER II.

THE REFORMATION IN GERMANY AND GERMAN SWITZERLAND.

CHAPTER III.

THE DISTINCTIVE DOCTRINES OF THE REFORMATION.

CHAPTER IV.

THE REFORMATION IN GERMANY (CONCLUSION).

CHAPTER V.

THE REFORMATION IN THE SCANDINAVIAN KINGDOMS.

CHAPTER VI.

CHAPTER VII.

CHAPTER VIII.

CHAPTER IX.

THE REFORMATION IN SCOTLAND.

THE REFORMATION.

CHAPTER I.

INTRODUCTION.

THE Reformation is one of the most important events in the history of the world. It has not only been a decisive turning point in the spiritual and moral life of the Christian Church : it serves as a great landmark in the intellectual, political, and social development of mankind. It marks the boundary line between the modern world on the one hand, and the Medieval world on the other. No sphere of human activity has escaped from its searching and penetrating effects. It has profoundly influenced European literature. It has profoundly affected social life. It has profoundly modified the political system of the civilized world. It has profoundly altered the problems, the methods, and the conditions of philosophical thought. The contrast between the " Summa Theologica " of Saint Thomas Aquinas and Kant's "Critique of the Pure Reason" is a type of the contrast between the Medieval and the modern mind. The contrast between the Holy Roman Empire, the Empire of the Othos and the Fredericks, in the plentitude of its power and influence, and the most marvellous and unique creation of the last hundred and fifty years, the United States of America, is a type of the contrast between the aims and theories of Medieval and modern politicians.

But the Reformation was primarily and above all a religious movement, and any estimate of it which disguises or misrepresents its religious significance must be imperfect or inadequate. If it has covered the whole field of human thought and action, the explanation is simple. In the Middle Ages the spiritual life and the ecclesiastical system of the Church were inextricably intertwined with every interest of Western Christendom from politics to art. It was impossible to touch a single stone of the vast and imposing structure without endangering the stability of the whole fabric. When the Reformers overthrew or undermined the power of the Medieval Church throughout a great part of Western Europe, it was inevitable that every department of human life should be directly or indirectly affected by the consequences of their victory. Art, literature, science, philosophy, education, law, political life, and social life were all cast into the potent crucible of change, and came forth largely altered or completely transformed.

The corruptions and abuses of the Medieval Church had excited the sorrow, the indignation, and the anxiety of religious, earnest, and thoughtful men long before the Reformation began. The reforming Councils of the fifteenth century had given expression to the universal feeling of Western Christendom. But their efforts had been fruitless: the greed of power of the Papal Curia, the selfishness of men who were interested in the maintenance of abuses, the unreasoning and conservative instincts of some of their members, and the precipitate and injudicious haste of others, the apathy of some temporal rulers, and the treachery of others, had riveted the Papal yoke more tightly than ever upon the neck of the Church, and had foiled all schemes of reform. Towards the close of the fifteenth century the evils which had been observed and lamented for more than a century were as rampant as ever.

Nowhere was this corruption more glaring and notorious

than in the centre of Christendom, the See of Saint Peter, and among the men who claimed most loudly to have inherited the sanctity and power of the Apostles. The immorality, the extravagance, the worldliness, the thirst for gold, the unscrupulous ambition, the selfish promotion of kinsmen, the theological ignorance, the indifference to the spiritual interests of the Church, which characterized the Popes during the thirty years preceding the Reformation, could scarcely be matched by the ecclesiastics of the tenth century. The moral indignation of men like Erasmus and Machiavelli, the scathing irony of satires like the " Julius Exclusus " and the " Utopia," testify more eloquently to the corruption of the Papacy than pages of historical narrative.   The men who called themselves Vicars of Christ and Heads of the Church were not ashamed to prostitute their most solemn and sacred duties to basest uses : they converted the nomination of Cardinals into a huge commercial transaction, and the Cardinals too often justified their promotion by becoming the most venal and corrupt of statesmen, the chief debauchees, spendthrifts, bullies, and bravoes of Europe. Adrian the Sixth might well write to the Diet of Nuremberg that in the Church of the sixteenth century there was none that did good, no, not one.   Yet, in spite of all this, the Popes did not abate one jot of their claims and pretensions to supremacy in State and Church.   Charles the Fifth and Francis the First did not set a higher value on their temporal sovereignty : Saint Chrysostom and Saint Augustine did not boast half so loudly of their spiritual gifts and prerogatives.   The example set by Rome was faithfully followed by the highest ecclesiastics in every part of Western Europe.   The famous satire, commonly called " The Burying of the Mass," gives a vivid picture of the vice, the worldliness, the boundless extravagance, the pride like Lucifer's, the indifference to all things spiritual, of Cardinal Wolsey.   His contemporary, Albert of Brandenburg, Cardinal and Metropolitan of Germany, was as worldly and pleasure-loving as Wolsey, without Wolsey's ability. An eye-witness has left an account of the Easter festivities at his Court : everything was covered with silk and cloth of gold ; a single cross used in the procession cost 80,000 florins ; the very grooms were intoxicated with the choicest wines. Philip of Burgundy, Bishop of Utrecht, alternated between the rigid observance of the Church's ordinances and the grossest sensual excesses. In Denmark, the Archbishop of Lund never went anywhere with a smaller escort than five hundred armed attendants : even the King was not surrounded with greater pomp. He possessed thirty-two estates in Schonen alone. The Bishop of Roskild owned a third part of Zealand, and the other Bishoprics were endowed in proportion. In France, the celebrated Cardinal of Lorraine, by accumulating rich ecclesiastical benefices, had amassed a revenue of 300,000 gold crowns, and was ironically termed by Pius the Fourth, "the second Pope." In one half of Western Europe the highest ecclesiastics exercised temporal power, called themselves " Princes," and ostentatiously displayed the sword by the side of the crozier on their scutcheons.* In course of time the spiritual office became merged and lost in the temporal. The canonical laws, as well as the spiritual duties of their ministry, were openly and defiantly set aside. More than one Prince Bishop of Geneva during the century preceding the Reformation was appointed to the bishopric before he attained the age of puberty. Herman von Wied was elected to the Archbishopric of Cologne when he was not even in Deacon's Orders, and received the Pope's permission to be ordained Deacon, Priest, and Bishop on the same day. Scarcely one in a hundred of these princely prelates deigned to discharge the duty of preaching. A candid speaker at the Council

---

* That Medieval abuses died hard is proved by the curious fact that even in England as late as the middle of the eighteenth century the sword appears with the crozier in the scutcheon of the " Prince Bishop" of Durham.

of Trent explained the reason of this omission. The
office of preaching, he said, was no doubt held in the
highest esteem in the Early Church. But the Council
should consider how complex a Bishop's life was in the
sixteenth century, and how numerous and varied were the
claims upon his time and energy. It was natural and
pious to desire that all Bishops should attain to St. Paul's
ideal; but, after all, Bishops were men and not angels;
it would be grossly unreasonable to require more than
could be fairly expected of them. A Bishop must have
acquired sufficient knowledge of the vast and intricate
subject of the Canon Law; as a temporal prince, holding
constant intercourse with other princes in the affairs of
this life, he needed the qualities of an able politician
and a skilful diplomatist. These indispensable duties
of spiritual administration and of temporal government
could not be discharged by anyone in his stead: but the
duty of preaching might be suitably devolved upon others,
who, undistracted by temporal cares, could devote their
whole mind and all their time to it. It was no wonder
that the Reformers indignantly complained in Milton's
words,

" The hungry sheep look up and are not fed."

If such was the example set by the most exalted
members of the ecclesiastical Order, it could not be
expected that the lower clergy would be distinguished by
sound learning, or spiritual zeal, or apostolic virtues, or
faithful discharge of their pastoral duties. The character
of the clergy in the archiepiscopal city of Cologne, one of
the most important cities of Europe during the first half
of the sixteenth century, may be taken as a fair type of
the secular and regular clergy in most parts of Western
Christendom. The members of the Cathedral Chapter
were bound by their constitution to live a common life,
but this obligation was systematically disregarded; and
that they might sufficiently discharge their chief duty of

representing the interests of the nobles, they made noble birth a condition of admission into their body. Of the twenty-four members eight priests performed the services of the Cathedral; the remaining sixteen for the most part appeared in the choir to draw the fees which were paid for attendance, lived the careless, unspiritual, luxurious life of the lay members of the German nobility, indulged largely in feasting, gambling and hunting, and courted the society of ladies who were beautiful but frail. Such being the character of the Cathedral clergy, it would have been surprising indeed if the rest of the clergy, secular and regular, had reached a high standard. Unfortunately there is unquestionable evidence that, in spite of noble exceptions, the demoralization among them was widespread. As far back as the year 1452 an old edict to ensure the regular convocation of Synods was renewed, but only to remain a dead letter. The prohibitions of concubinage, of luxury in dress, and of other abuses were in like manner renewed in vain. The Synod of the Province of Cologne passed a severe censure upon the three vices of the clergy—pride, avarice, and licentiousness, harmonizing in a significant manner with Colet's denunciation of the four chief vices of the clergy in his celebrated sermon before Convocation—the lust of the flesh, the pride of life, the intense devotion to worldly occupations, and covetousness. One competent witness bewailed the fact that scarcely a shadow of the old church life remained in Cologne : " No one does his duty after the manner of the days of old ; we have preserved the names of the offices, we do not perform the duties they entail." Another witness declared that most of the clergy were hirelings who cared not for their flocks : " The pastors are the first to enter, and the last to leave the tavern, and are always stout fellows at the drinking bout ; in their drunken orgies they often blurt out the secrets of the Confessional." The distinctive designation of " priests' children " was given to a definite class of the inhabitants of Cologne.

The life of the regular clergy was not a whit more blame-
less. Abbeys and monasteries had become institutions
where the children of noblemen, citizens, and peasants
could lead an easy life, exempt from the painful and sordid
struggle for existence, squandering in worldly ease the
wealth which pious founders had given for very different
purposes. One of the leading monks of Cologne sharply
censured the greed, avarice, shamelessness, sloth, and
worldliness of his brethren : " There are few who love the
study of Holy Writ and learning ; most of them care
more for the treasures of the kitchen than for the treasures
of the library." The city archives contain the records
of numerous nightly brawls in which drunken monks
played a leading and discreditable part, and of still more
flagrant offences against morality of which they were
guilty.

There can indeed be no question that the regular clergy
stood in even less estimation than the secular among the
nations of Europe. The mass of evidence on this point
is too vast to be contradicted. Erasmus, himself a monk,
never dips his pen into gall so bitter as when he is writing
of the monastic Orders ; and it is a significant fact that
the severest censures which he pronounced upon them
were written under the roof of so staunch a churchman as
Sir Thomas More. As late as the year 1577 Requesens,
the Governor of the Low Countries, in a confidential
letter to Philip the Second bewailed the lamentable ignorance, apathy, and sloth of the monastic Orders : the
Order of Saint Dominic, once so famous for its preachers,
had not now a single one in the Netherlands. In 1535
Duke George of Saxony, one of the most upright and
consistent among the Romanist princes, set on foot a
visitation of the monasteries in his principality. But so
little confidence had he in the trustworthiness of the
ordinary visitors that he conferred the office upon two
laymen, adherents of the Church of Rome, on whose
wisdom and impartiality he could rely. The report which

they handed in to the Duke contained a melancholy
picture of the decline of the monastic system : in many
houses the monks lived an unchristian life, others had
been deserted by their inmates ; in one monastery only
a single monk was left, in another there was nothing but
carousing and feasting, the abbot being a drunken fellow
much given to fighting with his peasants, and bearing on
his visage the scars of these rustic combats. In almost all
these monasteries there was gross extravagance and luxury,
two kitchens instead of one, an unnecessary number of
fires, even a special shoemaker and a special tailor for the
service of the monks : in the larger houses the monastic
income was wasted in the entertainment, not of poor
wayfarers and needy pilgrims, but of fine lords, who could
perfectly well afford to put up at an inn, but who preferred
to live at free quarters. One of the visitors angrily protested that the time which he might have profitably
employed in delivering lectures before the University of
Leipzig had been wasted upon a pack of useless, drunken
monks, who in some places had left Mass unsaid for such
a length of time that they did not even know where the
chalices of their monasteries were kept.

If anything could have increased the contempt into
which the clergy had fallen, or the indignation which their
conduct excited, it would have been the manner in which
they misused their spiritual powers. The terrible weapon
of excommunication, which had long ago been blunted
even in the hands of the Popes, had degenerated in the
hands of the lower clergy into a mere bugbear which could
not frighten children. Yet it was wielded as unscrupu-
lously as ever. In Scotland the poor husbandman, even
though he had not a groat in his pocket, was ruthlessly
excommunicated and debarred from the means of grace
because he failed to pay his tithes. In one of the chief
towns of the Netherlands, a year before the Reformation
began, the burghers quarrelled with the monks. The
latter had always enjoyed immunity from customs, and had

taken advantage of it to stock their cellar with casks of wine. The magistrates closed the cellar, and forbade the townsmen to assist the fathers in providing new supplies. The monks, wounded in their tenderest affections, persuaded the Bishop of Liège to liberate the costly contents of their cellar by laying the whole city under an interdict. In every country the immunity of the clergy from taxation was one of the greatest grievances of the laity; the wealthiest Order in the State, they cried, did not contribute a farthing towards defraying the expenses of the commonwealth. In every country the extortions which they did not scruple to practise provoked incessant complaints; at one time the Vicar seized a cow for each death in the family, at another the price of the Sacraments was raised; in the Low Countries the fee for the administration of Extreme Unction was doubled within three years. In Germany the loudest protest was raised against the Suffragan Bishops because they demanded fees for the consecration of tapers, bells, Eucharistic linen, and cowls; against pastors, chaplains, and vicars because they exacted payments for baptisms, hearing confessions, reading masses, vigils, prayers, preaching, unction, and publishing the banns of marriage; thus only could "the insatiable avarice of priests and monks" be checked. The clergy of the national Churches might, however, plead with justice that in all this they were only following the baneful examples set by the Roman Curia. The enormous sums of money which were sucked out of every European diocese by the leeches of Rome rose to a fabulous total every year. The diocese of Munster, one of the poorest in Germany, paid a sum of 60,000 marks within twenty-five years. One Danish Bishop had to pay the Pope 6,000 ducats for his "confirmation" in the Bishopric, another 7,800 ducats. For wealthier countries and richer bishoprics the sums were raised in proportion.

It might have been some compensation if the ecclesiastical Order had atoned for their vices by a fair show

of learning. But the ignorance of the clergy, whether
regular or secular, was the laughing-stock of the laity.
At the close of the fifteenth century the extent and depth
of the theological knowledge required of a candidate for
priest's Orders might be gauged by the questions which
he was expected to answer in the diocese of Brandenburg:
" How many Sacraments are there? Name them. Which
of them can be repeated, and which cannot? How are
they administered? How many Keys has the Church?
What do you understand by the Keys?" The most
learned theologians of France raised the cry that the knowledge of Greek and Hebrew was the root of all heresies:
and this cry was re-echoed by ignorant priests and monks
from furthest east to furthest west. Beza declared that
before the Reformation not one priest in a thousand had
read the Bible. Luther had never seen a Bible before he
entered the monastery, and was totally ignorant that the
portions appointed for the Epistles and Gospels did not
comprise the whole of Scripture. He has recorded his
testimony that, though in his childhood he was taught the
Ten Commandments, the Lord's Prayer, and the Apostles'
Creed, he received no instruction in them nor any explanation of them from the clergy: even when he was a
student at the University of Erfurt, he did not hear a
single truly Christian sermon or address, nor an exposition
of any portion of the Gospel or Psalms. In the University
pulpit at Oxford in the beginning of the sixteenth century
a violent preacher stigmatized all who favoured the Greek
language as " heretics," all who taught it or learnt it as
"devils." A Court preacher delivered a sermon before
Henry the Eighth in which he denounced the Greek
language and literature after the fashion of his Order;
when he was taken to task by the King for his ignorance,
he amended his previous statement by affirming that
Greek letters were derived from the Hebrew. As Erasmus
sarcastically observed, " they call everything which they
cannot understand Hebrew." The attack which was

made by the bigoted monks of Cologne on the famous
Hebrew scholar, Reuchlin, and which the Pope with
ignoble cowardice refused to condemn, opened the eyes of
all thoughtful men, who had the slightest tincture of
letters, to the unfathomable depths of ignorance and
stupidity in the clergy of the Medieval Church. But
Reuchlin was speedily and amply avenged : the " Letters
of Obscure Men," the work of his indignant Humanist
friends, one of the most effective and inimitable satires of
the sixteenth century, was received by the whole literary
world with peals of inextinguishable laughter, and remains
to this day the immortal monument of the unlucky monks
who fell beneath its lash. .

As was natural, ignorance became the fruitful parent of
superstition. The development of Saint worship which
we find at the beginning of the sixteenth century admir-
ably illustrates this truth. The Medieval Saints with
their various attributes and qualifications reproduced, as
Melanchthon observed, the leading ideas of Pagan mythology. Saint George, like Castor and Pollux, was the
patron of horsemen ; the Virgin Mary, like Venus, was
the goddess of the sea. One Saint worked the cure of
toothache, another of headache, another of diseases of the
eyes. Saint Louis healed horses, Saint Denys cattle,
Saint Anthony swine fever. In the Low Countries an
image of the Virgin was carried round the fields to make
the flax and corn grow; the maimed and cripples resorted
to Saint Cornelius ; his rival was Saint Koryn, who cured
bad legs ; Saint Remus was credited with the cure of
lunatics ; Saint Vincent healed those who had bad mouths.
Saint Adrian of Ghent was visited by thousands of the
sick and infirm ; the shrine of Saint Lievan of Houten,
" who carried her head in her hand," was frequented by
those who suffered from boils and blains. The strangest
legends were connected with the chief resorts of pilgrims.
At Einsiedeln in Switzerland, one of the most celebrated
of these holy places, the monastery had been built in the

tenth century in honour of the Virgin Mary, and, according to the popular legend, had been consecrated at
midnight by Christ Himself. Pope Leo the Eighth had
expressly forbidden the devout sons of the Church to
express a doubt of the truth of this legend.

The worship of Saints naturally led to the extravagant
veneration of relics. The multiplication of these relics,
the traffic in them, and the keen rivalry for the possession
of them, engrossed the attention of the Medieval Church.
The monastic Houses of England contained relics of
almost every known and unknown saint—the hand of
Saint James, the stole of Saint Philip, Our Lady's smock,
a part of the rock on which Christ was born, a part of the
Last Supper, the girdle of Mary Magdalene, the girdle of
Our Lady, a part of the coat of Saint Francis, a piece of
the shirt of Saint Thomas, the wheel of Saint Catherine,
and bones of numberless Saints in the English hagiology.
The Reformers commented sarcastically upon the ab-
surdities to which this accumulation of relics gave rise.
The dish containing the Paschal lamb at the Last Supper
was found at Rome, at Genoa, and at Arles. The cup containing the Eucharistic wine was found at two different
places. The pieces of the true Cross which had been preserved all over Christendom were sufficiently numerous
and large to build a man-of-war. The spear-head which
pierced Christ's side was shown at Rome, at Paris, in
Saintonge, and near Bordeaux. The sword and buckler
of the Archangel Michael were exhibited in France. Fourteen different places boasted the possession of different
portions of Saint John the Baptist's head. The body of
Saint Matthias was in three places, the body of Saint
Sebastian in four. At the famous city of Tours the chief
relic was called the " bouts Saint Martin," two little ends
of sleeves made of violet taffetas and set in crystal, which
the priests maintained had been brought from Paradise by
an angel to Saint Martin to cover his wrists when he
wished to elevate the consecrated Host. At the episcopal

city of Rodez in France a more grotesque relic still was exhibited and adored, the slipper of the Virgin Mary, called the " Saint Saboton," which was specially worshipped on Saturdays, as though there were some connection between the Latin word " sabbatum " and the French word " sabot."

During the latter part of the Middle Ages there was no more revolting form of popular superstition than the belief in " Bleeding Hosts." The extraordinary imposture designated by this name had originated in the doctrine of Transubstantiation. To justify the withdrawal of the Cup from the laity, and to prove that the communicant had received the Eucharist as fully in one kind as in both, unscrupulous priests invented this absurd miracle. Wilsnack, a village in the Electorate of Brandenburg, became about the beginning of the fifteenth century the most celebrated scene of this imposture. The fame of its " Bleeding Host " rapidly spread through the neighbouring lands, and drew a great army of pilgrims from a vast tract of country stretching from Bohemia and Hungary in the south to Denmark and Sweden in the north. The village expanded into a town, small houses were converted into thriving hostelries, and a great church was built with the offerings of worshippers. When the Cardinal Legate, Nicholas of Cusa, honourably distinguished among the churchmen of his age for his piety, learning and sincerity, visited North Germany in 1451, an appeal was made to him. He ordered the church which was the scene of the imposture to be closed, laid the Bishop who had countenanced it under the ban, and placed Wilsnack, which had prospered by the fruits of it, under an interdict. An appeal was instantly made to Rome against the unjust sentence of the Legate ; and Pope Nicholas the Fifth was induced to issue a Bull in favour of the " Bleeding Host." Thus after more than half a century the reign of superstition was again established, and the pilgrimages increased in frequency and were more numerously attended than ever.

All the vices, however, and all the corruptions of the
Church and her rulers were powerless to shake the faith of
the Medieval clergy in the infallibility of the See of Saint
Peter and in their own infallibility.   Their method of
dealing with heretics bore witness to this faith.   The
truth of the Church's doctrines was as clear as the noonday : the heretic, therefore, could not be troubled with
conscientious doubts, or justifiable scruples, or reasonable misgivings; he could only be guilty of wilful and
incurable obstinacy ; to argue with him was a waste of
time and a confession of weakness ; a far more summary
proceeding was needed.   Whatever may be said of the
Inquisition, it was only the living and visible embodiment
of these confident assumptions and beliefs of the Medieval
theologians, and it only retained its vitality so long as any
part of Europe was under bondage to the spirit which
animated the Middle Ages.   The unhappy heretic was
placed outside the pale of Christian society.   Like the
accursed race of Canaan under the Old Dispensation, he
was doomed to death—often a cruel and lingering death,
his property was confiscated, and the house which had
been polluted by his presence was demolished.   Even if
his soul was overawed by the terrors of impending dissolution, if in the agony of mortal fear he recanted his
false opinions and embraced the Roman Catholic faith,
he was doomed to a life-long imprisonment, was stripped
of all his property, and was deprived of the rights which
he possessed as a Christian citizen.   Nor were these views
confined to hard-hearted and brutal warriors, or to narrow-
minded and bigoted ecclesiastics.   Saint Thomas Aquinas,
one of the greatest theological and philosophical lights of
the Middle Ages, deliberately adopted and defended the
same principles.   He was forced, indeed, to allow that
several passages of the New Testament were against him,
notably the parable of the wheat and the tares, and that
Saint Chrysostom in his homily on this parable interpreted it in a sense adverse to his own.   He quoted Saint

Augustine's words, that a man can do everything else against his will, but cannot believe except with the consent of his will. Having thus refuted his own doctrine beforehand, the Angelic Doctor drew a distinction between Jews and Gentiles on the one hand and Christians on the other : the former of these two classes have never received the faith, and it would be a gross injustice to compel them to believe, because belief is an act of the will; the latter have once received the faith and still profess it; they must, therefore, be subjected to bodily compulsion that they may fulfil their promises and observe their pledges ; their acceptance of the faith was an act of free will, they were at liberty to accept it or to reject it ; but having once accepted it they must hold it fast, and therefore heretics must be compelled to keep the faith. What, then, is the nature of this bodily compulsion ? Saint Thomas does not leave us for one moment in doubt. The sin of the heretics is so deadly that they have deserved, not only to be severed from the Church by excommunication, but to be removed from the world by death. If, therefore, after the first and second admonition enjoined by the Apostle, the Church takes measures for the salvation of others by separating him from the communion of the faithful through the sentence of excommunication, she then leaves him to the secular judge to be rooted out by death. Thus the explicit teaching of Aquinas elevated intolerance into a cardinal principle of the Church's action, and expressly justified the system of the Inquisition. When Luther on the threshold of the Reformation laid down the maxim, " It is against the will of the Holy Ghost that heretics should be burnt," and when Leo the Tenth, following Aquinas, denounced this maxim in his Bull of excommunication, the spirit of the Middle Ages and the spirit of modern times clashed together in the lists of battle, never to cease from their struggle till the victory of the new principle had been finally assured.

Two documents of capital importance have been

preserved, both supplying unimpeachable evidence of the corruptions and disorders of the Medieval Church, both dating from the early years of the sixteenth century, which deserve the careful study of every one who would realize the impression made by the reckless folly of the Roman Curia upon devout and eminent Christians. The first is the list of Grievances drawn up by the temporal Estates of the Imperial Diet in 1523, and presented to the Papal Nuncio at Nuremberg. They expressly guard against the assumption that the list is exhaustive: they are careful to state that they have hastily put together "a few great and important grievances" selected out of a much larger number. They complain that Papal dispensations are sold for money; that marriages are forbidden at certain seasons unless permission is bought of the Bishops; that monks in their sermons threaten divine punishments and plagues to extort much money, "which is a sheer deceiving of the poor simple man"; that there are often two, three, or four kinds of Mendicants in a single district, so that the money which ought to go to the poor is withdrawn from them and given to the Friars; that temporal causes are taken to Rome to be tried; that Papal judges pass judgment in temporal matters which ought to come before secular judges; that Papal delegates and commissaries invade the temporal jurisdiction; that the rights of lay and clerical patrons are invaded; that the benefices of the clergy who die on the way to Rome are given to Papal favourites; that these favourites wantonly cite beneficed priests to Rome, who are forced to compound with them by a yearly pension; that the Roman Chancery empowers the clerics of Rome to get the spiritual fiefs of Germany into their hands, and that these are "reserved" for enormous sums, such as 1,000, 2,000, or 3,000 florins; that annates specially given for a crusade against the Turks are diverted to other purposes; that excommunication is recklessly pronounced; that secular property is seized by the clergy; that money is unjustly extorted from pilgrims at several places; that ecclesiastical judges and officials permit concubinage and usury in return for money payments; that a parishioner is debarred from the Sacraments if he is in debt to the pastor; that some of the clergy keep inns; that monks and priests persuade the sick, whom they know to possess money or property, to leave or bequeath their possessions to them after death, as though they could thereby avert divine punishment and buy the kingdom of heaven. Such are a few of the grievances: it would be tedious to give the whole list; and one, on the immorality of the clergy, it is impossible to reproduce.

There are, however, three Grievances, by which every country of Western Europe was in a greater or less degree affected, and which are, therefore, so important that they deserve to be quoted more fully, the third, the sixteenth, and thirty-sixth. The third bears the title, " The Great Grievance of the Papal Indulgence ": " Under cover of church buildings and other plausible pretexts, Indulgence for sins has been sold in Germany: and truly an indescribable sum of money has been drawn from Germany to Rome: thereby many a poor simple man has lost his substance, which he needed for himself: and, what is much more harmful, by this Indulgence, and by frivolous and unskilful preachers, Christian men have been moved and seduced to commit many grievous sins, perjury, blasphemy, murder, and others. And this Indulgence has been extended, not only to present and future sins of the living, but also to the souls in Purgatory, if money was paid for them to ensure their certain release. And although several times this Indulgence has been publicly preached, as though it were designed for war against the Infidel and for the saving of Christian men, yet this has not been done, but it has been perverted to other worldly and selfish objects, for the exaltation and maintenance of the Pope's friends and family; and this, together with the scandal and seduction of Christian men mentioned above, has spread such incredulity among Christian folk that,

when they are asked in the hour of need to give help
against the Turks, they suspect that this aid will be
misused in like manner. Moreover, the Pope and Bishops
keep and reserve certain sins for their own absolution.
And if such cases occur, they will not grant absolution,
save for a large sum of money. And so a poor man, who
has no money to give, is not absolved." The sixteenth
Grievance runs as follows : " All Prelatures and Livings,
or at least the best, are taken from the German nation,
and given to unlearned, unskilled, and frivolous persons :
so that many from foreign nations obtain Prelatures and
' God's gifts,' who are not of German tongue, and who
are unlearned ; these men, being unable to feed Christ's
sheep with Christian doctrine and instruction, bestow the
livings upon other unlearned and unsuitable persons, who,
instead of Holy Scripture, preach to the people useless
and unverified legends of the Saints, and other fictitious
and offensive heathen fables, and cannot do anything
better. Thus Christian people are led away by these
unlearned and unfitting administrations of the livings
from true Christian faith and trust in God, in which alone
consist our salvation and our souls' blessedness, to superstition and the works of man, which serve for the temporal
profit of the administrators of these parishes." The
thirty-sixth deals with a third grievance, which seems to
have pressed even more heavily upon Germany than upon
the rest of Western Christendom : " When priests are
presented to livings by laymen, and ask the Bishops and
their Vicars to institute them, some demand one or two
years' income for payment, half being demanded by the
Bishop and half by the Archdeacon. Besides, such
spiritual benefices are so highly and immoderately taxed
that the priests have not enough left for their necessary
maintenance : and so they indemnify themselves by selling
to the laity for money the Sacraments and other Christian
gifts, which according to the command of the Holy
Gospels they are bound to give for nothing." It would

have been difficult for any of the Reformers to draw up a
more formidable list of grievances, or to couch them in
language more pointed and more plain-spoken.

The other document emanated from Rome itself, and
was, if possible, still more extraordinary. At the request
of Paul the Third a Committee of distinguished prelates
drew up proposals for a reformation, and in their vigorous
denunciation of the corruptions of the Church re-echoed
all that had been said by the Reformers. In this paper,
published in Germany in 1537, it is asserted that Popes
with itching ears have listened to the voice of flatterers,
have been persuaded that they can do what they will
with their own and yet contract no guilt of simony, and
that the mere will of the Pope is the sole rule and
measure of all his actions; from unworthy Popes, as
the fountain-head, have flowed all the diseases of which
the Church lies sick even unto death; the Turk on this
account makes a mock at our Christian faith and religion;
and through the Roman Curia the name of Christ is blasphemed among the heathen. The Pope has sought for
money, gain, and advantage in the power of the Keys.
Inexperienced and unlearned men, youths of the lowest
origin and of infamous character, are recklessly ordained
and consecrated priests. All the shepherds have left their
flocks and entrusted them to hirelings, till a Christian man
who travels from country to country can behold no more
piteous sight than the desolation of the Churches. On
plea of reservation a benefice is stripped of everything
which ought to be given to divine service and the holder
of the cure. In the exchange of benefices simoniacal
agreements are made, of which the sole object is gain.
The poisonous vice of simony holds such sway in God's
Church that men have ceased to be ashamed of it. The
most stringent laws are mocked and defied by cures of soul
being converted into legacies and bequeathed by will, or
by the children of priests holding their fathers' benefices
as private property, or by Cardinals holding two or more

Bishoprics apiece to gratify their avarice, instead of setting
an example to all men of the holiness of their lives. Bishops
are hindered from punishing clerics for their wicked lives,
because the evildoers betake themselves to the Peniten-
tiaries, and get off scot-free by the payment of money.
The scenes of immorality which can be witnessed in Rome
in the full light of noonday, scenes in which the most
eminent of the Cardinals and ecclesiastics take part, have
no counterpart in any other Christian city. Such are the
confessions made by Prelates, some of whom were the most
illustrious of their time. In the face of these documents
it is idle to assert that the Reformers wilfully exaggerated
the abuses of the Medieval Church.

The Humanists, of whom Erasmus was by far the most
distinguished, were the pioneers of the Reformation. The
value of their work lay, not so much in the actual stores
of knowledge which they accumulated, or in the new fields
of thought and study which they opened out, as in the
critical temper with which they tested the fictions and
scattered the mists of the Middle Ages. Till the beginning
of the sixteenth century stories of consecrated Hosts being
mysteriously whisked out of the priests' hands and conveyed to bedridden sufferers, of angels presenting crippled
maidens with divine keys to unlock the secret shrines of
saints and be healed as if by magic, of departed spirits
moaning from the vaults of churches that they are suffering
the tortures of the damned because they had not been laid
in consecrated earth with the Medieval ceremonies, were
greedily swallowed by the credulous multitude; monastic
preachers filled their sermons with them in order to fasci-
nate the imagination, and to loose the purse-strings, of
ignorant parishioners, to magnify the greatness of the
Church, or to prove the miracle of Transubstantiation;
and whatever educated men may have thought of them,
not one in ten thousand dared or cared to impugn them.
But as soon as the Humanists appeared, all this was
changed. When Erasmus, the most learned, sagacious,

and witty among them, overwhelmed Medieval miracles, superstitions, and beliefs with his keen sarcasms, mocked at the idea that dying in the garb of a Franciscan could be a passport to salvation, jeered at the vows offered to Saints in the hour of danger, ridiculed the delusion that any number of pilgrimages could minister to the soul's health, scoffed at the most sacred of English relics, the milk of the Virgin, subjected the wealth and dominion of the ecclesiastical Order to a criticism more biting than Luther's, and even dared to deny that the Vulgate translation was inspired, the cause of Medievalism was irretrievably lost.   Compared with this work of the professed champion of the Church, the disproof of the most unquestioned historical beliefs of the Middle Ages, such as Laurentius Valla's exposure of the forged Donation of Constantine, was comparatively unimportant.

This was not the only result of the critical temper of the Humanists.   They rejected at once without hesitation the cumbrous system, the wearisome arguments, the interminable hair-splitting, the grotesque medley of theological doctrines and philosophical tenets, the absurd, useless, and irreverent questions, which were the delight of the Scholastic theologians during the Middle Ages.   Saint Thomas Aquinas, on the threshold of his great work, the "Summa Theologica," fills page after page with such questions as, "Is God composed of matter and form?   Is He composed of subject and accident?   Is God's knowledge discursive?   Has God a speculative or a practical knowledge of things?   Does God possess free will?   Is an angel composed of matter and form?   Do angels possess bodies naturally united to them?   Can an angel move?   Does an angel love himself by natural or elective love?   Were angels created in the empyrean?   Ought woman to have been made out of man?   Ought woman to have been formed out of man's rib?   Did the first man see God by his essence?   Did the first man possess the knowledge of all things?"   Yet Aquinas, even though he was a blind Samson, was still a Samson, immeasurably superior to the wretched drudges who toiled in the Scholastic mill. Erasmus, in his " Praise of Folly," has given a list of the profound and subtle questions which at the close of the Middle Ages were engrossing the attention of the schoolmen : " Is there more than one filiation in Christ ? Is the proposition, God the Father hates the Son, a possible one ? Could God have taken upon Him the form of a woman, of the devil, of an ass, of a cucumber, or of a flint-stone ? If He had taken the form of a cucumber, could He have preached, worked miracles, and been crucified ? What would Peter have consecrated, if he had celebrated the Eucharist while Christ's Body was hanging upon the Cross ? Could Christ at that time have been called a man ? Will it be possible for us after the resurrection to eat and drink, as we do now, to guard against hunger and thirst ? " This impious quibbling, the like of which the Christian Church has never seen before or since, received its death-blow from the Humanists.

The work of the Humanists would have been far less effective than it was, had it not been supplemented and propagated by one of the most powerful of human agencies —the printing-press. The close of the fifteenth century witnessed the firstfruits of this marvellous invention. The impulse which the Reformation received from it cannot at this distance of time be estimated aright. But in every European country knowledge was increased, truth was spread, falsehood was checked, deceit was unveiled, new views of nature and of man were brought to light by the humble sheets and the rude letters, which, countless as the sands of the seashore for multitude, fluttered over the face of the earth. More than ten thousand editions of books and pamphlets were published during the last thirty years of the fifteenth century. In several cities, such as Milan, Rome, Paris, Cologne, and Strasburg, they exceeded five hundred in number: in Venice they numbered nearly three thousand. Isolated facts will give some conception of the rapidity with which books were multiplied. In the first half of the sixteenth century a single bookseller sold at a single Leipzig fair fourteen hundred copies of different works of Luther. In the course of forty years a single publisher sold 100,000 copies of Luther's translation of the Bible, besides countless copies of the New Testament, of the Psalms, and of separate Gospels and Epistles. An irresistible weapon had been placed in the Reformers' hands, and they wielded it with resistless force : for the books which they published during the fifty years from 1517 to 1567 outnumbered their opponents' tenfold, and found their way into quiet villages, as well as into the great centres of learning and the crowded thoroughfares of populous cities.

If the Reformation was fostered by the intellectual conditions which modified European thought at the close of the Middle Ages, it was not less effectively fostered by the political forces which were at work in Western Christendom. The fifteenth century had witnessed the slow decay of Feudalism, which for centuries had retarded the growth of national life, and had been the mainstay of Papal and ecclesiastical dominion. In England the Wars of the Roses, and in France the policy of Louis the Eleventh and his successors, had broken down the power of the great lords. From the beginning of the sixteenth century nobles like Warwick and Charles of Burgundy, the makers and masters of Kings, disappeared from the countries where they and their predecessors had played so important a part. In their fall they dragged down with them the ecclesiastical Princes, who belonged to the same Order, who were often their near kinsmen, and who were guided by the same policy, governed by the same principles, filled with the same prejudices, and inspired by the same aims and motives as themselves. In Germany, Switzerland, and the Low Countries the rise of great cities, with keen intellectual interests, an exuberant political life, and a widespread commercial activity, had

been even more fatal to the undisputed dominion of the
Church.   Probably there was not a single town of any
importance in those countries which had not, at some
time or other during the fifty years preceding the Reformation, quarrelled with the ecclesiastical authorities within
their walls, and which did not eye with undisguised
jealousy the pretensions and privileges of men who insisted
upon their rights with the same persistency with which
they neglected their spiritual duties and broke their
canonical laws.   It was in these cities, the flower of
European civilization in the first half of the sixteenth
century, the heralds and the forerunners of the new
principles and the new life of modern times, that the
religious movement struck its roots most deeply and bore
its richest fruits.

It is a strange and unquestionable fact that the Heads
of the Church had no more suspicion of these momentous
changes, and of their vital influence upon the future of the
Church, than the humblest Curate who lived in the wilds
of Cornwall.   Not a word fell from the lips of the Popes
who reigned during the half century preceding the Reformation which betrayed the faintest consciousness that the
dayspring of a new age had dawned.   Like the Roman
Emperors at the rise of the Christian Church, like the
Bourbon Princes on the eve of the French Revolution,
they were unable to discern the signs of the times, blind
to the sights which met their eyes at every turn, deaf to
the sounds which filled the air around them, heedless of
the invisible currents which were sapping the foundations of their spiritual throne, engrossed in petty political
interests, squabbling and scheming for a few square miles
of Italian soil, while the spiritual power, which should
have been dearer to them than all the States of the Church,
had they been ten times greater than they were, was
slipping from their grasp.   Not one of the famous dynasties
of history has illustrated with more convincing truth than
the Papacy the terrible proverb, " The fathers have eaten

sour grapes, and the children's teeth have been set on edge."

The decline of the Papacy was accompanied by the decline of the great political institution which for centuries had been the complement and the rival of the Papacy, the Holy Roman Empire, or, to call it by its true and not its formal title, the German Empire. During the fifteenth century the halo of glory which surrounded it had become visibly dim. It is true that Cardinal Pole, just before the opening of the Council of Trent, described the Emperor as the royal Vicar of Christ, to whom the Head of the Church had delegated His kingly power, as He had delegated His spiritual power to the Pope: but this attempt to give life and substance to the shrunken and bodiless fiction of the Middle Ages deceived no one. Had it been possible on the death of Maximilian the First to elect an energetic, able, and patriotic German prince, who could have enlisted the national sympathies, and secured the loyal support of the whole Imperial Confederation, who would have devoted himself heart and soul to German interests, wise enough to reconcile the conflicting claims of States, Orders, and Cities, unselfish enough to sacrifice his personal and dynastic ambition to the common weal, the Empire might again have risen to the proud pre-eminence which the earlier Emperors had claimed and secured for it. But when the Electors were forced to choose between the Kings of Spain, France, and England—of whom it is difficult to say whether Charles, or Francis, or Henry was the most unfitted to be the Empire's Head—it needed no prophet to foretell that before long the irrevocable sentence of doom would be recorded against it. Before the Reformation had been checked in its victorious career, the mightiest political creation of the Middle Ages could be described in the poet's words:

> "Jacet ingens litore truncus,
> Avolsumque humeris caput, et sine nomine corpus."

CHAPTER II.

THE German Reformation in its beginning is little more than a biography of Luther. It is true that he was supported and aided by many able and devoted followers. But it is no disparagement to them to say that they could not have done the work which Luther did. Indeed, no one could have been better fitted for the accomplishment of the mighty task which he carried to a triumphant issue. As the son of a peasant he was familiar from his childhood with the character of his own people and the force and vigour of his mother tongue. As a monk he had wrestled with spiritual doubts and perplexities which seemed to undermine his religious faith, and had proved by a terrible experience the uselessness of going about to establish his own righteousness. As a Professor and Doctor of Theology he was drawn to the intense study of the Bible and of Saint Augustine, and his eyes were opened to the spiritual truths of which the Medieval Church had lost sight. As a pastor of souls he was brought face to face with the practical abuses which threatened to deaden the Christian conscience and to poison the very springs of the religious life.

It may be doubted if any of the religious leaders of the Christian Church since the days of the Apostles has been more richly endowed than Luther with gifts of the highest order. To him belongs the honour, which he shares with master-minds like Homer, Chaucer, and Dante, of having definitely fixed his native language and

set forth its richness, flexibility, and force. His translation of the Bible, even after every deduction has been
made, is one of the most remarkable books in the history
of the world. Nor was he less eminent as an original
writer. Often, it is true, his works were thrown off
with a haste which was fatal to careful and elaborate
composition. But on occasions when he could do himself
full justice he wrote with a directness and an eloquence
which proved irresistible. As a pamphleteer, he may
compare with some of the foremost names in European
literature—Swift, Voltaire, Burke, and Mirabeau. If he
was great as a writer, he was equally great as a speaker.
His freshness of thought, his mastery of the great truths
of the Christian faith, his profound and intimate knowledge of the Bible, the idiomatic simplicity and directness
of his language, his complete mastery of the resources
of his mother tongue, the vivid imagery which rose
unbidden to his lips, above all, his sincerity, earnestness,
fervour, and pathos, never failed to rivet the attention
of his hearers. And when his sermons were printed,
they deeply and permanently influenced a wide circle
of readers.

Scarcely less influential were his contributions to
hymnology. He was the first of the eminent hymn-
writers who discarded the Latin language and composed
hymns in the modern languages of Europe. After three
centuries and a half his massive hymn, " Ein' feste Burg
ist unser Gott," still retains the foremost place in the
services of the Lutheran Church. Even his bitterest
enemies, the Jesuits, were constrained to acknowledge that
he had slain more souls by his hymns than by his sermons
and writings.

Luther's religious character is most vividly illustrated
in a letter written to his friend, the Town Clerk of
Nuremberg, giving him directions for the painting of his
religious device or coat-of-arms. He wishes to have a
black cross, set in the centre of a heart which keeps its

natural colour. The Cross is to remind him that faith
in the crucified Lord saves us. And though the cross
is black as a sign of mortification and anguish, yet it
lets the heart retain its natural colour, because it does
not destroy nature but preserves it. "For the Just shall
live by faith, but by faith in the Crucified." This heart
shall stand in the midst of a white rose, to show that
faith gives joy, comfort, and peace; for white is the
colour of spirits and of angels. This rose must be placed
in a field of sky-blue, to show that this joy in the spirit
and in faith is a beginning of the heavenly joy of the
future, and is clearly grasped by hope but not yet revealed.
And in this field there ought to be a golden ring, to
show that this joy lasts for ever in heaven, and is also
precious above all joys and blessings, as gold is the
costliest metal.

This sacred joy, which Luther valued as a supreme
privilege and blessing, was constantly overcast by terrible
fits of melancholy and depression. How far this melancholy
was constitutional, and how far it had been aggravated by the
hardships of his early years, or intensified by the spiritual
struggles of his monastic life, it is impossible to determine.
But there can be no doubt that he regarded it as one of
the severest trials of his life. When he writes of it to his
friends we seem to be listening to the words in which the
Apostle of the Gentiles describes his thorn in the flesh.
It explains the tenderness with which Luther, more than
any of the other Reformers, entered into the anguish of
troubled consciences, sympathized with the sufferers who
were passing through the Valley of the Shadow of Death,
and pointed to the one hope which was set as an anchor
of the soul sure and steadfast. To one such sufferer he
wrote a few months before his death: "God has given us
His Son, Jesus Christ, that we may daily think of Him
and mirror ourselves in Him. For apart from Christ
everything is misery and death, but in Him is nothing save
peace and joy." He who would understand the secret of

Luther's spiritual greatness and religious influence may find the key to it in these words.

As a practical Reformer Luther was essentially conservative and moderate. This may seem a surprising statement to those who are only acquainted with his opinions on isolated subjects, or who have been startled by the unmeasured violence of his language in some of his writings. But anyone who impartially considers his whole work as a Reformer will recognize the justice of this estimate. No religious leader has been more careful to insist on the paramount importance and the sacred duty of holding with an immovable grasp to what is of vital importance, and of maintaining the utmost tolerance and charity where diversity is possible and desirable. Saint Paul's words, "All things are lawful for me, but all things are not expedient," were constantly on his lips. He saw the danger which besets all great changes, when men with intemperate haste and immature judgment clutch at the shadow and lose the substance. He dreaded above all things lest his adherents in their unwise zeal for the shape of a vestment or the form of a ceremony should sacrifice the Christian virtues of faith and love. "There are some matters" (he writes to his people of Wittenberg) "which God has bidden us observe, and which must be observed: no man on earth has power to change them, neither Bishop nor Pope. Some things God has left to our free choice, and has not forbidden or commanded any of them. These must remain free, and no man on earth, no angel in heaven, has power to force them upon us."

Unhappily Luther did not always act consistently with the large-hearted principle which he strenuously advocated. No graver misfortune could have befallen Evangelical Christendom than the dispute about the sacrament of the Lord's Supper, which divided the adherents of the Reformation into two hostile companies. It is needless to enter into this controversy, the most dreary, the most melancholy, and the most unprofitable, in the history of the

Reformed Churches. But it is impossible for any fair-minded and impartial student to acquit Luther of wilfully violating his own rule of action in his treatment of it. When he maintained that his interpretation of the language of Scripture was the only possible interpretation, that any doctrine except the doctrine of Consubstantiation was false, and that the divergence of opinion in the German and Swiss Churches raised up an impassable barrier between them, and was a fatal obstacle to active Christian intercourse, such language was unreasonable, unjustifiable, and uncharitable in the highest degree.

The real harm which was done by Luther's part in this dispute could only be revealed in all its magnitude as time went on. Not only did Luther seriously weaken his influence as the leader of the Reformation and gravely imperil the cause to which he had devoted his life; what was far worse, he lent the vast authority of his great name and example for the embittering of religious strife. For one disputant who has been willing to follow Luther in his wise counsels of moderation and mutual forbearance ten have been ready to imitate his violent and bigoted prejudice. As is usual in all great movements, those who followed were eager to outstrip those who led. It was scarcely to be expected that the Lutherans should be temperate where Luther had been grossly intemperate. The strife between the Reformers of Germany and Switzerland was the original source of the manifold theological disputes which have so grievously hindered the union of Evangelical Christendom and impaired the work of the Reformed Churches.

Luther's acceptance of a Professorship at Wittenberg in 1508, when he was twenty-four years old, marks the beginning of a new epoch in his life. The University had been founded six years previously by Frederick the Wise, when, in consequence of the division of the Saxon lands between the Elector and the Duke of Saxony, the University town of Leipzig had fallen to the Duchy.

The Elector was naturally proud of an University which was his own creation, and decided to increase its efficiency by every means in his power. In this way Luther came under the special protection of a Prince who, for cool judgment, practical wisdom, earnest desire to further his people's welfare, and sincere piety, was probably superior to any of his contemporaries.

Of the first years which Luther spent at Wittenberg we know little. But in 1511 he was sent on a mission to Rome to transact some business for his Order, and to this visit he looked back in after years as one of the decisive events of his life. The deep impression which was made upon him during his stay in Rome by the religious hypocrisy and the moral corruption of the Papal city turned his thoughts seriously to the abuses which prevailed in the Church, and to the urgent need of reform. When only six years later Tetzel, one of the sellers of Indulgences, visited Saxony and hawked his wares with all the shamelessness of his money-making fraternity, Luther was deeply moved by the reports which came to his ears. At first he was content to preach against the misuse of Indulgences.   But it was a different matter when his own parishioners in the Confessional declared that they would not put away their sins, and, on his refusing them absolution, produced their letters of Indulgence and went to complain of him to Tetzel.   Then his indignation rose to fever heat, and he resolved to take a decisive step. Availing himself of a practice which was usual in those times, when a theologian desired the expression and formation of opinion upon some question of general interest, on the eve of All Saints' Day, October 31st, 1517, he drew up ninety-five Theses for disputation. All Saints' Day was the anniversary of the consecration of the Church at Wittenberg; a large number of clergy and theologians from the surrounding district would attend the service; and thus public attention would at once be directed to the subject of Indulgences.   His anticipations were more than fulfilled. Within a month, according to a contemporary, the Theses had spread through the whole of Christendom, as if borne on angels' wings.

Had a wise and spiritually-minded Pope been seated at this time on the throne of Saint Peter, he might have been able to satisfy Luther, and to remove the scandal of Tetzel's proceedings. But the reigning Pope, Leo the Tenth, had few spiritual interests and little personal religion. The objections and arguments of Luther sounded to him like the accents of an unknown tongue. He had obtained his lofty position as the Head of Christendom chiefly because he was a member of the famous House of Medici. The saying with which he was credited on his election, " Now that we have obtained the Papacy let us enjoy it," was eminently characteristic. A wit, a scholar, and an epicure, he gave himself without stint to the pleasures of this life. When he was not engaged in pleasure, he was dabbling in politics, eager to increase the States of the Church, proud of holding the balance between the contending monarchs of France and Spain, and endeavouring to establish his reputation as a consummate diplomatist. To such a Pope Luther's attack upon Indulgences would only seem of importance in so far as it had dried up one of his sources of revenue. He could have no understanding whatever of its spiritual significance. Perhaps, if the question had rested with him alone, he would have taken no further notice of the daring monk who had ventured to call in question his prerogatives and his motives. But pressure was put upon him ; and he embarked upon that short-sighted, inconsistent, selfish, and vacillating policy which was distinctive of the Roman Curia during the period of the Reformation, and which injured the Papal cause as fatally as the attacks of the Reformers. At one time it was necessary to conciliate the Emperor, at another to curry favour with the Elector of Saxony. At one time a Papal minister was commissioned to intimidate Luther, at another an Emissary was dispatched to flatter

and cajole him.   Every month that passed strengthened
the Reformer's convictions and widened his views; the
arguments of his opponents passed by him like the wind;
and when the Pope, after a delay of three years, excommunicated him, Luther on December 10th, 1520, publicly
burnt the Bull with his own hands and flung the books of
the Canon Law, the most enduring monument of unscrip-
tural teaching and of Papal tyranny, into the same fire.

The year in which Luther hurled his defiance at the
Pope was memorable in the political as well as in the
religious history of Europe.   The Medieval Empire, one of
the mightiest names in the world's annals, which had
fascinated the imagination of poets and kindled the
enthusiasm of heroes; which traced back its unbroken
lineage to Julius Cæsar; which claimed to be the representative of the political unity of Christendom as the
Papacy was of the spiritual; which still overawed men's
minds by the dim splendours of its immemorial antiquity
and the imposing majesty of its titles, was entering, after
many vicissitudes, upon a final stage of impotence and
decay.   A few weeks before the burning of the Papal Bull
the youthful Charles the Fifth, heir to the Spanish,
Burgundian, Italian, and Austrian possessions of his
House, the potential Lord of the New World, had received
the Imperial Crown in the historic Cathedral of Aachen.
At this momentous crisis in the fortunes of Germany, which
might have perplexed the wisest and most gifted in the
long line of Emperors, the German people received as
their Head a Sovereign who could not speak their
language, who was profoundly ignorant of their ideas,
their grievances, and their aspirations, who had no
sympathy with their national character, whose whole soul
was centred in the greatness of Spain, who had been
brought up in the straitest sect of the Church of Rome,
and who regarded the Empire as a convenient instrument
for the execution of his ambitious plans.   To such an
Emperor the Reformer who had lit an inextinguishable fire

of religious faith and hope in Germany was nothing more than an insolent and irreverent monk, who had dared to strike at the most time-honoured institutions of Christendom, and had set himself up as the judge and censor of the Holy Catholic Church.

The scene of Luther's appearance at the Diet of Worms in 1521 is one of the most dramatic in the world's history. The peasant's son, standing before the heir of all the Cæsars, in the centre of the most splendid political assembly that Europe could boast, undauntedly justifying his words and actions, refusing to be intimidated by the Emperor's threats and the Church's thunders, turning from antiquated formulas and worn-out arguments to new and living springs of light and truth, confidently appealing to the voice of conscience, the claims of reason, and the clear testimony of God's Word, was the representative of a new order, spiritual, moral, political, and social, before which the old order of autocratic Popes and despotic Emperors, and fires of the Inquisition, and immorality cloaking itself under the garb of religion, and ecclesiastics claiming the powers and usurping the privileges of temporal rulers, was destined to vanish like the baseless fabric of a dream.

For the moment, however, the Emperor's attempt to put down heresy seemed to be successful. He persuaded the Diet to pass the Edict of Worms, which placed Luther and all who favoured him, as well as his followers and supporters, under the ban of the Empire: their property was to be confiscated, and all Luther's writings were to be burnt. Had it not been for the Reformer's powerful friends, he might have shared the fate of Huss. But the Elector of Saxony would not consent to be deprived of his great preacher and professor. While returning from Worms, Luther was seized by his Prince's orders, and conveyed to the Wartburg, one of the Electoral castles. Here he was detained in secure and solitary confinement till the immediate danger had passed by. In this lonely haven of peace and repose he was enabled to begin the great work which for nearly four centuries has made his name a household word in millions of homes, the German translation of the Bible.

The reader will probably gain a clearer and more vivid impression of the Reformation, if, instead of tracing its vicissitudes through the length and breadth of Germany, he fixes his attention on a single city, where he may study in miniature the vast changes which were taking place with more or less rapidity and completeness over a large portion of Central Europe.

Among the free and imperial cities of Germany none, with the exception of Augsburg, could rival Nuremberg in all the elements of civic greatness. Unlike most of the German cities it had never been an episcopal see, and had not suffered from the vexatious and harassing tyranny of the ecclesiastical powers. The early German poet and master singer, Hans Sachs, himself a citizen of Nuremberg, has given us a vivid picture of the city in the day of its greatness. He describes the innumerable houses with gleaming roofs and gables, the costly buildings ornamented in Italian fashion, the stately streets, the six great gates, and the eleven stone bridges which spanned the river. He dwells with patriotic pride upon the inhabitants, of whom no man can tell the sum, upon their industry, wealth, and power, the trade which has spread into every land, the market filled with all the wares that man's heart desires. "Here may be seen artisans who can print, paint, and smelt, foundrymen, sculptors, carpenters, and builders, whose like is not to be seen in any realm."

Nor was the intellectual life of Nuremberg less remarkable than its manufacturing and commercial activity. At the beginning of the sixteenth century it was the home of humanists, jurists, astronomers, historians, men of letters, and enemies of the Scholastic philosophy. The popular government of the city was exceptionally good: a contemporary Venetian statesman pronounced it to be the

best governed town in Germany.   The success of the
Reformation in such a city is a proof of the influence
which the new doctrines obtained in commercial and
intellectual centres.

Luther's connection with Nuremberg began through
Staupitz, his friend and monastic Superior.   Staupitz
came to stay at the monastery of the Augustines, and it
was natural that in the course of conversation he should
speak of the monk who had interested him so profoundly,
and for whom he predicted so great a future.   When the
Theses of 1517 were published, they were received with
enthusiasm by a select circle in the city; his subsequent
writings were eagerly read, and formed the subject of
daily talk.   The most eminent citizen of Nuremberg
became the devoted admirer of Luther.   Albert Durer
had at this time reached the zenith of his fame and
popularity.   Raphael had openly expressed his admiration of him; the cities of Venice and Antwerp had made
him princely offers; the most cultured circles of Nuremberg were thrown open to him, and the noblest of its
citizens were his daily companions.   It was natural,
therefore, that Durer should have taken a keen interest
in the new doctrines.   In truth, he was attracted to Luther
by an irresistible sympathy.   The moral strength and
religious depth of his character, which had already been
reflected in the highest productions of his artistic genius,
in the loving and devout portraiture of Christ's Person,
and in the reverent realism with which he depicted the
most solemn events of Christ's earthly life as though they
might have taken place in the Nuremberg of his own day,
harmonized in a remarkable manner with the moral and
religious characteristics of Luther's writings.   The Edict
of Worms excited strong feelings of repugnance in most
of the Imperial cities on account of the number and
enthusiasm of Luther's followers.   There was a long
debate in the Council of Nuremberg; but it was finally
decided to adopt a prudent policy, to publish the Edict,

and to forbid the printing of Luther's books. At the same time the strong leaning of the members towards the Evangelical doctrines was shown. Two city livings fell vacant, and both were filled by the appointment of avowed adherents of the Reformation, formerly students at the University of Wittenberg, one of them an enthusiastic admirer of Luther and a personal friend of Melanchthon.

In the autumn of 1522 the Imperial Diet met at Nuremberg. When the religious question was brought forward, it became evident at once how rapidly Lutheran opinions were gaining ground. The citizens of Nuremberg saw clearly that no serious attempt would be made to enforce the Edict of Worms, and urged the Town Council to permit the free preaching of the Gospel and to remove ecclesiastical abuses. The clergy began to proclaim the new doctrines with increasing boldness. What was a still more ominous sign, the reformed teaching began to penetrate into the monasteries. A preacher in the church of the Dominicans who denounced monastic vows, escaped from the monastery, and when the Prior demanded that he should be sent back, the Town Council refused to grant the request. In defiance of the Papal Bull and the Imperial ban, Luther's books were read more eagerly than ever; the printing-presses of Nuremberg were engaged in producing broadsheets which spread over the whole country; and itinerant pedlars and colporteurs sold Luther's works in every quarter and corner of the city. The Diet, in spite of all opposition, postponed the execution of the Edict of Worms, and renewed the demand for a Free and General Council. The favourable attitude which the majority of the Diet took up towards the Evangelical cause produced a great effect in Nuremberg. The Town Council felt that their hands were free, and that it was no longer needful to disguise the opinions which they secretly held.

A new Diet was summoned to meet at Nuremberg in the first weeks of 1524. Before it assembled, a momentous

change had taken place at Rome. Leo the Tenth's
successor, the reforming Pope, Adrian the Sixth, had died
after a pontificate of a few months, and with him expired
for many years the reforming zeal of the Church of Rome.
Clement the Seventh, his successor, resembled Leo the
Tenth in his indifference to the spiritual interests of the
Papacy and his desire for its temporal aggrandizement.
Cardinal Campegio appeared as Papal Legate at the new
Diet. In March, 1524, he arrived at Nuremberg, and in
a private interview with one of the chief citizens unbosomed
himself without reserve. The picture which he drew of
the state of Nuremberg is a striking proof of the progress
which the reformed doctrines had made in less than seven
years. "Everyone," he said, "held the doctrine of
Justification by Faith; Confession and the Mass were
totally disregarded; in nearly five hundred houses meat
was eaten on fast days; all the bookstalls were heaped
with Lutheran books." Matters at last came to such
a pass that Campegio was afraid to leave his house,
and the Bishop of Bamberg, in whose diocese Nuremberg
lay, was insulted by abusive ditties which were sung after
him in the streets. During Lent, 1524, in presence of
the Papal Legate and in spite of his express prohibition,
the Eucharist was administered in both kinds in the city
churches. What made a still greater impression, not
only upon the city, but also upon the members of the
Diet, was the news that Queen Isabella, wife of the
deposed King of Denmark and sister of Charles the Fifth,
had received the Eucharist according to the Evangelical
rite from the hands of the chief minister of Nuremberg.

Then the Town Council wrote to the Bishop of Bamberg: they urged that, on account of the strong Evangelical
tendencies which prevailed in Nuremberg, they could not
put down the innovations which had already been introduced without exciting a revolt among the inhabitants.
The Bishop's only reply was to lay the city under sentence
of excommunication, and Nuremberg retorted by casting

itself practically free from Episcopal jurisdiction. The Council saw that the time had now come for the final settlement of the religious question : they determined to follow an example which had already been set, and to hold a public disputation. By the Lutheran party this offer was eagerly accepted, by the Romanist party with great reluctance. On the sixth day of the disputation the Romanists sent a memorial to the Council, refusing to accept them as judges because they were not impartial, professing their readiness to obey the Bishop of the diocese in all things, and offering to submit to the decision of three Universities.

The immediate result of the disputation was that the Council openly ranged itself on the side of the Reformation, ordered the dissolution of the monasteries and nunneries, made all ecclesiastical persons subject to the supreme authority of the civic magistrates, suppressed all clerical immunities of every kind, compelled the clergy to enrol themselves as burghers, and forced them to pay taxes like all other citizens. When this question had been disposed of, another problem which presented graver difficulties pressed for a solution. How were the endowments which had been bestowed by the liberality of former generations to be dealt with ? On this point the Council had recourse to the wise and temperate advice of Melanchthon. He strongly urged that the income should be applied to the maintenance of the Evangelical clergy and of divine service, and the Council proceeded to act at once in accordance with this advice. The question of clerical marriage was decided in accordance with the reformed doctrine : all clergymen who had concubines were ordered to dismiss them within eight days, or to be united with them in lawful wedlock. The ecclesiastical laws of fasting, which had excited the greatest ill-will and the strongest opposition among the people, were abolished. Many of the holy-days which had fostered the tendency to saint worship were struck out of the calendar : of the numerous

festivals in honour of the Virgin only three were retained.
Still more important was the regulation of the marriage
laws : on the principle that these laws rightfully fell under
the cognizance of a Christian government of Christian
laymen it was decided that all legislation on this subject
belonged to the Council as the guardians of the common
weal.

Immediately after the definite establishment of the
Reformation at Nuremberg the Diet met at Spires in
1526.   Five years had passed since the Edict of Worms,
and heresy, instead of having been crushed, had waxed as
great as the Fame of the poet :

> " Ingrediturque solo et caput inter nubila condit."

The language of the disaffected members of the Diet
was bolder and more uncompromising than ever.   When
the leaders of the Reformation, the Elector of Saxony, the
Landgrave of Hesse, and the Dukes of Luneburg, entered
the city and rode through it in procession, they and their
attendants bore on their sleeves as the sign of their unshaken
resolve, conspicuously embroidered for all men to see, the
monogram V.D.M.I.E. ("Verbum Dei manet in æternum").
The Elector and the Landgrave had brought their chaplains
with them ; they used the courtyards of their hostelries
for religious services ; the doors were flung open ; the
people for miles round Spires flocked together to hear the
new doctrines ; one sermon was preached every day, and
two on holy-days, before congregations which sometimes
numbered thousands, in defiance of the Emperor's Vicegerent, the Electoral Archbishops, and the Bishops of
the Empire.   No such scene had ever been witnessed
within the boundaries of Germany : it is not surprising
that it created the most profound sensation through the
length and breadth of the country.

The Imperial cities pressed the most sweeping demands
upon the Diet.   But the most remarkable and significant
of all was that the Evangelical clergy should receive

permission to preach the Gospel without reserve throughout
the Empire, and that all members of the Diet should deal
with the ceremonies and usages of the Church according
to their good pleasure, until a free and impartial Council
should pass judgment upon them. This demand led to
prolonged discussions. It was impossible to reconcile it
either with the Bull of the Pope or with the Edict of the
Emperor. Yet so great was the strength of the Evangelical party and the bitterness against the Church of Rome,
that the most obstinate Romanists were compelled to give
way. It was resolved that all members should live and
govern in matters of religion as they hoped and trusted to
answer for their conduct to God and the Emperor. At
the same time it was decided that an embassy should be
sent to Charles to request him, in union with the Pope, to
summon as soon as possible a Free and General Council,
or, if this were impossible, a Free Assembly of all the
Estates of the Empire under the presidency of the Emperor.
Till this could be done, the Emperor should be graciously
pleased to suspend the execution of the Edict of Worms,
since some of the members could not enforce it on conscientious grounds, and others feared to excite a revolt
among their subjects if they made the attempt.

While the religious movement which originated with
Luther was shaking the German Empire to its centre,
Zwingli was the leader of another movement, essentially
the same in its character and objects, within the boundaries of the Swiss Confederation. Like Luther, the Swiss
reformer was pre-eminently fitted for his task. As a
Humanist, filled with the deepest admiration for the
master minds of Greece and Rome, he sympathized profoundly with the mighty intellectual movement in which
for the first time the spirit of liberty burst its Medieval
cerements and drew breath in an ampler air; and, like
Saint Paul, he sought even in the heathen writers for traces
of the divine revelation which God had vouchsafed to
Gentile and Jew alike—scattered rays of the Light which

lighteth every man that cometh into the world. As a
theologian he studied the Bible intensely, copying out
Saint Paul's Epistles in the original Greek to imprint
them more perfectly on his memory, imbibing from the
sacred writings a love of truth which became with him
an overpowering passion, and which moved him to exclaim
that nothing could make man more like God than the
truth ; for as he loved and honoured the truth more deeply,
he approached more nearly to God and resembled Him
more closely. As an assistant priest at Einsiedeln, one
of the most celebrated of the holy places of Europe,
frequented yearly by crowds of pilgrims, he was brought
face to face with one of the most practical abuses of the
Medieval Church, and was led to examine and set forth
with transparent clearness the Scriptural doctrine of the
forgiveness of sin. As army chaplain to the Swiss forces
in Lombardy during the campaigns of 1513 and 1515, he
learnt to realize all the evils of the mercenary system which
had induced the Pope, the Emperor, and the French King
to court the Swiss as assiduously as Cyrus the Younger in
the days of Xenophon courted the warlike Greeks, and
which drew the brave and simple-minded mountaineers
into the vortex of the dynastic and territorial struggles
of Europe.

It is interesting to observe how strongly the religious
life of Zwingli during these years contrasts with Luther's.
There is no trace in Zwingli of the torturing doubts, the
inward self-questionings, the ascetic striving after a perfect
life, the intolerable burden of an unquiet conscience, the
haunting sense of unworthiness and sin, which embittered
Luther's monastic life and which invest his struggles with
such a pathetic interest. Zwingli's spiritual development
advanced in an even course, moving from stage to stage
without hesitation and misgiving, without spasmodic
efforts and violent recoils. The intellectual difference
between the two Reformers corresponded to this
difference in their religious character. As a born leader

of men, able to sway their hearts by the magic of his
inspiration, entering into different moods and interpreting
diverse characters with an insight which none of his contemporaries could rival, possessed of the eloquence red
hot with passion which finds a natural expresion in
thoughts that breathe and words that burn, Luther displayed a genius to which Zwingli could lay no claim.
The special gifts of the Swiss reformer were of a different
order. With him clearness of thought and lucidity of
expression took the place of passionate and entrancing
eloquence. The incisiveness of his polemical writings
and the judicial power of his theological reasoning remind
the English reader at one time of Chillingworth and at
another of Hooker. He possessed the keen and logical
mind which detected at once the weak points in an
opponent's case and the flaws in an opponent's argument.
To this dialectical power he was beyond all question
largely indebted for his success as a reformer. No contro-
versialist of the sixteenth century except Calvin surpassed
him in argumentative readiness and force.

The reputation which Zwingli had acquired at
Einsiedeln led, at the close of the year 1518, to his election as priest in the Minster of Zurich. It was here that he
first acquired an European celebrity. For nearly thirteen
years he was identified with the religious and political
life of Zurich. His first object on entering upon his new
office was to set before the people fully and clearly the
teaching of the New Testament. In fulfilment of this
purpose he preached a series of homilies on the whole of
Saint Matthew's Gospel, on the Acts of the Apostles, on
the First Epistle to Timothy, and on the Epistle to the
Galatians. From Saint Paul he turned to Saint Peter.
From Saint Peter he turned to the Epistle to the Hebrews.
No such courses of sermons, so complete, so systematic,
and so masterly, had been preached in any Swiss church
within the memory of man.

It is a proof of the wise, temperate, and prudent spirit

in which Zwingli undertook his Reformation that up to
the close of 1522 no change had been made in the existing
ecclesiastical system, no abuses had been removed, and no
public step had been taken for the establishment of the
Evangelical Church. Zwingli was content to sow the
good seed, and to let it spring up day and night, men
knew not how. At last, after four years of his ministry,
Zwingli, faithful to his principle of leaving the responsibility for religious changes with the rulers of the people,
urged the Council of Zurich, in justice to himself, to hold
a public disputation on the religious questions at issue
between the two parties. After long deliberation the
Great Council resolved to adopt his proposal, and fixed
January 29th, 1523, as the date for the Conference.

This discussion at Zurich was one of the most marked
and visible signs of the change which was coming over
Christendom. It had nothing in common with the
theological disputations between learned Doctors in the
Middle Ages, confined to one or two theological questions,
carried on in a dead language, and referred for decision to
the theological faculty of an University. The practical
genius of Zwingli discerned at once how great would be
the value of a popular discussion, carried on in the vulgar
tongue, in which anyone might freely interpose with questions, arguments, and objections, held under the presidency
of eminent laymen who were profoundly interested in the
result, and decided by open reference to the Bible in the
original languages. He saw the immense advantage of
such a popular discussion and authoritative decision over
the appeal to a future Council which was the favourite
weapon of the German reformers, and which, in Zwingli's
contemptuous language, was likely to be realized when the
Parthian should drink of the Arar and the German of
the Tigris.

On the day of the disputation an audience of six hundred
persons gathered in the hall of the Great Council of Zurich,
including the members of the Council, a number of the

clergy and burghers, and three representatives of the Bishop of Constance. In the centre sat Zwingli, with Latin, Greek, and Hebrew Bibles open on the table before him. The proceedings were opened by the Burgomaster, who stated the object of the meeting. Then Zwingli spoke: he had been reviled as a heretic because for four years he had preached the Gospel of Christ which contained all truth : the sixty-five Theses which he had drawn up and published contained the sum total of his teaching, and he hoped to prove that they were in harmony with the Gospel. Faber, the Bishop's Vicar-General, followed with an evasive speech, in which he dwelt on old, praise-worthy customs and ancient traditions, on the meeting of a General Council of Bishops, and on the impossibility of deciding religious questions unless they were submitted to the learned faculties of Paris, Cologne, and Louvain. The discussion which followed was a discussion only in name, so few and feeble were the objections of the Romanists, so cogent and forcible were Zwingli's replies. At its close the Burgomaster adjourned the meeting to the afternoon. When the audience reassembled, the Burgomaster announced the resolution of the Council: " Since no one has been able to convict Master Ulrich Zwingli of error, we, the Burgomaster and the Lesser and Greater Councils of Zurich, after mature deliberation, have determined that Master Ulrich Zwingli shall continue to preach the genuine divine scripture according to the Spirit of God to the best of his ability. We also command all other priests, pastors, and preachers to preach nothing else in public except what can be proved from the Holy Gospel and the canonical Scriptures."

The example which Zwingli had set was recognized as a precedent in German Switzerland. In October, 1523, a second disputation was held at Zurich, and was followed by the removal of images from churches and by changes in the service of the Mass. In the summer of 1526 a disputation was held at Baden in Aargau. Zwingli was not present, but was represented by his friends with whom he kept up daily communication. The result was that Basle enrolled itself in the ranks of the reformed cities. At the beginning of 1528 a disputation was held at Berne, which lasted for eighteen days, and in which Zwingli by general consent was pre-eminently distinguished. The accession of Berne to the Evangelical cause produced a great effect. It gave Zurich a powerful ally in the Confederation, ecclesiastically as well as politically. But it also spread the influence of Zwingli's teaching over a wider circle, including French-speaking Switzerland and some of the Imperial towns of South Germany.

If we were to regard Zwingli as a religious reformer and nothing else, we should form a very inadequate conception of his work and character. The truth is that his political activity was little less important than his spiritual influence. Zwingli, like an Athenian or Roman citizen in ancient times, and like an inhabitant of Florence and Milan in the twelfth century, was compelled to form a thoughtful estimate of political forces and tendencies, and to pass an independent judgment upon urgent problems of civic life. Only a few years before Zwingli's birth the Swiss Confederates had won the glorious victories over Charles the Bold of Burgundy, which had filled Europe with their fame. Zwingli's youthful patriotism was inflamed by tales of heroic deeds which loomed as large in the imagination of the Swiss boy as the feats of arms at Salamis and Thermopylæ in the imagination of the Athenian or Spartan. He did not hesitate to denounce in the austere and lofty spirit of an Old Testament prophet the pernicious system of mercenary warfare which was decimating and demoralizing his beloved people. " Those who risk their life," he exclaimed, " in battle for truth, religion, righteousness, and country, are faithful and godly men. But as for these bloodthirsty and mercenary soldiers, who march to battle for filthy lucre's sake, I believe that there is nothing on earth more godless and

criminal than their conduct, and that such soldiers deserve
the name of freebooters and not of Christians."

The commanding personality of Zwingli and his fervid
expostulations soon wrought a change in Zurich. He
awakened the slumbering consciences of his fellow-
citizens; he opened their eyes to the national sins; all
that was pure and patriotic in the Canton started instinctively forward and ranged itself on his side. The first
sign of the new order of things was the unanimous rejection of an alliance which Francis the First proposed to
Zurich against the Emperor and the Pope. In 1521,
when Cardinal Schinner appeared to enrol troops
nominally for the defence of the Pope, according to the
terms of the treaty made in 1515, Zurich felt bound to
comply. "Rightly," cried Zwingli, in the bitterness of
his soul, " do the Cardinals wear red hats and red cloaks :
shake them, and red ducats and crowns fall out ; wring
them, and there runs out the blood of son, father, and
brother." At last he gained his object : clergy and laity,
rulers and citizens, took an oath to receive no more
presents, pensions, and gifts from foreign Princes. But
from this moment all the friends of the old system, all
who hankered after foreign gold, all that was sordid and
base in the Swiss Cantons, vowed enmity to the bold
patriot.

As the first ecclesiastical statesman of the Reformed
Churches, it was natural that Zwingli should attempt to
solve the momentous problem of the relations of Church
and State. In his opinion the principle of the Medieval
Papacy ought to be reversed; and instead of subordinating
the State to the Church, the Christian Church should be
merged in the Christian State, which was only the
Christian Church "writ large." The pattern for this
relation between Church and State was, he contended,
supplied by the sacred history of the chosen people.
Consistently with this principle he left with the Council
of Zurich the responsibility of deciding religious questions,

and constituted them the guardians of the Word of God.
It is evident that Zwingli's logical mind recoiled from no
consequences. He carried out the theocratic theory to its
uttermost results. The ruler in Israel, whether judge or
king, was bound to enforce at all costs the observance of
the divine laws of the heavenly King. The Mosaic law
made no distinction between a breach of the fifth or
seventh commandment of the Decalogue and a breach of
the sixth or eighth. If "citizen" was only another name
for "Christian," and "State" was only another name for
"Church," it necessarily followed that in Zurich, as in
Jerusalem, offences against morality must be treated as if
they were breaches of the State law, and that the same
measure must be meted out to sinners as to criminals;
and Zwingli did not shrink from the fullest application of
this startling theory.

The resolution of the Diet of Spires, in 1526, had
practically left the decision of religious questions to all
members of the Diet within their own dominions. It was
not long before the consequences of this decree were made
manifest. In Electoral Saxony, in the Margraviate of
Brandenberg, in the Landgraviate of Hesse, in Ulm,
Augsburg, and Strasburg, as well as Nuremberg, measures
were at once taken for organizing and endowing the new
Churches; and this example was followed in Luneburg
and East Friesland. In the dioceses of Schleswig and
Lubeck large numbers were won over to the Reformed
faith. One of the greatest changes took place in North-
East Germany. Albert of Brandenburg, Grand Master
of the Order of the Teutonic Knights in Prussia, and
brother of the Margrave of Brandenburg, became an
adherent of the Reformation, obtained the leave of the
King of Poland, his suzerain, to change his Grand
Mastership into a Dukedom, and married a Danish
Princess.

This ceaseless advance of the Reformed doctrines was
eyed with the greatest disfavour by those who clung to

the old faith, and filled them with serious alarm.   Yet no effectual measures were taken to check the new religious movement.   Isolated efforts were indeed made here and there to crush the Evangelical preachers.   But the voice of the Empire, represented by the Estates in the Imperial Diet, did not make itself heard.   A Diet had been summoned at Ratisbon for the year 1527, but the attendance of the Estates was so poor that no business could be transacted.   In the following year another Diet met at Ratisbon which was closed by the Emperor's command. Finally, in November, 1528, a new summons was sent out for a Diet at Spires in February, 1529.

On March 15th the new Diet was opened by a speech from Frederick, the Count Palatine, and the Emperor's mandate was read, " more severe " (wrote the Elector of Saxony) " than any which I or any other members of the Diet have ever heard."   A Committee of the Diet was appointed to consider this and to report upon it.   Meanwhile the scenes of the previous Diet of Spires were renewed.   An Edict had been issued forbidding all and sundry in stringent terms to attend the sermons in the Elector of Saxony's hostel.   The presence of a large number of ecclesiastical lords sufficiently accounted for the issuing of this Edict.   But it remained a dead letter. At each service on Palm Sunday the audience numbered about 8,000, and, if we may trust the Elector's account, there was a large attendance at every service during the whole time that the Diet was sitting.   The majority of the Committee, like the majority of the Diet itself, were devoted members of the Church of Rome ; they therefore drew up a decree to embody the views and wishes of Charles.   After referring to the decree of the last Diet of Spires and recapitulating its terms, they added that, as it had been completely misunderstood and made the pretext for the adoption of all kinds of new doctrines, it was determined that all who up to the present time had observed the Imperial Edict of Worms should continue to observe it, and that the other Estates who had adopted the new doctrines should as far as possible refrain from all further innovations till a General Council had met.

This decree was energetically opposed by the Evangelical party, but Archduke Ferdinand, the Emperor's brother and vicegerent, relying on the support of the majority, disregarded their protest. Only one course, therefore, was open to them. To justify their action in the eyes of Christendom they drew up and read publicly on April 19th the celebrated Protest against the decree of the Diet which gave rise to the world-famed name of Protestant. In this manly and dignified document they triumphantly vindicated their own consistency, and conclusively demonstrated the inconsistency of their opponents. "Either" (such was in effect their argument) "suffer us to remain as we are, or place us before the tribunal to which we, as well as you, are content to appeal. If a Free Council or a General Assembly of the German nation can alone decide the questions in dispute, it is grossly unfair to forestall their judgment and to treat us as though we had been already condemned. Three years ago, without a single remonstrance, you consented unanimously to treat the Edict of Worms as null and void: to-day you attempt to enforce it as the wisest and justest of legislative measures. Six years ago you recognized as fully as ourselves the manifold iniquities of the ecclesiastical system: to-day they are still unremoved, and yet you will not suffer us to test them by God's Word. We have, therefore, no option but to turn from your shifting opinions to the solid ground of Holy Writ on which we have long since immovably taken our stand." A few days later they drew up an appeal, recapitulating the main arguments of the protest, and laying stress on the fact that their opponents had attempted to bear them down by a numerical superiority: they declared in the most unqualified manner that in a question which concerned each individual member the voice of the majority had no binding force. They appealed, therefore, from the decree of the Diet to the Emperor, to a Free or National Council, or to any impartial or competent judge. The protest and the appeal were signed by the Elector of Saxony, the Landgrave of Hesse, the Margrave of Brandenburg, the Dukes of Luneburg, and the Prince of Anhalt. Among the Free and Imperial cities there was for the first time a division of opinion. Fourteen cities, situated for the most part in southern and western Germany, and headed by Strasburg, Ulm, Nuremberg, and Constance, openly avowed their faith in the Reformed doctrines, and united with the Princes in signing the protest and the appeal.

The events of the last eight years had clearly shown what a grotesque anomaly the Medieval Empire had become. At the greatest crisis in the history of the German people they had been deserted by their Head. The mighty Confederation which excited the wonder of contemporary historians as the most marvellous political fabric recorded in the annals of history had been left without the strong hand and the controlling will. Electors, Landgraves, and Margraves, Princes, Dukes, Counts, and Imperial Cities, had been suffered to follow their own devices. The authority of the Emperor had been defied, and his Edict, the most momentous edict which any Emperor had put forth for centuries, was openly set at nought. During all these years Charles had been absorbed in his ambitious schemes, engrossed by leagues and alliances, spinning the careful webs of his diplomacy in every country of Europe, endeavouring to win over England, straining every nerve to checkmate France, striving to make the Popes his vassals, enlarging his hereditary dominions in the Low Countries, wasting his time, his blood, and his wealth in the plains of Italy, the fatal Helen whose seductive charms had bewitched the Princes of Europe and had avenged her terribly of her conquerors. In the midst of these vast schemes he completely forgot the vital interests of Germany, allowed his imperial power to fade into a shadowy phantom, and neglected the duty of learning by personal observation, and checking by personal influence, the vast progress which heresy was making in the Holy Roman Empire. How, indeed, could a monarch whose first thoughts were for the greatness of Spain and for his own glory find time to dabble in the petty questions of religion and morality which were shaking Germany to its centre? How could a monarch whose troops had just stormed and sacked Rome unite heart and soul with the Pope for the defence of the Holy Catholic Church and the maintenance of the Holy Catholic Faith? How could a monarch who had just won the most glorious of victories, and had laid in the dust the power of his mightiest rival, turn aside to busy himself with the obscure doings of an obscure Elector, the patron of an obscure monk? At last the Diets of 1526 and 1529 startled him out of his self-satisfied composure. He began to realize that he no longer bore sway over an undivided Empire. He saw dimly that the day had gone by when the Imperial Diet would suffer him to deal with heresy in the simple and summary fashion of the fifteenth century, and that he might find more difficulty in bringing Luther to the stake than the Council of Constance and the Emperor Sigismund had found in burning Huss to death. He recognized the startling truth that the new-fangled printing-press might be more powerful than 50,000 veteran troops. He foresaw that the impalpable arms of conscientious conviction might be weapons more formidable than the fabled hammer of Thor in the northern legend. Whatever he did to assert his authority and to put down his disobedient subjects must be done quickly. The peace of Cambray had freed him from his European complications: he would go to Germany at once: he would preside at the next Diet in person: he would try the effect of gentleness and persuasion: if these failed, he would rally around him the orthodox members of the Empire, would rise in his might as the champion of the

Church, would vindicate his title as the Most Catholic King, and would smite this handful of heretics and disloyal subjects hip and thigh through the length and breadth of the land.   What chance was there that this scheme would fail, that the "protesting Estates" would persist in their protest when they saw him wielding his Imperial authority against them, that he who had forced the Pope to fly in ignominy and penury, and had seen the mighty King of France a prisoner in his Spanish capital, would be foiled by three or four German Princes ?

But if Charles was resolute, his opponents were more resolute still.   The fatal procrastination of Charles had given them ample time to sit down and count the cost of their great enterprise ;   Luther's appearance at the Diet of Worms had left an indelible impression :   his undaunted courage and burning enthusiasm had filled them with the same spirit as himself ;   argument and discussion had matured their opinions and deepened their convictions. Nor was this all.   The Reformation had spread like a forest fire : in Denmark, in Sweden, in the Low Countries, in the Swiss Confederation, in England, and in France, the bright flame was soaring heavenwards, piercing with its keen light the darkness of ages.   The torch of truth, as in ancient Greece, was handed from runner to runner, and the unbroken line stretched far as the eye could see.   The bold stand of the German Estates would cheer and nerve countless hearts beyond the limits of the Empire.   When Charles appeared at the Diet, they would present him with the articles of their faith; they would ask to have them read in the hearing of all men ; surely the words of truth would not be spoken in vain.   In this temper both parties prepared for the Diet of Augsburg in the summer of 1530.

The task of drawing up the Confession of Faith was assigned to Philip Melanchthon. Among the great Reformers Melanchthon holds a peculiar and distinctive place.   Born fourteen years after Luther, he had early acquired an

European reputation, to which the seal had been set by
the admiring eulogy of Erasmus. Through the recom-
mendation of the great Humanist and Hebrew scholar,
Reuchlin, whose near kinsman he was, he obtained the
post of Professor of Greek in the new University of
Wittenberg, and immediately gained the hearts of all who
heard him. No one was more enthusiastic in his praise
and admiration than Luther, who at one time described
himself as the Elijah destined to prepare Melanchthon's
way, at another as the rough forester compelled to hew
out the path along which Melanchthon, as the master
husbandman, planted, sowed, and watered. This admiration was fully reciprocated by Melanchthon, who recognized
at once the moral and spiritual greatness of his illustrious
companion. A close friendship sprang up between them
which was equally honourable to both. This friendship
was the more remarkable because there was a wide
difference between their characters. Melanchthon was the
shy, timid, retiring scholar who was ever sighing, like the
Psalmist, for the wings of a dove that he might flee away
and be at rest, or praying to be hidden in God's tabernacle
from the strife of tongues. On more than one occasion
he seems to have been betrayed into a serious error of
judgment by excess of consideration for his opponents, and
by his earnest desire for the things which make for peace.
On more than one occasion his extreme pliability exposed
him to the grave charge of having compromised the cause
of Evangelical truth. But these errors will be judged with
leniency by all who have realized how rare a gift it is to
preserve the golden mean in religious controversy, and
how hard it is for fair-minded men to reconcile generous
concessions to opponents with perfect justice and loyalty
to their own cause. Nor can it be doubted that
Melanchthon's moderation conferred inestimable benefits
on his party and on Evangelical Christendom at large.
It supplied a clear and indisputable proof that impartiality,
temperate statement, and measured argument were not

incompatible with the most fervent and unshaken adherence to the new religious doctrines. It conciliated men who were repelled by the vehemence and harshness of Luther. It carried dismay even into the ranks of his theological enemies, who confessed that it was easier to bear up against the ferocious attacks of Luther than to foil the " artifices and cunning " of Melanchthon.

The influence of Melanchthon was greatly increased by the knowledge that he was one of the most brilliant scholars of his day. In his intimate acquaintance with the language and literature of Greece as well as of Rome he had few rivals in Europe. At times his letters were sown as thickly as Cicero's with Greek words, phrases, and sentences. He shows a close familiarity with the most eminent of the Greek writers, and quotes in turn poets, dramatists, historians, and philosophers. Nothing can be more apposite (to give a single illustration) than his use of the profound maxim of Thucydides, ἀεὶ τὸ παρὸν βάρυ, to account for the melancholy change which had come over many who had welcomed with enthusiasm the first dawn of the Reformation. In his ardent zeal for the cause of education he was surpassed by none of his contemporaries. His colleagues in the University of Wittenberg bore touching testimony after his death to the stimulating effect of his presence and example, to the ardour with which he threw himself into their studies as well as his own, and to the generous and unselfish help which he was always ready to give them. The keen interest which he took in his pupils and the warm affection which he felt for them were cordially reciprocated, and the students who attended his lectures frequently numbered fifteen hundred.

But Melanchthon's work in his University was only part of his work. Among his correspondents were the crowned heads of England, France, Poland, Sweden, Denmark, and Hungary, as well as a number of lesser Princes. Henry the Eighth and Francis the First, in turn, sent pressing requests that he would come to their Courts to confer with them on religious questions, and Cranmer begged him to fill the chair of theology at Cambridge. Indeed, the theology of Melanchthon may be traced unmistakably in the Articles of the English Church, of which Cranmer was the principal author. Not only the Princes and leaders of Christendom, but cities, universities, churches, preachers, and laymen, wrote to consult him on the most diverse subjects. At times he almost sank down in despair beneath the unintermittent stress of work. " What the poets write of the toils of the damned in Tartarus " (so he complained to an intimate friend) ". is mere child's play compared with those which bow me down."

One more feature of Melanchthon's work must not be passed over in silence. It was of the utmost importance that a religious movement which emphasized the claims and rights of the Christian laity, in opposition to the sacerdotal exclusiveness of the Medieval Church, should have a Christian layman as one of its most eminent representatives, and should prove that an earnest, pious, and learned Christian, even though he were not a minister of the Gospel, was capable of handling the deepest religious questions with a mastery which had not been attained by any contemporary Pope or Cardinal. It is this vindication of the rights of the Christian laity which gives Melanchthon his peculiar claim to the respect and admiration of Evangelical Christians. Probably no layman since the beginning of the Dark Ages has so deeply influenced the theology of Christendom.

The Confession of Augsburg, the earliest and in some respects the most important of the Protestant Confessions, falls naturally into three parts. Some Articles treat of the doctrines on which there was practically no difference between Protestants and Romanists ; some set forth the distinctive doctrines of the Reformation which will be examined in the following chapters ; four of them deal

with the practical abuses of the Church of Rome, which
were regarded by the German Reformers as the most
dangerous and the most offensive.   The twenty-third
Article, on the marriage of priests, gives utterance to the
grievous complaint of all classes and orders that priestly
celibacy has borne fruit in gross immorality and flagrant
vices, that in spite of God's commands, the practice of the
Early Church, and the scandals which an enforced celibacy
causes, priests are put to death for the fictitious crime of
entering into lawful wedlock.   In the twenty-seventh
Article, on monastic vows, Melanchthon draws attention to
the shameful practice by which boys and girls were inveigled
into taking the vows, nay, sometimes were even forced
to take them, before they had attained the canonical age ;
and declares that on this ground alone the vast majority
would be amply justified in quitting their monasteries.
The twenty-sixth Article, on the distinction of meats,
briefly summarizes the evils arising from the general
belief that the observance of the laws of fasting was a
good work which served to earn grace and to make satisfaction for sins, and that the neglect to observe them was
a deadly sin.   Closely connected with this is the twenty-
eighth Article, on the ecclesiastical power.   What is the
origin of this error that men by observing ecclesiastical
traditions can make satisfaction for sins or merit grace
and justification, and that by neglecting to observe them
they infallibly incur damnation ?   It has its source,
Melanchthon answers, in the arrogant claims of Popes and
Bishops to supreme and undisputed sway over the Church
of God ; in their assertion that by the laws which they
invent they can bind men's consciences with adamantine
chains ; that it is in their power to heap holy days upon
holy days, to add ceremonies to ceremonies, to multiply
fasts indefinitely, and to prescribe incessantly new traditions ; and that these human laws are as divine as the
laws of God.   It is a noteworthy fact that these four
Articles take up as much space as all the remaining

Articles put together. Such was the general character of the Confession on which Melanchthon spent weeks of intense labour, weighing every word and every phrase for fear of saying too little or too much, softening down every expression which might cause needless irritation, and avoiding even the mention of any name which might jar upon the listener's ear.

CHAPTER III.

THE DISTINCTIVE DOCTRINES OF THE REFORMATION.

THE services which the Reformers rendered to theology were very great. The mere bulk of their writings fills us with amazement, when we remember that they were not only students, toiling with uninterrupted assiduity in the peaceful seclusion of monastic cloisters or University libraries, but great ecclesiastical statesmen, inaugurating, directing, and controlling a new religious movement, over-whelmed with the care of all the Churches, admitted to the Councils of Princes, confronted with practical questions and unforeseen problems of supreme difficulty, surrounded by watchful and powerful enemies, checked by lukewarm and faithless friends, at one time wandering into exile, and at another carrying their lives in their hands. Yet, in spite of these hindrances to their literary activity, they were able to pour a flood of fresh light upon almost every branch of theological science, upon exegesis, dogmatic theology, pastoral theology, and Christian ethics. Even after the lapse of three centuries and a half, the student who turns to their writings is astonished at the power and originality which are stamped upon countless pages of their volumi-nous works. In many points they not only widened and enlarged the borders of Christian truth, but completely transformed the current opinions of the Christian Church. In their treatment of almost every doctrine they sowed the seeds of new ideas and of fresh conceptions of divine truth, some of which have only within the last century sprung up and borne fruit abundantly. To attempt a complete and impartial estimate of their labours would be a task of surpassing magnitude, for it would cover the whole field of Christian thought. But it may be possible within a moderate compass to give a clear idea of the most important and distinctive of the Reformed doctrines, of their wide divergence from the teaching of the Medieval theologians, and of their antagonism to the existing Church system.

The Reformers on the very threshold of their labours laid down, in opposition to the Medieval theologians, the great principle which has been retained throughout Evangelical Christendom to the present day as the foundation of Evangelical theology, that the Bible as the Word of God is the primary and absolute authority for the fashioning of the Christian's faith and the guiding of the Christian's life. The Bible was the voice of God Himself speaking through His servants, the foundation and rock on which the Church was built upon the chief Corner-Stone, the one unfailing rule and test of all doctrine, all godly living, and all worship of God, containing fully and perfectly all that is needful and serviceable for man's justification and salvation. Indeed, the reason for this supremacy of Scripture was obvious: so prone was the human mind to forget God, so inclined to every kind of error, so bent on devising new forms of faith and worship, that a sacred and inviolable depository of truth was imperatively needed to secure it from being blotted out through the neglect, or overlaid with the errors, or corrupted by the presumption, of men.

The Reformers, therefore, put aside without hesitation all decrees of Councils and opinions of Fathers as imperfect, fallible, and erroneous, unless they were in harmony with the Bible. Nay, even the collective Christian Church may err and fail for a time, though it cannot permanently continue in error or in sin. Conscious of her ignorance and weakness, of her manifold errors and failings, the Church knows that she must bring them to the touchstone of God's Word to be corrected and removed. If, therefore, any doctrine or ordinance of the Church is adduced, unsupported by the authority of God's Word, it is worthless, and no Christian can be bound by it. The clearest proof of this principle was found by the Reformers in St. Paul's words to the Galatians : " If any man preach any other Gospel to you than that ye have received, let him be accursed." Here St. Paul (they urged) places himself, the angels of heaven, and all teachers and masters on earth, in subjection to the Bible : the Bible alone shall rule, and all others (let them bear what name they will) shall submit to its sway, shall not be its lords and judges, but only its witnesses, pupils, and confessors.

At this point the Reformers were met by a serious objection. " How can the Bible," argued their opponents, " discharge the duty which you assign to it of judge and expositor of the Christian faith, when it is a patent fact that its language is ambiguous and obscure, when every error and every heresy that has marred and divided the Christian Church can be traced to its source in the dark sayings of the Bible ? Marcion and Arius, the Donatists and the Pelagians, all alike appeal to Scripture in support of their tenets. How would this be possible if the meaning of its words were as clear as daylight ? How could we know what the teaching of the Bible really is, if it were not for the decisive interpretations of Councils, Popes, and Fathers ? And if the ultimate decision rests not with the simple text but with the interpreters of the text, if it is they alone who can still the ceaseless strife of tongues and bring harmony out of chaos, what becomes of your boasted principle that Scripture is our sole and infallible guide to religious truth ? "

To this objection the Reformers returned a threefold answer. In the first place they denied the obscurity of Scripture. Was there a single syllable in Holy Writ to countenance the belief that the Father of lights flung the inspired writings upon the heavenly board of the Church, like the famous apple in the heathen mythology, to breed

discord and dissension among the children of the Kingdom?
Did not the language of the Bible itself supply the clearest
refutation of this monstrous suggestion? The Father bade
us hear His beloved Son. But to what purpose should we
hear Him, if He came to scatter utterances as ambiguous
as the ancient oracles? The Psalmist spoke of God's
Word as a lantern to his feet and a light unto his path.
But how could it give him light, if it was itself encompassed with triple shades of darkness? St. John expressly
told his converts that they needed not that any man should
teach them, seeing that they had an unction from the Holy
One which taught them all things. But why should he have
written this misleading statement, if the Spirit's teaching
was valueless without the comments and interpretations
of human teachers?

In the second place, they denied that the Fathers claimed
any such authority over the Bible as the adherents of the
Church of Rome claimed on their behalf. The Fathers
ceaselessly confessed their dependence upon Scripture;
they quoted Scripture in order to explain and illustrate
Scripture. If they found any passage of the inspired
writings dark or difficult, they resorted to other passages
in order to solve the difficulties or illumine the darkness.
They confessed that their Commentaries had no value
and no authority, except in so far as they were faithful
interpreters of the divine meaning. Nothing could have
been further from their intentions than to force their
opinions upon Scripture with an imperious dogmatism.

Lastly, they contended that errors, divisions, and heresies
had their root, not in the obscurity of God's truth, but
in the perversity of men's minds. Men came to Scripture
with their prejudices, not to correct them, but to confirm
them. They framed their doctrines beforehand, and then
ransacked the Bible for any text, no matter how absurd
or impossible, which seemed to give them the faintest
shadow of support.

The Bishops of the Middle Ages wished to establish

their right to temporal sovereignty. What was simpler than to take St. Peter's words, " Ye are a royal priest-hood," and to distort the passage which invested all Christians with a spiritual pre-eminence into a sanction of episcopal arrogance ? The Pope set himself pre-sumptuously above the Emperor. What was more obvious than to take the Psalmist's description of the " greater light to rule the day and the lesser light to rule the night," to declare that the first part applied to the spiritual and the second to the temporal power, and to bolster up the Papal domination with words which were designed to extol the glory of God ? The Medieval Priest-hood coined the fiction of Purgatory. What could be more convenient than to wrest St. Paul's warning, " He shall be saved, yet so as by fire," from its natural context and its obvious meaning, and to misuse the precept of the wise master-builder for ministering to the sordid greed of Mass Priests ? No doubt, if Holy Writ were treated after this fashion, anything and everything might be proved from its words, and Christendom would soon be rent in twain for ever.

The Evangelical doctrine of Justification by Faith was in its practical results as important as the Evangelical doctrine of Holy Scripture. For in this doctrine the eternal problem, which every religion after its own fashion has attempted to solve, " What must I do to be saved ? " was stated afresh by the Reformers, and received an answer which carried conviction to the hearts of myriads, and brought peace and consolation to thousands of troubled consciences.

The Reformed doctrine of Justification by Faith was based upon the explicit words of St. Paul, that no man is justified by the works of the law, but by faith in Jesus Christ. But this faith was not a mere outward and formal profession such as St. James denounced—a faith like that of the devils who believed and trembled ; a faith which hovered upon the lips, but had no abiding seat in

the heart.   It was a conviction so profound, a confidence
so complete, an assurance so mighty, that death, and
hell, and the power of sin, and the accusing voice of the
Law, and the doubts of an anxious heart, and the terrors
of an evil conscience, could not prevail against it.   Nor
was it a mere historical faith in the truth of the Gospel
history, such a faith as might be placed in the Commentaries of Cæsar or the Chronicles of Froissart.   It rested
wholly upon God's grace ; it cast anchor with an unshaken
trust upon God's blessed promises; it riveted its gaze
upon the Cross of Christ ; it had ever upon its lips the
Psalmist's cry, " Enter not into judgment with Thy
servant, O Lord, for in Thy sight shall no man living be
justified "; it recognized the imperfection even of its best
works ; it fled from the throne of God's justice, where
all men must stand condemned, to the throne of God's
grace, where all sin is blotted out, as a drop of water
vanishes in the noonday heat of the sun ; it knew that
shortcomings, weakness, and sin were covered with the
Saviour's robe of righteousness ; it fell at Christ's feet,
not shrinking from Him as the stern and wrathful Judge,
but clinging to Him as the tender and loving Mediator,
ever ready to spread over the sinner the glorious heaven
of His mercy and forgiveness.   " The reason why faith
justifies," exclaimed Luther, " is that it lays hold of, and
has ever before it, the costly and glorious treasure which
is Christ.   And thus the Christian's righteousness is Christ,
Who is apprehended and dwells in the heart by faith ; for
which righteousness' sake God deems us to be righteous,
and accepts us as such, and gives us eternal life."

The Reformers could speak bitterly from their own
experience of the terrible results which had followed the
neglect of this doctrine.   Monks who had lived the strictest
lives, who had macerated their flesh with watchings,
fastings, and scourgings, till they were worn to mere
skeletons, were haunted at the approach of death with
such terrible misgivings, that hardened murderers faced

their end with more composure than these monastic
saints. Indeed, what assurance of salvation could men
have who spent their lives in laboriously piling up good
works, in feverishly scanning the lengthening catalogue
of their sins, and in anxiously reckoning whether they
had done enough, or had done it well enough, to obtain
acceptance with God ? Nor was this all. The speculative
consequences of ignoring this doctrine were as serious as
the practical. The Scholastic theologians had actually
taught that there was a righteousness which was the fruit
of the natural reason, and had pretended that the unre-
generate man, even without the help of the Holy Spirit,
could love God above all things. They went so far as
to assert that a man could earn forgiveness of sins by
his own works, and that God was obliged to give His
grace to men who did these works. " If this is Christian
righteousness," exclaimed Melanchthon, " what difference
is there between philosophy and the teaching of Christ ? "

But with this statement of the doctrine of Justification
by Faith the task of the Reformers was only half completed.
For religion is not a more essential part of Christianity
than morality. If Christianity, on the one hand, is the
absolutely perfect religion, revealing the nature of God
with unerring completeness, and proclaiming the only true
relation in which man can stand to Him, it is, on the
other hand, the highest morality, setting up the supreme
standard for the moral life, supplying the supreme motive
of moral action, gathering up into itself, and subordinating
to itself, the manifold forms of human activity in the
Family, in Society, and in the State.

Since the Reformers, in accordance with Scriptural
teaching, rejected the meritorious value of good works,
and declared that they had not, and could not have, any
lot or part in the believer's justification, what was the
place which they assigned to them in the Christian
system ? On what did they ground the necessity of good
works and the obligation to perform them? In answering

this question the Reformers followed five main lines of thought.

In the first place, they maintained that good works were the necessary fruits of faith. The faith which contented itself with profession without service, with words without deeds, was a spurious and not a genuine faith. If faith was no vain delusion or idle dream, but a divine work of the Holy Spirit within the man, mortifying the old Adam within him, transforming his character, and changing his heart and life, it was impossible that he should not ceaselessly do good works. " The man, without compulsion or constraint, is ready and willing to do good to all, to be the servant of all, to endure every kind of suffering for the love and praise of God Who has bestowed such mercy upon him. It is, therefore, as impossible to separate works from faith as to separate light and heat from fire."

In the second place, the Reformers insisted upon the necessity of good works as a test and proof to assure the believer of the reality of his faith, and as an outward and visible sign to make his faith manifest to men. The fruit does not make the tree good, but proves and reveals its goodness. In like manner the fruits which spring from faith bear witness to the reality of faith. The passion of love is one proof of our faith, the readiness to forgive is another, the kindly heart is another, the helping hand is another. In this lay the significance of the Scriptural example of Abraham, the father of the faithful. Though his faith was reckoned unto him for righteousness, God willed that he should be convinced of it by an irrefragable proof; and his obedience to the divine command manifested his faith to himself and to all men, moving them to glorify God on his behalf, and spurring them on to emulate his example.

In the third place, the Reformers maintained that good works necessarily spring from the changed relation in which the justified sinner stands to God. It is one aspect of this changed relation that the Christian is freed from the dominion of the Law. While we are under the power and dominion of the Law, we work by constraint and not willingly : we fulfil the Law, not by living to the Law, but by dying to the Law. Then faith assumes its sovereign sway : then a new power, a new light, and a new fire enters the heart, which works all righteousness, and fulfils all obedience, and mortifies the lusts of the flesh. It is another aspect of this changed relation if the believer's good works are described as the necessary consequence of his adoption by God. It is the mark of slaves to demand pay for their work. But faith has made the believer the son of God : he is an heir by adoption, and not by works : he needs not to toil for the reward, for the reward is already his ; and as a son he forestalls his Father's commands, and anticipates his Father's wishes, and labours with unwearied joy in his Father's strength.

In the fourth place, according to the Reformers, the obligation to moral action was implied in the Christian's relation to his fellow-men. So far from the Christian living for himself alone, it is more true to say that he should live for others alone : since he does not need his works for his own salvation, he is bound to lavish them all the more generously upon others. This is the true Christian motive for care of the body, that our health and strength may enable us to benefit our fellow-men, caring for one another, and bearing one another's burdens, serving our neighbour willingly, without thought of recompense, in joy and love.

In the fifth place, the Reformers emphatically denied the possibility of passing judgment upon good works in the abstract, and insisted that they only possessed value if they were done in faith. It is not the deed which matters, but the source and spring from which it flows. The most trivial act of the humblest believer, if it be done in faith, rivals in lustre the most heroic action of the greatest saint. The noblest work, if it be done from vain glory, or selfishness, or the love of praise, or the hope of receiving as much again, is marred by an ineradicable taint, and is abomination in the sight of God. Viewed in the light of faith, all the believer's works, whether they be great or small, whether they be few or many, are of equal worth, for the informing principle is the same in all. Faith is like the stamp on the coin which determines its value, like the crown on the monarch's head which distinguishes him from his fellow-men.

Thus, not content with rejecting the popular religious and ethical standards of their day, the Reformers laid down a most important principle which naturally followed from their doctrine of Justification by Faith and of Good Works, which revolutionized the current ideas of the later Middle Ages, and which justly entitles them to be called the apostles of common life. They maintained that the divine character of ordinary, homely, household works was clearly taught in God's Word, that such works were immeasurably superior to the so-called life of perfection, or " Angelic life," and that the believer who plied these works humbly and diligently had attained far more nearly to the fulfilment of the divine commandments than the most rigid ascetic.

The doctrine of the Church acquired a peculiar importance in the Reformers' eyes on account of the relation in which they stood to the ecclesiastical system of the Church of Rome. Their opponents were never weary of reiterating the charge that they had apostatized from the Church of Christ, that they had forfeited the supernatural means of grace, that they had cut themselves off from the fellowship of the Saints, and that they had sunk to the level of a heretical sect. The Reformers felt these charges keenly: they were firmly convinced of their injustice; and they were, therefore, led to examine and to state with fulness and precision the true doctrine of the Church.

If God had given men an inestimable treasure of truth in the inspired writings; if those writings needed no addition and no correction; if no doctrines, no laws, and no constitutions could be imposed upon men as necessary for the believer's eternal welfare, which were not enjoined in Holy Writ; if all other authorities, however ancient and however imposing, were as dust in the balance when weighed against the lively oracles of the Most High; if Councils, Fathers, and Saints could do nothing against the truth but for the truth; and if humble submission to God's revealed will was the most unfailing test of the Christian's faith: it was clear that the Church could only be found among those who accepted the Word of God with their whole heart, and clave to it with all their strength. To love this Word as the Word of her divine Spouse, to take it as the guide of her steps, to look to it alone as the touchstone and measure of all her words and actions, this is the supreme mark by which we may recognize the Holy Catholic Church. Wheresoever the Word is, there is the true knowledge of God, and there may the Church be found; there we may be assured that God is dwelling in her, and is speaking and working through her. The Church, therefore, may be defined as "the congregation of believers in which the pure Word of God is preached." To this definition the Reformers added another. The divine Founder of the Church had Himself ordained two visible channels and signs of spiritual union and invisible grace—the Sacrament of Baptism as the mark of the believer's admission into the Christian fellowship, and the Sacrament of the Lord's Supper as the pledge of his continuance in it. None might add to these sacred ordinances, nor alter them, nor tamper with them: they were coeval with the birth of the Christian Church, and could not pass away until faith had been changed into sight, and hope had given place to fruition in the perfected Kingdom of God; and therefore "the due administration of the Sacraments according to Christ's institution" was the second proof of the true Church.

But this definition of the Church was supplemented by an important distinction. The Church was no airy dream, no unsubstantial vision, stored up somewhere in the heavens, like Plato's ideal Republic. The Church, like every earthly polity, was evident to the sight and the hearing ; it possessed a local habitation and a name, visible signs of fellowship, visible assemblies for prayer and praise, visible places for the meetings of the faithful, visible Ministers, visible Courts for the determination of disputes and the administration of discipline. But this visible Church, even though she were the dwelling-place of the Holy Spirit and the depository of God's gifts of grace, was, like her individual members, liable to be seduced by false teachers and misled by evil counsellors : she might fall into partial apostasy and grievous sin : her virgin purity might be sullied, and her treasure of divine truth buried beneath manifold corruptions. Yet, however low she had sunk, there were ever in the midst of her the seven thousand who had not bowed the knee to the Baal of iniquity and error, who, like the Prophets of the old dispensation, held aloft the undimmed lamp of true faith and knowledge to rebuke a wicked and gainsaying generation.

Indissolubly connected, therefore, with the visible Church stood the invisible, the Church of the Elect from the beginning of the world, of the First-born whose names were written in heaven, who were Christians not by out-ward profession but by inward faith, known to the all-searching gaze of God alone. It was this invisible Church in which Christians professed their belief when they repeated the Article of the Creed, " I believe in the Holy Catholic Church " ; for in Scripture faith was always opposed to sight, and if the Church was an object of faith, it could not be an object of sight.

This distinction enabled the Reformers to answer the question, How far the Church of Rome, from whose communion they had deliberately separated, and whose teaching and system they openly denounced, deserved the name of Church ? Both Luther and Calvin allowed that the Roman communion was a Church, even though an erring and a faithless Church. For she called herself by the name of Christ, she possessed God's Holy Word, she administered the Sacraments of Baptism and the

Eucharist, and she proclaimed to her members the forgiveness of sins. But still more than this, she contained
within her pale all the holy and humble men of heart who
were members of the invisible Church; and wherever the
invisible Church was found, there, in whatever measure
and degree, the visible Church must also exist.

There were three charges in particular which the
advocates of the Church of Rome brought against the
Reformed Churches: they had forfeited the supernatural
grace of their services and sacraments by rejecting
the Apostolical succession in their Ministry; they had
refused to accept the decrees and decisions of General
Councils, which from the earliest ages had been regarded
as the inspired legislators of the Church; and they had
broken the unity of Christendom by quitting the fellowship of the "Vicar of Christ," the divinely appointed
Head of the Church.

The answer of the Reformers to the first charge turned
upon the double meaning of the phrase "Apostolical
succession." "There are," they said in effect, "two
kinds of succession—the succession of persons and the
succession of doctrine. What comparison can there
possibly be between the value of the two? What loss
is it to be without the former if we possess the latter?
Now, as in the days of the early Church, it is the true
Church which makes the lawful Ministry, and not the
lawful Ministry which makes the true Church. Of what
avail is it to have Bishops who can trace their lineal
descent from the Apostles, if they reject the doctrines
which the Apostles held, and hold the doctrines which the
Apostles rejected? What are they better than the false
prophets and the ravening wolves against which Christ and
St. Paul warned us? We reverence above all things the
writings of Prophets, Evangelists, and Apostles; we search
in their words for the pure and undefiled well of truth; we
refuse to swerve a hair's breadth from their precepts and
commandments; we cast aside, as they have bidden us,

the traditions of men and the fancies of a vain imagination. Which, therefore, approach most nearly to the true Catholic Church—you with the material succession of persons, or we with the spiritual succession of doctrine?"

The Reformers were all the more careful to meet the second charge because they repeatedly appealed during twenty-five years to a General Council for the settlement of religious differences, and refused to quit their ground within the Church till such a Council, lawfully summoned and lawfully held, had decided against them. It was essential, therefore, that, in their own justification, they should clearly state what they conceived the nature, the conditions, and the powers of a General Council to be.

At the outset they absolutely rejected the doctrine which had been laid down in the fifteenth century, and had been unquestionably accepted till the Reformation began, that a General Council, lawfully assembled, was under the direct inspiration of the Holy Spirit, that it could not err, and that the decrees and resolutions which it passed were as absolutely binding upon all Christians as the laws of God. Such a doctrine was completely at variance with the Reformers' doctrine of the supremacy of Scripture; it was completely refuted by their study of Church history. On the one hand, they found that the decisions of Councils had been partial and fragmentary; on the other hand, they had been purely negative. Not one of the Councils had even attempted a complete enunciation of the Christian faith; the four principal Councils had only decided four points of doctrine; and if all the decisions of all the Councils were put together, they would make a most imperfect summary of the Christian creed. Further, when their decisions were carefully examined, it was found that they did not increase the sum of Christian truth, but simply defended the old truth against the new errors of Arius or the new fancies of Nestorius and Eutyches. What, then, might General Councils fitly and legitimately do? They might condemn

new errors which threatened the foundations of the faith,
or new vices and superstitions which were undermining
the spiritual life; or they might ordain ceremonies in
accordance with St. Paul's precept, " Let all things be
done decently and in order." But they had no power
to enact new Articles of faith without the warrant of
Holy Writ, nor to order " good works " which are not
expressly ordered in the Bible, nor to impose new ceremonies to be observed on pain of mortal sin or on peril of
the conscience, nor to interfere in any way with temporal
laws and government, nor to establish in any form the
ecclesiastical tyranny of Bishops and Prelates. In short,
the Reformers recognized only two alternatives : Either
the decisions of the General Council conformed in letter
and spirit to God's Word, and therefore served for the
confirmation of the faith ; or its decisions clashed with
the teaching of Scripture, in which case they were null and
void, even though all the Apostles and all the Fathers had
been present in it. If an appeal was made to Christ's promise
to be in the midst of those who assembled in His Name, it
was replied that this was the very point which needed to be
proved by the results ; for it was just as easy for wicked
and dishonest Bishops to conspire against Christ, as for good
and honest Bishops to meet in His Name. And what
the character of some General Councils had been, how
iniquitous were the decrees which they had passed, and how
the few wise and upright members had been overpowered and
silenced by the many ignorant and unscrupulous members,
might be sufficiently learnt from the pages of history.

The Reformers dealt with the third charge in a still more
trenchant and uncompromising fashion. What were the
claims and what the proceedings of the Popes which justified their assumption of the awful title " Vicar of Christ " ?
The Pope claimed the sole right and power of electing,
ordaining, confirming, and instituting all Bishops and
Pastors, of making any laws that he pleased for the regulation of divine worship, of sanctioning changes in the

administration of the Sacraments, and of prescribing
alterations in Christian doctrine.   He demanded that all
his statutes and ordinances should be placed on an equality
with the Articles of the Christian faith and with Holy Writ,
so that they could not be disobeyed without mortal sin,
and added that all men, on pain of the loss of eternal
salvation, must believe in his power to do this.   Further,
the Pope did not confine his usurpations to the ecclesiastical
sphere; he encroached upon the rights and prerogatives of
the temporal power.   Pope Boniface, in his Bull " Unam
Sanctam," and the parasites of the Papacy in many passages
of the Canon Law, maintained that the Pope by divine
right was Lord over the Kingdoms of the world.   Acting
upon this principle, he filled all Europe with disorder,
seizing Principalities and Kingdoms, setting up and
deposing Emperors and Kings, branding them with
unrighteous excommunication, and stirring up unjust
wars against them.   Worse than this, he even attempted
to palliate his presumptuous sin by pleading Christ's
commands, interpreted the Keys of Heaven to mean the
possession of temporal sovereignty, and made the salvation
of souls depend upon the recognition of this impious claim.
Lastly, he claimed the right to alter the doctrines which
Christ Himself had delivered, and arrogated to himself
the power to bind and to loose not only in this world but
also in the world to come; he would not suffer that anyone
should judge him, but set himself above General Councils
and above the whole Church, asserting his superiority over
all Councils, and his ability to annul at pleasure all their
decrees.   This principle the Canon Law shamelessly
asserted, and upon this principle the Pope had shamelessly
acted.   Thus the Reformers, so far from acknowledging him
as the Vicar of Christ, recognized in him the three marks
which St. Paul ascribed to the Antichrist, that he bears
rule in the Church of God, that he teaches a doctrine
opposed to the doctrine of Christ, and that he makes
himself equal to God.

If, however, neither General Councils nor Popes were infallible, did it follow that there was no infallibility vested in the Church, and that an eternal atmosphere of doubt would brood for ever over the Christian community? " Not so," the Reformers answered ; " if God's Word is infallible, and the Church's very existence is linked to that Word, the Church draws her infallibility from the divine fountain-head, and no man may impugn it or take aught from it. The divine Founder of the Church has said that He knows His sheep and is known of them, because the Father has given them to Him, and they are all taught of God. These are the sheep who cannot err, who hear their Shepherd's voice and will listen to none other ; for he who is of God hears God's Word, the others do not hear it because they are not of God. This is the Church which cannot fail, the Church which follows the voice of the Good Shepherd, which draws all her light from the Father of Lights, and is taught by His Holy Spirit, and judges all things, but is herself judged of no man. This Church renounces her own authority, and discards her own wisdom, and mistrusts the inventions of her own reason, and is guided into all truth by the Spirit of Truth, Who brings to her remembrance whatsoever her King has said unto her."

In the doctrine of the Sacraments the Reformers no less decisively modified or repudiated the teaching of the Medieval Church. They began by drawing up a new definition of Sacraments. A Sacrament according to them must have been instituted by Christ Himself, and must be binding upon all members of the Christian Church. The first part of this definition excluded the Sacraments of Penance, Confirmation, and Extreme Unction ; the second part excluded the Sacraments of Matrimony and Ordination. It followed, therefore, that the seven Sacraments of the Medieval Church were reduced to two, Baptism and the Lord's Supper. Further, they denied that the mere administration of the Sacraments was of any value, or that they conferred grace, according to the technical expression of the Schoolmen, "Ex opere operato." On the contrary, they asserted in the strongest terms that Faith was a necessary condition of sacramental efficacy, and that the measure of spiritual grace which the Sacrament conferred depended absolutely upon the greater or less degree of faith in the recipient. In support of this view they were never weary of quoting St. Augustine's words that it is not the Sacrament, but faith in the Sacrament, which justifies. Again, they refused to encumber the Sacraments with the fantastic rites and ceremonies which the superstitious reverence or the superstitious credulity of the Middle Ages had gathered around them ; and they, therefore, unanimously rejected the exorcism of the Evil Spirit, the spittle, the salt, and the oil in Baptism, which had been added to the original institution of Christ and His Apostles. Lastly, they refused to recognize any distinction in the importance of the Sacraments, and discarded the tacit or avowed depreciation of the Sacrament of Baptism, in comparison with the Sacrament of the Eucharist, which had been prevalent in the Medieval Church.

But it was in their treatment of Eucharistic doctrine that the Reformers were most diametrically opposed to the teaching of the Medieval Church. Unhappily, the divisions which broke out among the adherents of the Reformation on the subject of the Eucharist have obscured and thrown into the background the important principles upon which all the Reformed Churches were agreed, and which separated them collectively from the Church of Rome. Those principles were seven in number.

In the first place, they rejected on Scriptural, historical, and theological grounds the doctrine of Transubstantiation, or the change of the Bread and Wine at the moment of consecration into the actual Body and Blood of Christ, though the accidents of the bread and wine remained ; and they ridiculed the metaphysical absurdity of a substance without accidents, and of accidents without a substance.* In the second place, they maintained that the consecrated elements only retained their sacramental efficacy during the sacramental service, and therefore condemned the reservation of either or of both the elements. In the third place, as a consequence of this, they condemned the practice of carrying about the consecrated wafer in solemn procession on Corpus Christi Day, and the adoration which was paid to it on such occasions. Fourthly, they denied that the Mass was a sacrifice in the Medieval sense, to be offered for the living and the dead; the only sacrifices which they recognized were the Communicant's sacrifice of praise and thanksgiving, and the sacrifice of the Communicant's body, soul, and spirit as a lively offering, holy, acceptable unto God. Fifthly, they denounced with equal vehemence the profane misuse of the Eucharist as a superstitious charm for averting the cattle plague and the swine fever, or for ensuring a good harvest and a successful haul of fish. Sixthly, they pronounced the refusal of the Cup to the Laity to be contrary to the plain words of Scripture, and to the known practice of the Early Church. Lastly, they indignantly reprobated the practice of selling Masses for the benefit of the living or the dead, as though a Christian's special privileges could be dependent upon his temporal advantages, or as if the shortening of his pains in Purgatory could hang upon the emptiness or fulness of his purse. These comprehensive and fundamental differences were of infinitely more moment than the differences which separated the followers of Luther from the followers of Calvin, and the followers of Calvin from the followers of Zwingli.

The difference of opinion between the Reformers and the Medieval theologians on the subject of the State was as

---

* According to the Scholastic theologians, the taste, colour, smell, &c., of the Bread and Wine were the "accidents," the Body and Blood of Christ were the "substance."

profound as the divergence of their views on the subject
of the Church.   The idea of the State in the Middle
Ages had been deeply coloured partly by the teaching of
St. Augustine, partly by the desperate struggle which had
been waged for generations between the Papacy and the
Empire.   St. Augustine laid down the doctrine that the
State, as the Kingdom of this world, has its living principle
in the realm of sin, and that it cannot be brought into
harmony with the divine ordering of the world except
by submitting to the guidance of the Church.   Nothing
could be more characteristic than the way in which Hildebrand applied St. Augustine's teaching.   "Who knows
not," he wrote, "that the kings and rulers of this world
derived their origin from those who, in ignorance of God,
by pride, by rapine, by perjury, by homicide, in short, by
almost every kind of wickedness, at the instigation of
the Devil, the Prince of this world, claimed to rule over
their fellow-men with blind concupiscence and intolerable
arrogance?"   A theory so convenient for the deadly
opponent of the Empire could not lie fallow.   Innocent the
Third trod faithfully in the footsteps of his great predecessor.   "To the Pope," he said, "not only the sovereignty
over the Church, but over the whole world also has been
given by Christ.   To the Bishop of Rome all lands and all
who dwell in them are subject.   Only the Episcopate has
a divine origin ; temporal sovereignty is a purely human
institution."   No Pope before him had adopted so calmly
the favourite Medieval theory which took the sun and the
moon as the images of the spiritual and temporal Powers.
Even the express words of Scripture did not discompose
Innocent.   When he was confronted with St. Peter's
words, "Submit yourselves to every ordinance of man,"
this intrepid advocate of the Papacy quietly observed
that the Apostle meant, of course, every one except the
Priesthood.

It might have been imagined that it would be difficult to
improve upon Innocent's theory.   But Boniface the Eighth

proved equal to the task. In 1302 he issued the Bull "Unam Sanctam." It sums up the avowed and unexpressed beliefs and aspirations of all devoted admirers of the Papacy during the Middle Ages. It is the high-water mark of the pretensions of the See of Rome. In this Bull, Boniface asserted that both swords are in the power of the Church, the spiritual and the material. But the one sword must be subject to the other, the temporal authority must be subject to the spiritual Power. Therefore, if the earthly Power swerves from the right path, it will be judged by the spiritual Power. This spiritual authority, however, although it has been given to man and is wielded by man, is not human but divine. Whosoever, therefore, resists this Power thus ordained of God, resists the ordinance of God.

Accordingly, when the Reformers broke decisively with the Medieval doctrine of the State, the impression which they produced was so profound that it almost revolutionized men's ways of thinking. Now, for the first time since the fifth century, great spiritual leaders came forward to lay the axe to the root of the Papal theory of the State. With a power and an eloquence which riveted men's attention and convinced their reason, they scattered to the winds the foolish claims and the grotesque arguments which had accumulated in the Decretals of Popes and the folios of Canonists. Rejecting the view that the State originated in the arbitrary will of man, and is devoid of any higher nature or purpose, disclaiming the theory that the temporal Power must of necessity derive its sanction from the Church, and that without this sanction it will inevitably fall under the sway of the Prince of this world, contending that the State is a divine ordinance which possesses a moral nature and is animated by a moral purpose, applying this doctrine to heathen and to Christian, to Jewish and to Gentile Kingdoms, illustrating it from Nebuchadnezzar as well as from David, from the Empire of Julius Cæsar no less than from the Empire of Charles the Fifth, they laid down the chief lines of the modern theory of the State.

The Reformers began by expressly denying Gregory the Seventh's theory. " The supreme power with which Kings and Rulers are endowed is not the result of human perversity, nor does it proceed from the will and device of men, but from the dispensation of divine Providence and the decree of Him Who has willed that the affairs of men should be thus ordered. For this reason the Bible gives Magistrates the title of ' Gods,' because they have a commission from God, because they are invested with divine authority, because they are Vicegerents of the Most High. They are the Ministers of the divine Justice, the very image of the divine Benevolence and Goodness, the guardians and vindicators of public innocence, honour, and tranquillity. For the establishment and maintenance of peace is the greatest blessing which God can bestow on the children of Adam, and this blessing, with all that follows from it, the happiness of hearth and home, the enjoyment of the fruits of our industry, the training of children in the fear of God, is ensured to us by the civil Power. He who is disobedient to Rulers encroaches upon God's office ; for the sword has been placed in their hand by God, and the sentence which they execute is God's sentence. Who, then, can doubt that civil authority is not only sacred and lawful in God's sight, but is the most sacred and the most honourable of all the stations to which God has called men in this mortal life ? Indeed, if the temporal Government were an unrighteous estate, how could Christ, speaking of a heathen Emperor, have said, ' Render to Cæsar the things which are Cæsar's ' ? How could the great Patriarch have consented to be the chief Minister of a heathen King, serving as an example of fidelity and obedience among a strange people ? Why should the King of Kings and Lord of Lords in His earthly life have submitted to pay the tribute which was demanded of Him ? "

With equal energy the Reformers cast to the winds the delirious dreams of Medieval ecclesiastics, and tore to shreds the incongruous reasons with which they had skilfully draped the temporal sovereignty of the Church. Christ had expressly declared that His Kingdom was not of this world; He had solemnly rebuked St. Peter for drawing the sword on His behalf; He had emphatically disclaimed the office of judge and divider over men; He told His disciples that He sent them as His Father had sent Him; He forbade them in the clearest terms to exercise authority and dominion like the Kings of the Gentiles. What shadow of justification, then, could be found for these Prince-Bishops, Electoral Archbishops, Cardinals, and Popes, who governed Principalities, nego- tiated treaties, made peace and war, marshalled armies to the field of battle, were immersed in affairs of State, pre- sided over Courts of Justice, and paraded in their scutcheons the crozier crossed by the sword? They claimed and obtained immunity from the custom of tribute which their poorer fellow-citizens were compelled to pay, and weakened the sinews of the State by this unjust exemption. They claimed and obtained a preponderating influence in the Councils of great nations, to the lasting detriment of the spiritual life and the weakening of the temporal Order. They maimed the civil government in the most solemn and responsible of all its functions, the administration of justice, by setting up special Courts of ecclesiastical jurisdiction. Such were the abuses which had been fostered or tolerated by the weakness of Kings and the grasping ambition of Prelates. It may be doubted whether this terrible indictment of the ecclesiastical government, standing side by side with the exaltation of the temporal Power, did not weaken the influence of the Church of Rome with thoughtful men as much as the religious doctrines of the Reformation. But nearly three centuries were to pass before the remedies which the Reformers so loudly demanded were effectively applied;

and more than three centuries had passed before the last
survival of the Medieval system which they had so fiercely
denounced disappeared for ever from the map of Europe.

But what gave peculiar force to these arguments of the
Reformers were the practical consequences which they
deduced from them. If during the centuries which preceded the Reformation the ecclesiastical Power had
successfully invaded the domain of the temporal, in the
following centuries the balance was more than redressed
in favour of the civil Power. In the forefront of their
practical reforms the Reformers placed the question of
education. They maintained that education was of
supreme importance for the rising generation to enable
them to become profitable members not only of the Church
but also of the Commonwealth. They impressed, therefore, upon all Rulers, whether of Cities or of States, the
imperative necessity of providing an adequate number of
schools and an efficient staff of teachers. In a remarkable
letter which Luther addressed to the Elector of Saxony in
the early years of the Reformation, he came forward as
the first advocate in modern times of free and compulsory
education by the State; and after nearly 300 years Europe
tardily entered upon the path which his pioneering genius
had pointed out. But this was not all. The Reformers
freed education from the ecclesiastical trammels by which
it had been hitherto fettered. That the Laity as well as
the Clergy belonged to the universal Priesthood of
believers, that in the words of St. Peter and St. John they
had been made a royal Priesthood, Kings and Priests
unto God, and that the duty of teaching which was one
of the chief marks of the priestly office, was as incumbent
upon them as upon the Clergy, this was one of the new
truths with which the Reformers boldly startled the
awakening mind and conscience of Christendom. In
accordance with this principle they refused to imitate
the Medieval Church, which had carefully guarded the
teacher's office with the most watchful jealousy, and had

confined it within the most arbitrary bounds. They
unhesitatingly threw down the barriers which the usage
of centuries had created. That a Layman like Melanchthon
should address hundreds of students in one of the most
famous Universities of Europe on religious and theological
subjects, marked in the most impressive manner the
passing away of the old order of things.

Even more important was the attitude which the
Reformers took up towards the question of marriage and
divorce. If the State was an institution not a whit less
divine than the Church, if the purity and integrity of
family life lay at the very foundations of the well-being
of the State, and if matrimonial relations necessarily
affected every part of the civic and social fabric, it was
evident that the State could not, without endangering
the safeguards of its own prosperity and independence,
resign to the Church the control of marriage and divorce,
as had been the practice in the Middle Ages. The
Reformed State, while fully acknowledging the right of
the Church to put forth her interpretation of God's will
and God's law, and frankly conceding to her authorized
Ministers and her representative Assemblies the free
expression of their opinion, transferred at one blow the
ultimate decision and jurisdiction in these vital matters
from the ecclesiastical to the temporal Power. Here, again,
the Reformation anticipated the drastic reforms of modern
times, and the most Catholic governments of the nineteenth century have been compelled to act upon the
principles which the Reformers laid down.

Lastly, if the Prince was the ambassador, the representative, and the vicegerent of the Most High, it was
impossible that he could stand by as a passive and subservient spectator, and leave to the Church the exclusive
decisions on the most momentous of all questions, the
question of religious belief. On the contrary, as the chief
among the Priests of God he had the chief voice in deter-
mining what the faith of his people should be. The

Reformers expressed this truth by saying that to Rulers was entrusted the guardianship of both Tables of the Law. Not only were they bound to punish murder, theft, perjury, and all evil-doing which marred and hindered the material security of the State; they were equally bound to punish the idolatry, superstition, unbelief, blasphemy, and contempt for the clear teaching of God's Word, which undermined its spiritual life. The transparent fiction by which the Church took exclusive cognizance of spiritual offences and handed over the offender after conviction to the secular Power for condign punishment, was ruthlessly brushed aside by the Reformers. The Christian Rulers of the State were as vitally affected as the Heads of the Church by the spiritual evils from which their members suffered; and the duty and responsibility of obviating or repressing those evils devolved upon them even more clearly and more directly. By the acceptance of this principle the spiritual centre of gravity in the State was completely shifted: henceforth the support or the toleration of any and every form of religious belief rested wholly with the sovereign power; and in this point again the Reformers anticipated the great principle which separates the modern conception of the State from the Medieval by an impassable gulf.

There is another doctrine which it is impossible to pass over in silence, because it occupies so important a place in the Reformed theology, and because it has drawn down so much undeserved obloquy upon the Reformers. This is the famous doctrine of Predestination. Indeed, so distinctive has this feature of the Reformed theology appeared to many that the term Calvinism has been widely applied to the religious system which sets the doctrine of Predestination in the forefront of its teaching. Those who use this term ignore or overlook the fact that the doctrine, so far from being peculiar to Calvin, is common to all the leading Reformers. But what is still more persistently ignored or overlooked is the fact that the doctrine, in the form which it assumes in the theology of the Reformation, originated with the greatest Father of the Western Church, St. Augustine, and that the foundation on which Calvin rested his defence of the doctrine is as purely scriptural as St. Augustine's.

The truth is that the Reformers' adoption of this doctrine is an additional proof how powerfully they had been influenced by St. Augustine, and how strictly in conformity with Scripture they found his teaching to be. The great Father was in their eyes a perpetual argument, a constant protest, against the theological system which had been established in the Church by the close of the Middle Ages. This held good not only of such doctrines as sin, grace, good works, and forgiveness, but also of such doctrines as free will, predestination, election, and final perseverance. When they found that St. Augustine's doctrine had no real place in the system of the Church of Rome, they naturally denounced her apostasy from the world-famed teacher whom she honoured with her lips while her heart was far from him, and bent all their energies to the restoration of his neglected teaching.

In its broad outlines St. Augustine's doctrine of Predestination is identical with Calvin's. There is, it is true, an apparent distinction between the two theologians. In St. Augustine's unsystematic treatises the tenet may seem less harsh and less repulsive than in the measured march of Calvin's systematic theology. But if they are compared step by step, it will be evident that this is a difference of form and nothing more. Indeed, Calvin uses the remarkable expression, " Were I disposed to frame an entire volume out of Augustine, it were easy to show the reader that I have no occasion to use any other words but his."

Like St. Augustine, Calvin starts from the Fall of man as the foundation of his doctrine. As with Augustine, the most awful result of original sin is the slavery of the Will. From this state of hopeless bondage Calvin, following St. Augustine, represents man as delivered by the grace of God.   But it is as clear to Calvin as to St. Augustine that the gift of grace is not bestowed on all, and to explain the difference he, like Augustine, falls back on the doctrine of Predestination.   In answering the objections to it he again follows St. Augustine.   Like Augustine, he uses St. Paul's question, " Who art thou that repliest against God ? "   Like Augustine, he adduces the examples of the great Patriarchs of the chosen people.   Like Augustine, he appeals to the patent facts of Christian life.   Finally, Calvin, like Augustine, assumes that God gives to His elect the crowning gift of Perseverance.   We are sufficiently taught by experience itself that calling and faith are of little value without perseverance, which is not a gift bestowed on all.   But Christ has freed us from anxiety on this account, for He says that His sheep shall never perish, neither shall any man pluck them out of His Hand.

To anyone who with an attentive and unprejudiced mind examines the twofold presentation of this doctrine by the two theologians, it will be evident that Calvin and St. Augustine agree in all the essential features of their teaching on the subject of Predestination, and only differ in such unimportant modifications as might be expected from two powerful minds, dealing with the same subject and separated by an interval of ten eventful centuries.   It must, therefore, be regarded as the result of theological ignorance or theological prejudice if Calvin is made exclusively responsible for doctrines of which he was not the author but the interpreter, which he did not assert in a harsher or more peremptory manner than the great Western Father, and which he, like St. Augustine before him, found written on the pages of the New Testament in characters so plain that in his judgment he who ran might read them.

Yet one admission must be frankly made to Calvin's opponents.   However defective their historical or theological insight may have been, in this case their instinct has guided them aright.   For it is through the agency of the great Reformer of Geneva that Augustine's doctrine has influenced Europe so widely and so deeply for three centuries. But for him, the dogma of Predestination might have slept undisturbed in dusty folios on the shelves of public libraries, or might have served only as theses for disputations in the schools of divinity. If Augustine's teaching suddenly became a living and powerful principle in the historical development of Europe, if it exercised an unprecedented influence in the formation of individual character, if it has been enshrined in the immortal master-pieces of modern literature, this was due to the energy with which it was grasped and enforced by Calvin, and through him permeated the Evangelical Churches which looked up to him as their founder and their chief.

It is easy to see why this should have been so. For the dogma of Predestination has a twofold aspect; it is partly theoretical and partly practical. Except among a handful of religious bigots or logical students of theology the dogma on its theoretical side exercised an influence which was scarcely appreciable, and which faded away into a shadowy phantom before the light of common day. But over a countless host of anxious believers, longing to cast anchor upon some shore where the waves of doubt would break in vain, the faith in God's Election had an influence which was incomparably potent. The vast majority of Evangelical Christians who accepted the doctrine thought of it, not as involving the doom of the unbelievers, the impenitent, and the reprobate, who stood outside the pale of God's mercy, and had closed against themselves the gate of eternal life, but only as it affected the personal assurance of their own salvation. Upon them it acted as a mighty spiritual tonic, deepening their faith, sustaining them in disaster, cheering them in despondency, nerving them with an indomitable resolution, and enabling them to pass through life's dangers and trials with the echo of the Apostle's words ceaselessly ringing in their ears, " If God be for us, who can be against us ? "

CHAPTER IV.

On June 15th, 1530, Charles reached Augsburg. No man living could remember anything equal to the magnificence of his entry. At no previous Diet had there been such a gathering of Electors and Princes, spiritual and temporal. Their escorts of nobles and knights blazed with parti-coloured garments and costly trappings. King Ferdinand alone, who had succeeded to the crowns of Hungary and Bohemia, had brought with him more than a thousand knights from his wide dominions. Cardinals on white mules, and ambassadors of Kings swelled the long procession. It might have seemed as though at this critical moment in the history of his Empire and his Church Charles wished to strike an awe into the hearts of the heretics by such an imposing display of the Imperial guardian of the Church in the plenitude of his power.

But if this was his expectation he was doomed to a grievous disappointment. At every step he was foiled by his resolute and wary subjects. When he wished to stop the Evangelical sermons, he was forced to pledge his word that the preachers who took their place should avoid all controversial topics by filling their discourses with long passages from the Bible, " purely textual preachers," as the Protestants ironically termed them. When he invited the Protestant Princes to join in the solemn and official procession on Corpus Christi Day, they bluntly refused on conscientious grounds. When he asked them to give him a copy of the Confession before it was read to the Diet,

they successfully evaded the request.   When the Diet met
in solemn session on June 25th, and he asked them to read
the Latin version of the Confession, the Elector of Saxony
intrepidly demanded that, as they were met on German
soil, they should be allowed to use the German language,
and Charles was forced to give way.

The impression which the Confession made upon friends
and foes alike was great.   Many stories in proof of this
were current among the Protestants.   Duke William of
Bavaria frankly confessed to the Elector of Saxony that
the Evangelical doctrines had never yet been set before
him in this light.   Duke Henry of Brunswick invited
Melanchthon to dinner, and avowed that he could find no
fault with the Articles on the Communion in both kinds,
on the marriage of priests, and on the distinction of meats.
Some of the Romanist Princes were plainly told by their
Councillors that, if it came to a declaration of war, they
could not answer for the loyalty of their subjects.   Scarcely
less impression was made upon some of the prelates.   The
Cardinal Archbishop of Salzburg was reported to have
said that he, too, wished for a reformation of the Mass, of
the laws about fasting, and of other human ordinances ;
but what was intolerable was that a single monk should
undertake to reform them all.   The Bishop of Augsburg
exclaimed in a private conversation, " The Confession
which has been read is true, it is the pure truth ; we cannot
deny it."

But the effect which had been produced was not confined
to the city of Augsburg and the members of the Imperial
Diet.   The news of this memorable day spread far and
wide.   Cardinal Campegio had the Confession translated
into Italian and sent to the Pope, who was a wretched
Latin scholar.   One Imperial secretary translated it into
French, and another into Spanish.   Translations into
English and Portuguese were made, as well as into the
Bohemian and Hungarian languages.   Copies circulated
throughout Germany with great rapidity during the sitting

of the Diet.   It was a remarkable comment on the verse
of the 119th Psalm, which was prefixed as a motto to the
Confession, " I will speak of Thy testimonies even before
Kings, and will not be ashamed."

The Confession having been read, and handed to the
Emperor, the next step of Charles was to get it refuted.
The Papal Legate undertook to find theologians fitted for
the congenial task of crushing the heretics.   The theologians were easily found ; but unfortunately their language
was as strong as their arguments were weak.   Charles, who
was too able a man not to recognize the folly of answering
Melanchthon's measured and temperate language with
unmeasured invective and railing, peremptorily ordered
them to do their work over again.   Even after more than
one revision the inherent feebleness of the original version
remained.   A single instance will show what the united
genius of these incompetent theologians could produce.
The administration of the Eucharist in one kind was
defended by the example of the descendants of Eli, who,
it was prophesied in the Book of Samuel, would beg for a
piece of bread ; from this it was argued that the laity ought
to be content with the bread alone.   On August 3rd this
Confutation was read before the assembled Diet; the
Emperor informed the Princes and Estates who had presented the Confession that their arguments and doctrines
had been completely answered and refuted, and that nothing
was left for them but to recant.   The "protesting Estates,"
who had listened with scarcely concealed contempt to the
grotesque arguments and theological jargon with which
they had been overwhelmed, naturally declined to take
this view, and denied that a single one of their doctrines
had been shaken by their opponents' Confutation.   At
this point the proceedings of the Diet would have come
to an abrupt termination, had not the more moderate
Romanists suggested a conference, at which representatives
of both parties should discuss their differences in a friendly
spirit.   Charles gladly adopted the suggestion ; but it was

soon clear that, whatever advantages such a conference might have, it certainly would not unite in religious harmony the severed fragments of the Empire. Not a whit daunted by their ill-success, the advocates of conciliation pressed for a second conference with fewer representatives on each side : but the results of the second conference were as unsatisfactory as the first. At last the representatives of the Evangelical party made a definite and final offer : if they were allowed to retain the marriage of the clergy, the Communion in both kinds, and their own way of administering the Eucharist, till the meeting of a Free and General Council, they would order their clergy to render all due obedience to the Bishops, and would not hinder the Bishops from exercising the jurisdiction which they might rightfully claim. The magnitude of this concession will be apparent when it is remembered that all the Free and Imperial cities which adopted the Reformed doctrines had cast off the authority of their Bishops and viewed the restoration of it with the utmost repugnance. Yet even this concession failed to propitiate their opponents, and the conference came to an end.

Then Charles made up his mind to fall back on his former policy. At a meeting of the Diet on September 7th he referred contemptuously to the numerical insignificance of the Evangelical members, expressed his astonishment and regret that they had formed a new religion, and assured them that he would use his utmost efforts to procure the meeting of a Council, but only on the condition that they would undertake, till the Council met, to live in harmony with the majority on religious questions. It was only fitting and reasonable that the minority should yield to the majority ; and, compared with the Pope, with himself, and with the rest of the Princes, they were a mere handful. If they had any further offers to make or terms to propose, he would spare no pains and trouble to meet them halfway ; if not, he must act as befitted the Protector of the Church. To this haughty and threatening speech the Evangelical party returned an elaborate answer, plainly declaring at the close that they could not conscientiously make any further concession. The clearness and vigour of this reply showed Charles how little chance there was of shaking the resolution of his opponents. He determined, therefore, to take a decisive step. On September 22nd the Diet was summoned to hear the draft of the decree which the Emperor submitted for their approval. After declaring that the Confession of the Protestants had been confuted by conclusive arguments out of Holy Writ, Charles gave the " protesting Estates " till April 15th to return into the fold of the Church, forbade them to print or sell heretical books, ordered them to replace the regular and secular clergy in their monasteries and domains, commanded them to restore the Mass and the Communion in one kind, and prohibited every preacher who had not been licensed by his Archbishop or Bishop. This led to a prolonged discussion, which was closed by the declaration of the Protestants that they could not accept the Imperial decree; as for the Confession, they believed that it was so firmly established on Holy Scripture that the gates of hell could not prevail against it. After this the Evangelical Estates conceived that no further purpose would be served by a longer delay, and left the city.

The Emperor's perplexity was very great. Numerically ndeed the Protestants were weak, but their material and moral power was out of all proportion to their numbers. Six of the chief cities of the Empire, which could not be matched by an equal number on the Romanist side, and two of the leading temporal Princes had ranged themselves against Charles. The Ottoman power in eastern Europe was pressing restlessly forward into the heart of Ferdinand's dominions. It might have been some compensation if the Emperor had been assured of the devoted support of his own party. But here, as he indignantly complained to the Pope, he was confronted by apathy and indifference : " They care only for their own selfish interests." In one case he encountered positive dislike : the powerful Dukes of Bavaria were intensely jealous of the might and advancement of the House of Hapsburg, and suffered their hostility to Charles and Ferdinand to outweigh their fidelity to the old Church.

The importance of the Diet of Augsburg is evident at a glance. Not only has neither of the rival Churches receded from the position which it then took up, not only have the Reformed Churches as a whole held by the Confession of Augsburg in every material point of doctrine and of practice; there was a further reason why the Diet marked a turning point in the history of the Reformation. The wording of the decree made it impossible to doubt that Charles had resolved to suppress heresy throughout the Empire by force of arms. This avowed purpose wrought a complete change in the relation between the Estates of the Empire and their Head. Hitherto the new movement had been almost exclusively religious : for the first time after the Diet the religious question was permanently transferred to the political sphere. This important change, which for more than a century was fruitful of results affecting the whole history of western Europe, may be clearly seen in the leader of the German Reformation. Up to this time Luther had advocated the doctrine of passive obedience with the zeal and vehemence of a believer in the divine right of Kings. The events at Augsburg profoundly modified this view. In one of the most effective of his pamphlets he declared plainly that, if the Emperor made war against the Protestants and summoned his German subjects to join him in the crusade, no man ought to obey him : " Let him be assured that in such a case he is stringently forbidden by God to render obedience to the Emperor." The League of Schmalkald was the direct result of this exhortation. In accordance with the summons issued by the Elector of Saxony the Evangelical

Princes and cities met at the close of the year 1530. The
League was designed for mutual defence against all attacks
" on account of God's Word, the Evangelical doctrine, or
our holy faith." Its weakness was apparent. What power
of combined resistance or attack could a Confederation
possess whose members were scattered over a vast territory
extending from the Baltic Sea to the confines of Switzerland ? The truth was that the strength of the League lay
in the weakness of its adversaries. On every side Charles
encountered insuperable difficulties and obstacles. In
spite of the peace of Cambray, in spite of the marriage of
Francis the First to the Emperor's sister, Charles could
count as little as ever upon the real friendship of France. The
French King scarcely concealed his intention of crossing
the Emperor's policy as soon as a favourable opportunity
offered itself. In this attitude of hostility he was seconded
by Pope Clement the Seventh. A Free and General Council
was regarded by the Pope with unfeigned repugnance and
dread. He could not forgive Charles for joining in this
unwelcome demand. Why had not the Emperor, instead
of doing this, drawn the sword at once and boldly cut out
heresy by the roots ? Clement was not indeed moved to
take this view by any fervent zeal for orthodoxy : he gave
it as his private opinion that the Confession of Augsburg
was after all not so bad, and saw no objection to making
sundry concessions to the foolish and unreasoning prejudices of the Protestants. But a Council he could not
and would not have. Accordingly the Pope professed the
greatest eagerness for a Council, and at the same time
piled up impossible conditions which must be fulfilled to
the letter, before he would consent to call it.

The day fixed in the decree of Augsburg, before which
the Protestants were to send in their submission to the
Emperor, was April 15th, 1531. But so gloomy was the
aspect of affairs in the East, and so despairing the strain
in which Ferdinand wrote, that on April 3rd Charles confessed to his brother that it would be necessary to make

concessions to the heretics. While negotiations were being carried on with the League of Schmalkald, Charles was exposed to fresh humiliations by the Romanist Estates at the Diet of Ratisbon. They haggled with the unhappy Emperor as if they had been pawnbrokers or money-lenders, raked up all their grievances against the Imperial government, complained bitterly of the preference given to Spaniards over Germans, of the exorbitant taxes which had been recently levied, and of the unfair partiality which Charles and Ferdinand showed to Austria because it was the hereditary possession of the House of Hapsburg. At last matters came to a climax. Charles, provoked beyond endurance, spoke out his mind in the plainest language. The Estates with equal heat rejoined that such language had never been heard from an Emperor before, and that they could only set it down to his foreign Councillors, to their hatred of the Germans, and to their ignorance of the German language.

After this quarrel it was clear that, unless Charles could make peace with the Evangelical Estates, it was vain to hope for any effectual resistance to the Sultan. He therefore commissioned the Electors of Mentz and the Palatinate to come to an understanding with the Princes and cities of the League as soon as possible. On July 22nd, 1532, the offers of Charles were formally accepted; on August 3rd he proclaimed the religious peace. In the preamble he stated his conviction that no effectual resistance could be made to the designs of the Turks unless a general peace were established in the Holy Roman Empire. Till a Free and General Council, or a General Assembly, had met and had decided otherwise, no member should injure any other on account of his faith, but all should live in friendship and true Christian love.

If we compare the position of Charles at the Diet of Worms in 1521 with his position after the Religious Peace of Nuremberg in 1532, there can be no doubt that it had greatly changed for the worse. He had lost the general

confidence and respect which he enjoyed on his accession
to the Imperial throne. He had permanently forfeited
the affection and trust of his Evangelical subjects. The
League of Schmalkald was an open defiance of his
authority as Emperor, a standing menace to his government of the Empire. Even among the Romanist Estates
he was regarded with suspicion and distrust; some were
completely estranged from him; upon none, except upon
his brother, could he reckon with absolute certainty for
help and support. From the East the danger was more
imminent than ever. To stem the advance of the Ottoman
power he had been compelled to sacrifice his dearest
religious prejudices. What probability was there that,
hampered by these disadvantages, he would be able to
crush out heresy, or even to check its rapid growth ?
Luther might well quote in triumph one of his favourite
maxims, " Principiis obsta." Had Charles acted upon
this principle with unswerving energy from the beginning
of his reign, he might not have found himself forced to the
humiliating task of parleying with subjects who had openly
renounced the authority of the Church, and had definitely
refused obedience to himself. Even now, had he been
content to stay and to give his whole attention to the
settlement of the religious question, he might at least
have arrested the further progress of the Reformation.
But in spite of the earnest entreaties of his brother and of
his most faithful friends, he turned his back once more
upon Germany, and did not revisit it for another period
of nine eventful years.

Shortly after the conclusion of the Religious Peace of
Nuremberg the question of a General Council again came
prominently forward, and may be said for the first time to
have assumed a definite form. Clement the Seventh had
passed away in 1534; his successor, Paul the Third, had
no such horror of a General Council as had filled the soul of
Clement. Indeed, so far was he from opposing the scheme
that one of the earliest acts of his pontificate had been to

send his nuncio, Vergerio, into Germany to intimate to the
members of the League of Schmalkald that he intended
to convoke such a Council. It became necessary, therefore, for the Evangelical Estates to define once for all what
they understood by a General Council, and how far the
Council which the Pope proposed harmonized with their
wishes or was at variance with them.

The Protestant Estates began by declaring once more
their desire to see a Council assembled, and their readiness to take part in it, because, if ever a Council was
needed, it was needed now. After this prelude they
replied to Vergerio's intimation that the Pope had settled
Mantua as the place for the Council by curtly expressing
their conviction that the Emperor would give effect to the
decrees of previous Diets, which fixed the place of meeting
in Germany and not in Italy. This they deemed to be an
essential condition, "in order that these matters may be
rightly and duly discussed, and that every one may speak
freely." They then passed on to a still more important
point. They were informed that in this proposed Council
there was to be no discussion about the manner and order
of the proceedings, but that the determination of these
matters fell entirely within the Pope's province. To such
a statement they vouchsafed no further answer than the
emphatic comment that "this was not granting them a
Free Council." Even this, however, was not all: the
Pope by advancing such a claim set himself up as the
supreme judge. On what principles of equity could this
pretension be justified? Was it not a notorious fact that
the Pope had repeatedly condemned the Evangelical
doctrine? Was it not, therefore, plain that he was one of
the contending parties in this great spiritual lawsuit? And
with what justice could one of the parties in a case arrogate
the right to pass judgment upon it? How could the
prosecutor be also the judge? It was evident to every
fair-minded man that this duty must be left to others,
to the Emperor, to Kings, Potentates, Princes, and

Estates of all realms, who should select competent and impartial persons out of all classes to discuss and to decide these disputed questions in accordance with God's Word. "For Councils ought not to embody the judgments of the Popes alone, but also of all other classes and men in the Church. It is a crime and a tyranny to exalt the power of the Pope over the power of the whole Church. In Councils, therefore, the Emperor, Kings, Princes, Potentates, and Estates, as well as pious, Christian, honourable men, ought to have their due weight; and competent people shall be chosen to take part in them, especially in those matters in which the faults and errors of the Popes are attacked. These matters concern the whole of Christendom, and Kings and Princes are bound to provide for a proper discussion of them." It could scarcely be expected that the Pope would assent to this line of argument. How could a Pope, whose predecessor only a few years before had been hailed by an Œcumenical Council as "a second God upon earth," consent to appear as defendant before a Council presided over by earthly sovereigns, and listen with bowed head and on bended knee to the arraignment of obscure heretics who had been cast out by a Papal Bull from the fellowship of the Christian Church? But if this was so, the demands of the Reformers were in hopeless and irreconcileable opposition to the utmost concessions which the Papacy would make, and the meeting of a General Council in which all western Christendom should take part faded for ever into an airy vision as unsubstantial as the mirage of the desert.

In the meantime the Reformation had been making steady and decisive progress throughout Germany. But of all conquests which it made none were of more capital importance for the present fortunes and the future destinies of the Evangelical Church than the gain of the Duchy of Saxony and the Electorate of Brandenburg. In 1485 the division of the Saxon lands into the Ernestine and Albertine had taken place. Ernest, as the elder brother, retained the Electorate of Thuringia ; the younger brother, Albert, took as his portion Meissen, which was henceforward known as the Duchy of Saxony. Frederick the Wise succeeded to the Electorate on Ernest's death : Albert was followed in the government of the Duchy by George. As soon as the Edict of Worms had been issued it was published in the Duchy. But George soon saw to his bitter mortification the hateful poison of heresy penetrating every part of his dominions, and nowhere working with more deadly effect than in Leipzig, his greatest city, at that time, as at the present day, one of the most important of German towns, the seat of an University and a centre of European commerce. The three yearly markets of Leipzig were largely attended by Lutheran merchants, who found many opportunities of disseminating the new doctrines without attracting notice. Wittenberg was only a day's journey from the gates of Leipzig, and it was inevitable that there should be constant intercourse between the two University cities. But what made the Duke's position especially difficult was the close proximity of Electoral towns and villages, some of which could be seen from the walls of Leipzig, and whose inhabitants went to and fro between the Electorate and the Duchy for purposes of business and of pleasure.

When George died without male heirs, he was succeeded by his younger brother, Henry, who was a decided Protestant. The intelligence of the Duke's death was received with the greatest joy at the Elector's Court. The religious division of the Saxon lands was now at an end. It was well known that the majority of Henry's subjects would on religious grounds welcome his accession with delight, and that it was only the personal influence and authority of George which had propped up the cause of the falling Church. Luther attended his Elector on a visit to Leipzig, when the new Duke entered his capital for the first time. The great Reformer, prematurely aged by the excessive austerities of his early years, by the incessant conflicts and unsparing labours of his later life, and by the wasting effects of painful maladies which had more than once brought him to the very gates of the grave, was able to preach on Whitsunday to a congregation which filled the sacred edifice to overflowing. It was within a few days of twenty years since he had last preached, under widely different circumstances, in the famous city at the beginning of his great career. No preceding twenty years in German history had witnessed changes so vast, so marvellous, and so enduring.

The Reformation of Brandenburg was even more important than the Reformation of Ducal Saxony. No one, indeed, could at that time have foreseen that within less than two centuries the Electors of Brandenburg, by the adoption of a bold and consistent policy, would have laid the foundation of the Kingdom of Prussia, still less that the Kingdom of Prussia before the close of the nineteenth century would have become the centre of a splendid and mighty German Empire. But even in the early part of the sixteenth century the Elector of Brandenburg had great weight in the councils of the Empire. Elector Joachim was not only, like Duke George of Saxony, a sincere and consistent defender of the Church of Rome; he had also a special and personal interest in maintaining her rights and prerogatives unimpaired; for it was through his exertions that his younger brother, Albert of Brandenburg, had obtained the most splendid prizes of the German Church, the Archiepiscopal Electorate of Mentz, the Archbishopric of Magdeburg, and the Primacy of Germany. At the Diet of Worms Joachim took a leading part in the opposition to Luther, and welcomed the Edict with enthusiasm. On the first appearance of Luther's translation of the Bible he considered the matter important enough to justify him in issuing a manifesto and warning his people against it. This manifesto was issued at the beginning of 1524. In the summer of the same year he republished the Edict of Worms, alleging as the reason that the preaching

of the Lutheran doctrine had increased to an alarming
extent.   But in spite of all his efforts the Reformation
continued to make way in the Electorate.   His wife and
his eldest son were won over by the new doctrines.   The
younger Joachim, when he was still a boy, had made
Luther's acquaintance, and had fallen under the spell
of the mighty enchanter.   But though the Reformer's
teaching made an indelible impression upon him, years
passed before he openly professed the Reformed faith.
The younger son, Margrave John, held opinions more
decidedly Evangelical than his brother.   As soon as the
Elector had breathed his last, John, to whom the new
March and other territories had been bequeathed, proceeded in the summer of 1535 to introduce the Reformation
into his lands, and on Easter Day, 1538, publicly communicated according to the Reformed rite.   His brother, Elector
Joachim the Second, naturally of a cautious and hesitating
temperament, disinclined to unite with extreme partisans
and reluctant to identify himself exclusively with one
system, took up a neutral attitude, and suffered events to
run their course.   It soon became clear to which side the
majority of his subjects inclined : the monasteries of the
Electorate were almost deserted, or compelled through
poverty to dispose of their possessions ; Lutheran ministers
were everywhere introduced to take the place of the old
clergy ; the Medieval service in Latin was replaced by the
services in the vulgar tongue, and the Roman Mass by the
administration of the Communion in both kinds.   In
1538 the Elector invited Melanchthon to visit Berlin in
order to assist him with his advice.   The Council and
burghers of the capital unanimously petitioned for the
establishment of the Evangelical Church in Berlin.   A
similar bequest came from some of the Nobles, and from
the cities of Frankfort-on-the-Oder and Spandau ; and in
1539 a committee of theologians was appointed to draw
up an " Ordering " of the Evangelical Church.

It was chiefly owing to the Elector of Brandenburg that

the Diet of Ratisbon in 1541 took up again, after an
interval of eleven years, the task which the Diet of
Augsburg had abandoned in despair. Once more a Conference was held, in which Melanchthon took part as
the leader of the Protestant theologians, and Cardinal
Contarini, one of the noblest and purest prelates of the
sixteenth century, as the leader of the Romanists. That
such an attempt should have failed completely was only
natural. Even the most sanguine optimist in his wildest
day-dreams could scarcely imagine that, after the experi-
ences, the arguments, the discussions, the dissertations,
the struggles, the victories, and the defeats of more than
twenty years, men's prejudices could be broken down, or
their convictions shaken, or their difficulties removed, or
their opinions changed, by the controversial intercourse
of a few days. The Emperor, his great minister,
Granvella, and the Elector Joachim really seem for some
weeks to have cherished this hope: Luther, Calvin, and
Melanchthon could only smile in scorn at their delusion.
Even had the disputants agreed, they knew that the
Roman Curia would never have sanctioned the agreement. Nothing remained, therefore, but to give up the
attempt, and in the decree of the Diet to parade once
more the shadowy phantom of a General Council or a
National Assembly.

If, however, the Diet of Ratisbon had no religious
importance, its political importance was great. During
the time that the Diet lasted, Charles had ample opportunities of watching the restless intrigues of France and
of gauging the strength of the League of Schmalkald.
At any moment an alliance between the League and his
life-long rival might endanger his position in the Empire.
What more effective scheme could be devised for counter-
acting this policy than a close connection between the
Protestant Princes and the Head of the Empire? Of all
the Evangelical Princes, Philip of Hesse appeared the
most formidable to Charles and Granvella, and an alliance

with him the most desirable of all. On June 13th the
negotiations came to a close. The Landgrave undertook
to reject any alliance with France, to prevent France
from receiving any support in Germany, to reveal to
Charles any intrigues which the French King carried on
with German Princes, and to render the Emperor military
service in the war with France. Philip's son-in-law, the
young, energetic, and ambitious Maurice, who had succeeded his father as ruler of Ducal Saxony, was included
in this treaty. Six weeks later another treaty to the
same effect was made with Joachim of Brandenburg.
Had Charles consistently and warily persisted in this
new policy, had he bound the more influential of the
Protestant Princes to himself by the powerful motives
of self-interest, had he wisely rejected the evil counsels
of Rome and frankly abandoned his design of imposing
the Papal yoke again upon a reluctant nation, German
Protestantism as a political force would have ceased to
exist, and Charles might have ended his days as the
arbiter of Europe, the honoured sovereign of an United
Empire. It was the fatal error of his reign that he
recklessly sacrificed the advantages which he had gained,
suffered his personal feelings to override the dictates of a
wise caution, estranged his staunchest supporters by a
course of wanton folly, threw them into the arms of his
watchful and implacable foe, and atoned at last for his
political sins by the reverses and humiliations of his
closing years.

Immediately after the Diet of Ratisbon events occurred
in Cologne, one of the three great Electoral Archbishoprics, which filled men's minds throughout the
Empire with hope or alarm. Herman von Wied, the
Archbishop of Cologne, had been one of the most energetic
opponents of Luther, had ordered Luther's books to be
burnt, had strongly approved the Bull of excommunication, had strictly forbidden the new preachers to enter
his diocese, and had executed two heretics in his Cathedral

city. But gradually a change came over him : he became
suspiciously active in the reformation of abuses, used
language which savoured of heresy, associated with
heretics, persuaded the Electoral Estates to consent to
a reformation, and invited Bucer, the Reformer of Strasburg, to assist him in carrying it out. In the struggle
which followed, the temporal Estates of the Electorate
sided with Herman, the spiritual Estates, headed by the
Chapter of Cologne, opposed him. In the spring of 1543
Melanchthon joined Bucer, and in his letters to friends
drew a melancholy picture of the superstition, the ignorance, and the spiritual destitution which he found in the
Electorate. At this point the Pope and the Emperor intervened. Charles pressed the Archbishop to dismiss Bucer
and Melanchthon and to defer his scheme for reforming
the diocese. He had indeed good reason to be seriously
alarmed. The Elector was the near neighbour of his own
provinces in the Low Countries, and the Low Countries
were seething with heresy. Accordingly the Emperor, to
weaken and isolate the Elector, redoubled his gracious
favours to the Protestant Estates of Germany, confirmed
the religious peace, professed the utmost zeal for a
Christian Reformation, talked vaguely of a matrimonial
alliance with the Elector of Saxony, and dangled before
the eyes of the Landgrave of Hesse the dazzling bait of
the supreme command in the war against the Turks.
Supported by the whole forces of the Empire, he brought
the war with France to a successful issue by the Peace
of Crespy.

Suddenly a new subject of difference divided the
Emperor from his Protestant subjects. At the beginning
of 1545 the Pope summoned the Council which had been
so constantly demanded and so long postponed. Charles
pressed the Protestants to recognize the Council; the
Protestants would not hear of any Council in which the
Pope presided, and in which the decision rested with
his sworn bodyguard, the subservient Bishops. Their

obstinate refusal suggested to the Emperor a new move. Nothing had militated more against the pacification of Christendom than the suspicions, the insincerity, and the hostility which had estranged the two Heads of western Europe from each other.   The Emperor had not done what the Pope wished, and the Pope had not done what the Emperor wished : each had thwarted the plans of the other.   But since the Pope had complied with the Emperor's request, and had summoned a Council to meet on German soil, it was surely time that this disastrous policy should give place to a firm alliance.   If the Protestants refused to attend the Council which the Pope had summoned and the Emperor had approved, it was manifestly incumbent on Pope and Emperor to compel them to come in.   Paul the Third received the overtures of Charles with delighted surprise : he could not pay too highly for a war which should crush the insolent heretics and restore the shattered authority of the Holy See to its full pre-eminence in Germany.   He gladly accepted the Emperor's offers.

The resolve of Charles to ally himself with the Pope was probably strengthened by the formal admission of the Reformation into the Palatinate at the close of the year 1545.   The Elector was childless; and his heir, who exercised considerable influence over him, strongly urged him to admit the Reformed doctrines into his territories without delay.   Permission was accordingly given to celebrate the Mass in the vulgar tongue ; any one who had scruples about using the Canon of the Mass or the forms of service appointed by the Medieval Church was at liberty to make such alterations as he thought fit.   This change in the Palatinate had a far-reaching significance : three of the seven Electors were now Protestants; if the Archbishop of Cologne joined them, it would be possible to revolutionize the Empire by electing a Protestant Emperor.

But if Charles had lost by the defection of the Elector Palatine, he had gained far more than he had lost by a

close alliance with Maurice, the young ruler of Ducal
Saxony, the most brilliant, the most ambitious, the most
daring, the most resolute, and the most clear-sighted of
the German Princes. The offers which Charles made
him were tempting in the extreme. He appointed him
Protector of the Sees of Magdeburg and Halberstadt,
delivering over to him their lands and subjects during his
good pleasure; and if for any reason he deprived the
Elector of Saxony of his Electorate, he undertook to
bestow it, with the lands appertaining thereto, upon
Maurice. The Duke on his part promised to protect
the Imperial interests and to co-operate with the Emperor.
Yet even these negotiations might have opened the eyes of
Charles to the difficulties of his position, if he had not
been wilfully blind. Granvella urged Maurice to return
to the faith of the Church and of his forefathers, assuring
him that such a step would unquestionably redound to his
highest honour and profit. Maurice's answer was simple:
He had been brought up in the Confession of Augsburg,
and his conscience would not suffer him to renounce the
Evangelical doctrine ; but, even if he had no conscience,
self-interest would deter him from acting upon Granvella's
suggestion, for his subjects would certainly rebel against
any change in the Evangelical faith. On a second point
Granvella received a similar rebuff. He pressed Maurice
to acknowledge the Council, and to pledge himself to
submit to its decrees. The Duke promised to obey a
Free, Christian, General Council, but with the momentous
reservation that the Conciliar decrees should be in accordance with Holy Writ, a condition which Maurice probably
anticipated would not be fulfilled before the Greek Kalends.
If the warmest friend and closest ally of Charles in
Germany proved so uncompliant in questions of vital
importance, what probability was there of his ultimate
success ?

Relying on his three confederates, the Pope, Joachim,
and Maurice, Charles dropped the mask and laid the

Elector of Saxony and the Landgrave of Hesse under the ban of the Empire. He charged them with every kind of crime, wanton violence, grasping covetousness, reckless ambition, irreligion, insolence, arrogance, disloyalty, and rebellion. Such was the language in which the Head of the Empire deemed it becoming to describe the Princes whom a few weeks before he had been courting with adulatory smiles and hypocritical professions of friendship. The answer of the Elector and Landgrave to the Imperial manifesto was simple: Their religious faith was the one unpardonable sin which had provoked the united maledictions of the Emperor and Pope. When Maurice and Joachim proffered their services as mediators, the outlawed Princes indignantly reiterated their charge. They were branded with the crime of disobedience for this reason alone, because they refused to remain in the Church of Rome. If it were not so, why did Charles condemn and outlaw them without a trial? Why did he not give them the opportunity of making a public answer to the charges which he had heaped up against them? "We are accused of making alliances with foreign powers, we who have helped the Emperor against the French and the Turks, and the only reward of our fidelity is that we have been treated as though we were Turks ourselves."

The events of the war showed how greatly Charles had over-estimated his own strength and underrated the strength of his opponents. In spite of the advantages which he enjoyed, he was more than once in imminent danger of defeat. But incapacity, irresolution, selfishness, and disunion dogged the steps of the League, and irremediably weakened its forces. Instead of relying upon themselves, the Elector and the Landgrave frittered away priceless hours in futile negotiations with Henry and Francis. But the apathy of the Evangelical cities was of far more fatal import to the success of the League than the indifference of England or the vacillation of France. At that time the great cities of Germany were the wealthiest in Europe.

Yet these great cities, at the crisis of their fortunes, when none of the able men who directed their destinies could be blind to the consequences of the Emperor's victory, made an ostentatious parade of their poverty. The Confederates were compelled to disband the fine army which they had mustered from sheer inability to scrape together the paltry sum required for a month's military expenses. It was a just retribution that Charles, in the hour of his triumph, extorted from them at the sword's point the sums which religion and patriotism could not induce them to advance.

In the spring of 1547 the Elector was surprised at Muhlberg by Charles and taken prisoner. The cities one after another hastened to make their submission and were compelled to surrender their artillery, probably the finest in Europe, to pay an enormous war indemnity, and to receive Spanish garrisons. A still greater triumph awaited him in the voluntary submission of his most dangerous opponent, Philip of Hesse. Maurice felt a sincere respect for his father-in-law, very different from the unconcealed contempt with which he regarded his worthy and incompetent cousin. He persuaded the Landgrave to throw himself on the Emperor's mercy, relying upon his own influence with Charles to secure favourable terms for his father-in-law. To his bitter mortification, Charles paid no heed to his intercession, disregarded the promises which had been made to Philip, and kept his enemy a close prisoner. Instead of wisely endeavouring to propitiate Maurice and the Landgrave by a generous and considerate leniency, he gave the reins to his vindictive hatred. The high-spirited Prince was subjected to every kind of studied indignity and gratuitous outrage by his brutal Spanish gaolers. His spirit was completely broken, and he suffered seriously in health. At last, goaded to despair, he attempted to escape. Then the Emperor's ferocity redoubled. In his eyes the Landgrave was an incorrigible scoundrel on whom all pity and consideration were wasted. He so far forgot what was

due to himself as well as to his prisoner that he even
threatened to put him to the torture. No vanquished
Prince had received such treatment since Bajazet had been
dragged about in the train of Timour's victorious army.

The humbling of the League of Schmalkald was not
the only check which the Reformation received in
Germany. The fall of the Elector and the Landgrave
involved the fall of the Archbishop of Cologne. The
excommunication pronounced by the Pope in 1546 had no
terrors for him until it was enforced by the power of the
Emperor. When victory had crowned the Imperial arms
in South Germany, Charles took action against the Archbishop without delay. He ordered the Coadjutor Bishop
to be ready to take over the duties and privileges of the
Archbishopric: if any resistance was threatened, Charles
bade him apply for assistance to the Imperial general.
But Herman had no intention of entering upon a hopeless
struggle : he retired into private life; and Charles had
the satisfaction of seeing the Electorate fall once more
under the power of Rome.

While Charles was asserting his sovereignty in the
Empire, the Council had met at Trent, and had amply
justified the refusal of the Protestants to take part in its
proceedings. Œcumenical, in any true sense of the word,
it certainly was not. At many of the most important
sittings the Bishops present did not exceed in number
those who had seats in the Imperial Diet alone. Nor was
the quality superior to the quantity. Calvin, who had
ample opportunities of knowing, described the Bishops
who came from France as ignorant and incapable beyond
all belief. The dependence of the Council upon the
Roman Curia was as marked as the paucity of its
members and their lack of ability. Nothing was done,
nothing was decided, without consulting Rome ; and the
Protestants ironically observed that the inspiration of its
members depended on the couriers who travelled to and
from the Pope. As soon as the Council met it condemned

the chief reformed doctrines.   In the decree on the Bible
and Traditions, it was stated that Christian truth and
discipline were contained, not only in Holy Writ, but in
the unwritten traditions of the Church.   These traditions,
preserved by an unbroken succession in the Catholic
Church, whether relating to faith or morality, the Council
declared to be absolutely on an equality with the inspired
writings of the Old and New Testament.   At the same
time, the Fathers carefully abstained from giving the
slightest clue to the character, the subject-matter, and the
number of these traditions.   With whom they originated,
in what Churches they were handed down, and what
proofs of their " unbroken succession " could be adduced—
these were questions on which the decree maintained a
discreet and absolute silence.   To compensate for this
silence the Council decreed that no one should interpret
Scripture in defiance of the opinion of the Church, " to
whom alone it belongs to judge of the true meaning and
interpretation of the Scripture."   The real object of this
decree was set in the clearest light by the preceding discussion.   Bishop after bishop rose in his place to denounce
the audacity of laymen who dared to interpret the Bible :
" the Church alone may interpret the words of Christ " :
" all, especially the Laity, should be forbidden to interpret
Holy Writ " : " laymen should be forbidden to interpret
Scripture, since that office belongs to ecclesiastics " : " the
Laity should be absolutely excluded from the interpretation of Holy Writ " : such were the speeches made
by leading members of the Council.   Had the Fathers
of Trent been able to have their way, the lips of
Melanchthon would have been sealed for ever.

If the hostile attitude of the Council towards the
reformed Churches was illustrated by the decree on
Scripture and Tradition, it was emphasized beyond all
possibility of question by the decree on Justification.   The
very form of the Evangelical Article on Justification con-
trasted strongly with the elaborate and laboured prolixity

of the Tridentine decree. Instead of the plain and perspicuous statement of the doctrine which might be found
in the Reformed confessions of faith, and which was
intelligible to clergy and laity, to simple and learnèd alike,
the Roman theologians drew up a series of statements
and definitions, overlaid with verbose detail and bristling
with scholastic subleties, as unintelligible to the ordinary
reader as a lemma of Newton or a chapter of Kant's
Critique of pure Reason. It is needless to examine this
decree at length; but it is important to notice a great
difference of form between the Evangelical Article and
the Tridentine decree on Justification. The Reformers in
their doctrine of Justification never lost sight of the fact
that they were writing for the vast multitude of Christian
believers who had been brought up amid the ever-present
and immeasurable influences of the Christian community.
Their doctrine was intended as a practical answer to the
practical question—"How may I, a Christian believer,
a baptized member of the Church, who am striving to
live a Christian life, be assured that I am justified in
God's sight?" The Fathers of Trent, on the contrary,
began by describing the manner in which "the ungodly"
attains to Justification, as if they were compiling a
theological handbook for the use of Mahometans and
Brahmins. In this respect the incontestable superiority
of the Reformed doctrine is evident at a glance.*

Far more important than this difference was the difference of opinion about a doctrine inseparably connected
with the doctrine of Justification—the doctrine of the
assurance of salvation. The teaching of the Reformers
was perfectly simple and consistent. "The Christian,"

---

* This is made clear by the language of the Anglican Article—
"We are accounted righteous before God. . . . Wherefore that we
are justified by faith only . . ."—the "we" being *ex hypothesi*
the Christian believers who have already been made in baptism
"members of Christ, children of God, and inheritors of the Kingdom
of Heaven."

they argued, "who is justified by faith is in a state of salvation, and, after his mortal course is finished, receives from God the gift of eternal life. Justification, salvation, and eternal life are all alike the gift of God. But precisely for this reason, because they are freely bestowed by God upon the penitent and believing sinner, because they are in no way dependent upon his own fitful efforts, upon the inconsistencies and shortcomings of his Christian walk and conversation, he may hold to them and rest upon them with an unshaken faith and an unwavering assurance, confident that He Who has begun a good work in him will perfect it unto the end." Again and again the Reformers pointed to this religious consequence of their doctrine of Justification as the only true solace for the troubled conscience of the doubting or despairing believer. The justified Christian was not only warranted in believing that his salvation was assured, he was bound to believe it, if he would comprehend with all Saints the love of Christ which passeth knowledge..

This truth which lies at the very root of the spiritual life was completely maimed and marred by the Roman doctrine. The Fathers of Trent drew up a special section of their decree against " the empty confidence of heretics." To be assured that our sins are forgiven us is "a vain and ungodly confidence" : we must not assert that those who are truly justified ought to hold, without a shadow of doubt, that they are justified; " for no one can know with the certainty of a faith which is free from all possibility of error that he has obtained the grace of God." Indeed, the Fathers of the Council seemed to be so bent upon the refutation of the heretics that they took no pains to bring the different parts of their decree into harmony. Accordingly we are bidden by the Council to believe that the justified Christian's meritorious good works are sufficient to gain for him eternal life, but are insufficient to warrant his assurance that he is among the number of God's elect. This twofold statement is as inconsistent from the theological point of view as it is unfounded from the religious point of view.

While the Pope was busily engaged in laying the new doctrinal foundations of his Church in Italy, the Emperor was emulating his theological activity in Germany. The friendship between the ill-matched yokefellows had been of short duration. The Pope soon became jealous of the Emperor, the Emperor was soon offended with the Pope. Charles wished to dictate the order of proceedings at the Council, and Paul would not submit to his interference. Charles had expressly stipulated that the Council should be held on German soil, and Paul to show his independence sanctioned the transference of the Council from Trent to Bologna. The spiritual and temporal potentates exchanged revilings and recriminations with the energy of troopers ; and Charles, determined to take his revenge on his treacherous ally, assumed the character of a new Constantine or a new Justinian. He issued in 1548 a theological work called the "Interim," in which the familiar dogmas of the Middle Ages had been refurbished with a superficial varnish of Evangelical doctrine, and called upon the whole Empire to accept it. It is difficult to say whether the staunch Romanists or the staunch Protestants were most irritated by this proceeding : the former were indignant that the Emperor, a mere secular person, should presume to usurp the powers and prerogatives of Pope and Council; the latter were indignant that the worst dogmas of the Medieval Church should be foisted upon them under a transparent disguise which deceived no one. Distichs, anagrams, and acrostics, in elegiac, hexameter, and sapphic verse, were written against the book: a special coin, called the "Interim," was struck, bearing as a superscription the significant words, " Render unto Cæsar the things which are Cæsar's, and unto God the things which are God's." One poem was a scathing satire, entitled " The Holy Lady, St. Interim "; another was composed in the words and with the imagery of Isaiah. In one writing the Bible narrative of Aaron's golden calf was adapted " to the controversy of our times " ; in another, Christian folk were bidden to make no change in the Church to please the devil and Antichrist; a third was thrown into the form of questions and answers, " What part of speech is Interim ? An adverb. What is an adverb ? The word of Satan linked to the Word of God for the deceiving of souls " ; a fourth gave a pretended genealogy of the Interim, " My mother is the woman of Babylon, beauteous beyond measure, decked with purple, silk, and gold : Kings and princes have dalliance with her, all their desire is for her." Insolent ecclesiastics, supported by ruthless soldiers, swept through the land, driving the Protestant ministers by hundreds from hearth and home. In many parts of Protestant Germany the heavy hand of Charles was so greatly dreaded that no resistance was offered to his despotic will : but in the north the spirit of religious liberty and enlightened patriotism could not be quelled, and the great city of Magdeburg raised the standard of revolt.

The rebellion of Magdeburg would have mattered little if Charles had gained the support of the Empire by a conciliatory and prudent policy. But, with a short-sightedness as fatal as that of the famous Emperor who two centuries and a half later trod in his footsteps, he assumed that Germany had been humbled for ever, and that " the mad, drunken Germans," as he contemptuously termed them, had neither the wit nor the energy to throw off the Spanish yoke. With a violence as arbitrary as Napoleon's, but with even less justification than Napoleon could plead, he violated the constitutional rights of his subjects, and treated them as though they were conquered enemies. In defiance of his election oath and the protest of his Imperial Diet, he quartered his brutal Spanish soldiery in all parts of the Empire, till the whole of Germany rang with tales of their excesses and outrages. When the government of Free and Imperial cities was too democratic for his taste he forcibly changed it, and infused the measure of aristocratic leaven which he judged to be fitting. It was currently reported that the Spanish troops had threatened to put to the sword every man, woman, and child in Augsburg who resisted the Imperial will. The courtiers in attendance upon Charles were described by patriotic Germans as bloodsuckers; the celebrated Duke of Alva alone was credited with having plundered Germany of more than a million and a half of florins. In Franconia Charles broke the solemn promises which he had made to knights and nobles, and his conduct gave rise to the alarming rumour that a register was kept of the name and property of all persons of distinction who disputed his commands. The accounts which were sent by the deputies to their princes spoke of nothing but the intolerable arrogance of the Spaniards. A letter sent from Brussels conveyed the gossip of the Imperial Court : " It would never be well with the German lands until the pride of the German princes had been lowered; it was far better for Germany to have one lord than a host of petty tyrants, who only plagued their subjects with hunting and fighting, and did not apply themselves to a single matter in earnest." These opinions, it was added, were only natural, because the majority in the Council of the Empire and in the Emperor's Council were priests, "and therefore one wolf howls just like another." Flushed with his success, Charles had conceived far-reaching plans : he wished to make the Imperial crown hereditary in his family, and sent for his son Philip to attend the Diet that he might secure the succession for him. The Emperor's ministers and courtiers looked upon the consent of the Electors as a foregone conclusion. " When the Electors have reassembled," such was the account of the deputies of Brandenburg, "the matter will be finished out of hand. As soon as they see the Emperor's face and hear his winning words, as soon as he feasts them at splendid banquets, pledges them in the flowing grace-cup, and sets them down at the gaming table, they will be as docile as lambs. The Spaniards think they are masters of the Empire, and can lead the Germans by the nose as a buffalo. Only give them feasting, drinking, hunting, and gaming enough (such is the Spaniards' cry), and they will not trouble themselves about the government and affairs of the Empire. So low have we sunk that we, who once were dreaded by all nations, are now despised and mocked." The German princes read these scornful words with swelling hearts. Charles had arrayed against himself the most powerful motives which can influence mankind—the passion of religious faith, the love of political freedom, and the keen sense of personal honour. It is no marvel that his fall was so swift and so complete.

The policy of Charles would have been rash and fool-hardy if he had been face to face with Germany alone; but he was surrounded by enemies who were prepared at any moment to throw their weight into the balance against him. The Turks were as formidable as they had ever been. The hostility of the Pope was all the more dangerous because it was concealed under a fair exterior. The young King of France was as vehement in his opposition to the House of Austria as his father had been twenty-five years before. His ambassador was closeted with the Pope to devise ways and means "for bleeding the Emperor to death without seeming to make him bleed." In Germany Charles had not a single warm friend except among the Bishops, who rested upon him their hopes for the restoration of their jurisdiction and the restitution of ecclesiastical property. He could not bring himself to believe that any danger threatened his authority within the confines of the Empire. Yet at the very moment that he was indulging in this confident assurance the most dangerous plots were in progress against him.

Of these plots Maurice of Saxony was the soul. With the watchful eye of a born statesman he accurately noted the currents and eddies of thought and feeling in the world around him. With the sensitive temper of a proud and high-spirited German prince, he instinctively discerned how galling the Emperor's conduct must be to the proud and self-reliant people who had deigned to elect him as their chief. He could brook as little as his neighbours the swaggering insolence of the Emperor's ministers, who treated the German nation as if they were Roman pro-consuls hectoring and bullying the wretched provincials of Syria and Egypt. He saw what Charles, blinded by his religious and dynastic prejudices, had never been able to see, that the Reformation was a great fact in the history of the world and the development of human society, and that to talk of crushing it was as idle as to dream of levelling the Alps. But if Maurice was influenced by these statesmanlike considerations, he was no less influenced by personal emotions. Charles did not betray the slightest intention of liberating the Landgrave, for whose liberation Maurice had made himself responsible. How could the Elector remain unmoved by the touching appeals which were addressed to him, at one time by his father-in-law, at another by his brother-in-law? How could he hold up his head in the German Diet, while men whispered of him that he had betrayed his near relation and his dearest friend into the toils of the Spanish double-dealer?

Yet Maurice's task was far from easy. The price at which he had sold his support and alliance to Charles had drawn down upon him a greater storm of obloquy than any German prince of the sixteenth century had success-fully braved. The news that he had been invested by the Emperor with the Electorate of Saxony was received throughout Protestant Germany with bitter indignation. No Protestant could forgive him for his conduct to the Elector, his own cousin and the tried champion of the Evangelical cause. Men declared him guilty of the heinous sins of irreligion and ingratitude in their most aggravated forms. A flood of invectives was poured forth against him. In the contemporary literature he was denounced as the Judas of the Evangelical cause, who could play the traitor for filthy lucre in a masterly fashion, who was the devil's pupil and had laid his lessons to heart, who to his eternal disgrace had brought in the Italians to waste and persecute his fatherland, and the Spaniards to outrage man and woman with their cruelty and lust.   Even those who were disposed to judge him most leniently looked askance at the Epicurean who made a mock of religious faith, at the perjured kinsman and false traitor who was ready to pledge his very soul for wealth and honours, like the Faust of Medieval legend.   It was only with the greatest difficulty that he could surmount the ineradicable suspicions of his brother princes, could convince them that he was completely estranged from Charles and perfectly sincere in his hostility to him, or could induce them to let him open negotiations with the French King for the preservation of the Protestant Churches and of the Empire's liberties.

The siege of Madgeburg gave Maurice the opportunity for which he was watching.   Charles had appointed him commander-in-chief, to wreak his vengeance on the rebellious city.   While he was professedly engaged in this task, he was quietly gathering up the threads of his intrigues with the German princes and with France, completely blinded Charles and Granvella by his diplomatic skill, lulled to rest the suspicions of his watchful enemies, and with a secrecy and energy which proved irresistible swooped down upon southern Germany and forced the Emperor to flee for his life like a thief in the night.   No powerful Emperor had suffered so deep a humiliation since Henry the Fourth stood in a penitent's garb amid the snows of Canossa.

Maurice's success had been complete.   He had revealed to the world the impotence of the great monarch whose gigantic power had overshadowed Europe for a quarter of a century; he shook off at once the hatred and the calumny which for four years had clung to his steps, and

was celebrated throughout Protestant Germany as a hero
and a patriot. In the negotiations which followed, he
took by general consent the leading part, forced Charles
to liberate the Landgrave, drew up a terrible indictment
which set forth all the Emperor's crimes and misdemeanours, required as an indispensable preliminary the
establishment of religious toleration and a religious peace,
drove the foreign Councillors in headlong flight, compelled
the alien troops to withdraw, won over Ferdinand, the
Emperor's brother, to support his demands, and demonstrated by the clearest of all proofs that the whole of
Germany was banded together as one man in hostility to
the policy of Charles and the domination of Spain.

Maurice did not live to see the accomplishment of the
work which he had commenced with such brilliant success.
When the Diet met at Augsburg in 1555, the young Prince,
who even at an early age had displayed such remarkable
gifts, was no more.   The chief conduct of the negotiations
fell to Ferdinand ; for Charles could not bring himself to
appear before the princes who had humiliated him so
deeply, nor to sacrifice the convictions of a lifetime at the
bidding of heretics.   Three important questions awaited
an answer at the Diet : First, should there be a religious
peace ?   Secondly, should this religious peace be permanent and unconditional ?   Thirdly, with what limitations and restrictions should it be granted ?   The answer
to the first question would not have been doubtful but for
the action of the Papal Curia.   The agents of Rome,
faithful to their well-worn policy, were busily engaged in
sowing distrust, dissension, and hatred among the members
of the Diet.   It was fortunate that at Augsburg, as so often
since, the sound common sense and political wisdom of
statesmen turned a deaf ear to the cry of ecclesiastical
bigotry.   The answer to the second question was not as
simple as the answer to the first.   Up to this time every
religious peace had been in reality a religious truce.   It
was only valid till the meeting of the General Council, or

till the meeting of the next Diet, or till the religious dispute
had been settled.   In 1552 Maurice had recognized that
no religious peace could be satisfactory unless it contained the pledge of its own permanence; and though
Maurice had passed away, his Evangelical kinsmen were
the heirs of his principles and his policy.   Before the Diet
had been sitting many weeks, the princes of Saxony,
Brandenburg, and Hesse met at Nuremberg, and renewed
the hereditary alliance between the three Principalities,
pledging themselves to adhere to the Confession of Augsburg, and declaring that they would not recognize the
decision of the majority in the Diet as binding.   These
stipulations made a deep and instantaneous impression.
In the words of one of the Hessian Councillors, "they have
produced a greater effect than all the Councils, Colloquies,
and Diets which have been held up to the present day."

The unconditional and permanent religious peace was
in this way secured.   Should it be fenced in by any limitations and restrictions?   Some points were settled with
comparative ease.   Foremost among these was the vexed
question of ecclesiastical property, which had been hotly
debated for many years.   It was now decided that all the
property of which the Roman clergy had lost possession
before the year 1552 should be adjudged and held to belong
of right to the adherents of the Confession of Augsburg.
On the other hand, the question of individual toleration
was decided against the wishes of the Evangelical Estates.
The plan which the members of the Reformed Churches
had put forward for corporate toleration (if the phrase may
be coined) had been unreservedly conceded by their opponents.   All the Estates of the Empire should leave each
other in peaceful and quiet enjoyment of their religion.
But the further demand that, whatever the religion of the
prince might be, any one of his subjects who held different
opinions should be at liberty to obey the dictates of his
conscience, was hotly opposed: on this question the most
powerful of the temporal princes, Austria and Bavaria,

were at one with the spiritual princes.   The prospect was
in truth alarming.   In those parts of the Empire where
the Church of Rome was still dominant, the secret friends
of the Reformation were growing in numbers from year to
year.   It was notorious that the Austrian hereditary lands
were honeycombed with heresy.   The concession of individual toleration would intensify the evil tenfold ; and
twenty years hence the Emperor might be actually ruling
over a minority of orthodox subjects in his own territories.
Ferdinand declared in the most explicit terms that he
would rather let the whole peace fall to the ground than
give his consent to this clause ; he would rather mount his
horse and ride home, and leave the Diet to its own devices.
In the face of this opposition the Protestant Estates per-
ceived the uselessness of persisting in their demands, and
withdrew the Article.   Yet even Ferdinand and the Bishops,
though they stubbornly refused to adopt the broad views
of toleration put forward by the Evangelical Princes, had
been constrained to make a vast concession to the new
principle which the Reformation had introduced into
western Europe, had been forced to discard publicly the
principles of the Middle Ages, and to recognize, however
reluctantly, the necessity of putting the new wine into
new bottles.   It unquestionably redounds to the honour
of the Evangelical deputies that they were the first band
of responsible statesmen who asserted, however imperfectly, the fruitful principle of religious toleration and
liberty of conscience.   If they failed to carry the new
principle to its logical conclusion, if they halted halfway
between absolute intolerance and complete toleration, it
would be unjust on that account to make light of the
measures which they advocated.   The pioneer who is the
first to clear the virgin forest may claim his due meed of
praise as justly as the architect who raises stately palaces
upon the space which has been cleared.

   The second question on which the Evangelical Estates
were defeated affected the future prospects of the two

Churches.   The rights of the principalities and cities which had already embraced the Reformed faith were effectively secured.   But it was possible that in the years to come the Protestant Estates would receive further accessions from the Estates which still remained in their allegiance to the Church of Rome.   Should this be expressly sanctioned by the terms of peace ?   And if so, should the permission be absolute or conditional ?   Both parties at the Diet were fully prepared to concede this liberty of choice to the temporal Estates.   But the possible conversion of the spiritual princes was a very different matter, and this question was debated with a heat and a violence which had never been surpassed at any previous Diet.   Ferdinand was even less disposed to give way on this point than on the preceding.   He and his ministers were filled with alarm as they contemplated the possibility of a Protestant holding an Electoral Arch-bishopric.   Ferdinand as King of the Romans might become Emperor, but only on sufferance, the candidature of his son might be rejected, and the House of Austria might be permanently excluded from the Imperial throne. Only with the greatest reluctance and after a prolonged struggle did the Protestant princes make up their minds to yield to Ferdinand's demands, that every member of the ecclesiastical Order who joined the Reformed Church should at once resign his office and emoluments.

Finally, in all Free and Imperial cities where both Churches were already established Ferdinand granted the individual toleration which he had refused to concede in the Romanist principalities : clergy and laity, whatever their creed, should live side by side in peace and quiet ; neither party should presume to suppress or abolish the religion or divine worship of the other.   It might be urged that the votes of the majority ought to prevail, but it would be " not a little grievous " if the minority in many of these cities were forced to change their religion by the will of the majority ;   " for equals have no power over each other, especially in this high and weighty matter of faith and religion." This concession was a remarkable proof how far Ferdinand had advanced along the path of toleration under the influence of altered circumstances and of the lessons which the Reformation had taught him.

The irony of history was never more curiously illustrated than by the action of Ferdinand in 1555. The heir to the Holy Roman Empire took a foremost part in undermining the foundations of his splendid inheritance. What, indeed, was left of the royal Vicar of Christ when half of his subjects were separated from him by an impassable gulf on the most vital of all questions, when he had of his own free will legalized the existence of heresy, and had sealed a covenant of unchangeable friendship with those who branded the spiritual Vicar of Christ with the terrible name of Antichrist? The overthrow of Charles had been the overthrow of the Medieval Empire : and on the day when Ferdinand signed the religious peace of Augsburg, the crown of Charlemagne, of the Othos, and the Henries, and the Fredericks, had fallen into the dust for ever.

CHAPTER V.

THE REFORMATION IN THE SCANDINAVIAN KINGDOMS.

THE founding of the Reformed Churches in the Scandinavian Kingdoms was contemporaneous with a memorable event in their political history. By the Treaty of Calmar at the close of the fourteenth century Denmark, Norway, and Sweden were united under one sovereign. It is possible that under more favourable circumstances this union might have proved as durable and beneficial as the Confederation of the Swiss Cantons or the union between England and Scotland. But the Swedes were suspicious and restive ; the Danes were overbearing and inconsiderate. At last, in 1520, after the relations between the two countries had been strained for many years, Christian the Second, a reckless and unprincipled king, destitute of any real ability as a statesman, by a shameful act of perfidy and cruelty, the more shameful because it was cloaked under a transparent show of legality, made an irreparable breach between the northern and the southern kingdoms. The same misgovernment and incapacity which had cost Christian the crown of Sweden cost him the crown of Denmark also. In 1523 the nobles of Jutland renounced their allegiance to him, and offered the crown to his uncle Frederick, Duke of Schleswig and Holstein. Christian stooped to temporize with his nobles and the Duke, and when his attempts failed fled in despair. In August Frederick accepted the terms which the Danes dictated, and in December Copenhagen, which had fought fiercely for Christian, surrendered.

By the terms of his compact with his new subjects Frederick undertook to maintain all the rights of the Clergy, and to prevent any heretics or disciples of Luther from teaching doctrines at variance with the principles of the Medieval Church. These clauses were not inserted without good reason, for the new teaching had already found its way into Denmark. The two Duchies of Schleswig and Holstein formed the connecting link between Denmark and Germany. The trade with the great Hanse towns, Hamburg, Lubeck, Rostock, and Stralsund, was active and ceaseless. Scarcely less important was the trade with the Netherlands. The intercourse between the merchants and seamen in these parts and in the seaboard towns of the Scandinavian Kingdoms led to a constant interchange of ideas. The wave of the new learning had spread from Germany over Denmark, and young Danes attended the famous Universities of Rostock, Leipzig, Cologne, and Strasburg. In the two years preceding the Diet of Worms nineteen Danes matriculated at the University of Wittenberg, attended the lectures of Luther and Melanchthon, listened to the sermons of the great Reformer, and read the books which had exercised an influence unparalleled for its extent and its power in the literary history of Europe.

It was not, however, in the inherent power of the new doctrines alone that the strength of the Danish Reformation lay. In no part of Europe, except perhaps in Rome itself, had the Medieval Church sunk lower than in the Scandinavian Kingdoms. The Danish prelates were among the most ignorant, the most unspiritual, the most worldly, the most tyrannical, the idlest, and the richest in Christendom. The lower Clergy did not possess any virtues to atone for the vices of the higher Clergy. The monks were hated by the poor because they diverted the stream of popular charity into their pockets. So little had been done for the spiritual enlightenment of the people that sermons were preached only once a month, that three priests were considered sufficient to minister in twelve Churches, that Canons held six or seven benefices apiece, that the higher offices in the Church were regarded as the exclusive perquisite of the nobility, irrespective of any literary or spiritual qualifications, that the people were taught nothing but fables by ignorant priests appointed by bishops no less ignorant, that vendors of Indulgences hawked their wares under episcopal patronage, and that no part of the Bible, not even the Epistles and Gospels for Sundays and holy days, had been translated into the vulgar tongue.

Under these circumstances it would have been little short of a miracle if the new doctrines had not spread in Denmark. In fact, the Reformation was more completely the result of a popular movement in the Danish Kingdom than in any other country. The most remarkable of the leading reformers in Denmark was Tausen, a peasant's son like Luther, who had felt himself drawn to a monastic life like the German reformer, and had entered the monastery of Antwerskow, one of the richest in the kingdom. Far inferior to Luther in originality, in genius, in eloquence, and in emotional power, he resembled Knox in his hortative and argumentative gifts, and in the clearness and directness of his style. His residence in the monastery opened his eyes to the doctrinal errors and the low moral standard of the Medieval Church; and having obtained leave of absence in 1517, when he was twenty-three years of age, he visited Cologne and Louvain, and finally Wittenberg. In Wittenberg he remained for two years, sitting at the feet of Luther and Melanchthon, and in 1521 returned to his native land a convinced Protestant. In Holy Week, 1524, he preached for the first time on the doctrine of Justification by Faith, excited the displeasure of his Prior, was removed to another house of the Order at Wiborg, but continued his teaching there, and converted several of the brethren. Still more angry, his superiors imprisoned him; but he was able to preach to his friends through the window of his cell, and the reports and summaries of his sermons were carried into all the burghers' houses.

Hitherto Frederick had done nothing. He had not much energy and decision of character; his liberty of action had been fettered by the terms of his agreement; and he lay under an obligation to the Danish prelates who had greatly exerted themselves to procure him the crown. But his course of action had clearly shown with which side his sympathies were. Soon after he had mounted the Danish throne he had given permission to the Evangelical preachers to labour undisturbed in Schleswig. In 1526 he had married his daughter to the Duke of Prussia, one of the most Protestant Princes in Europe. He began to receive the Eucharist in both kinds, and to disregard the Medieval laws about fasting. He had sent his son Christian to the Diet of Worms, and the young Prince had returned full of enthusiasm for Luther, and full of zeal for Evangelical truth. In 1527 and 1528 Christian had devoted himself to the furtherance of Lutheranism in his own domains in North Schleswig, had organized the New Church under the supervision of German theologians, and had in this way given a fresh impulse to the Reformation in Denmark. The popular sympathy with which the Evangelical preachers were greeted seems to have decided Frederick to drop the mask and to take a bold step. In the autumn of 1526 he appointed Tausen to the post of Court Chaplain, and gave the Town Council of Wiborg orders to protect him in his office of preacher, in spite of the Bishop's prohibition. At the same time Jensen was allowed to open a public school in Wiborg, and to train young men for the ministry of the New Church. It was a still bolder measure that the King in 1527 summoned at Odense the first Diet which had been held in Denmark to settle religious questions, and delivered an uncompromising speech to the assembled prelates. He pointed to the vast religious changes in Germany, and to

the revelation of Papal deceit and imposture, reminded
them of their duty to feed the flock of Christ with the
pure Word of God, repeated the complaints of thousands
that, instead of teaching the truth, they drew from muddy
fountains the most absurd traditions, fables, and miracles,
and declared that, as the Reformation had struck root so
deeply, it was his will that the free profession of both
creeds, the new and the old, should be allowed to all
his subjects.

From this moment the religious movement advanced
with giant strides. The whole clergy of Denmark could
only put forward one champion of real ability and learning,
Paul Eliesen, Reader of Theology in the University of
Copenhagen, and afterwards Provincial of the Carmelites.
Eliesen was one of the many Romanists who were clear-
sighted and fair-minded enough to recognize the errors
and abuses of the Medieval Church, but who shrank from
the rejection of the Papal supremacy, and dreaded the
results of the Reformers' teaching. No Lutheran could
have spoken more strongly of the wealth, the sloth, the
ambition, the deceit, the luxury, the vanity, the licentiousness, the pride, the avarice, and the tyranny of ecclesiastics.
But the reformation for which he longed was purely practical and moral ; with a religious reformation he would
have nothing to do. Naturally he satisfied neither party,
for he condemned both, and by the popular voice he was
nicknamed " turncoat," though he deserved the title as
little as Erasmus. With voice and pen he defended the
doctrines of the Medieval theology, and his controversial
writings are valuable as an indication of the lines on which
sober and enlightened Romanists during the first half of
the sixteenth century defended the traditional faith. They
are also exceptionally interesting as the voice of one crying
in the wilderness, the utterance of the only Dane who
boldly attempted to roll back the advancing Reformation.

The important town of Malmo was the first to introduce
the Reformation. The Archbishop of Lund, in whose

diocese Malmo lay, prohibited the Lutheran preacher ;
but the Burgomaster defied the Archbishop, and assigned
a meadow which belonged to the magistrates for the
open-air Lutheran services. This was in June, 1527.
Then Frederick intervened, and gave the preacher one of
the churches. This proved too small for the crowds which
flocked to hear him, and he was allowed to preach in a
larger building. Soon after, Mass was read in the vulgar
tongue, hymns were translated into Danish, and the
numerous editions of these hymn-books testified to their
popularity. Private Masses were abolished ; monks of
evil life were expelled from the city ; at the request of the
burghers the King allowed them to found a hospital,
endowing it with the lands and houses bequeathed to
altars, guilds, and vicariates, to maintain a Reformed
Minister, to establish a school with teachers qualified to
give instruction in the Scriptures, and to defray the
expenses from ecclesiastical property. Before the close of
1529 the Reformed Church in the city had been organized,
and the old system had disappeared. Many cities followed
the example of Malmo, and every fresh victory made the
next easier. Tausen was summoned by Frederick from
Wiborg to Copenhagen, and placed as minister in the
chief church of the city. He introduced a Danish hymn-
book, read Mass in the vulgar tongue, and advocated the
removal of images from churches. Within a year two
more parish churches in the capital were handed over to
the Reformers, and only one was left to the Catholics.

The triumph of the Reformation led to an outburst of
literary activity. Before the Reformation most of the
Danish publications had issued from German and French
printing-presses. In 1528 a German publisher from
Stuttgart set up a printing-press in Wiborg, and at the
same time another was erected in Malmo. Within four
years from that date about forty books in Danish had
been published. Of these the most important by far was
the translation of the New Testament and the Psalms by

Petersen, a Canon of Lund; for in Denmark, as in other countries, the advent of the Reformation brought the knowledge of the Bible to all classes of the community. A Danish version of the New Testament had already been made under the patronage of Christian the Second, and had been published at Wittenberg by the publisher of Luther's Bible. But the great defect of the earlier translation had been that the language in which it was written was neither lucid nor idiomatic. In both these points the translation of Petersen was far superior. He recognized the principles which must guide the translator, and avoided the twofold danger of a version which reproduced the original word for word, and a version which attempted to follow servilely the Greek idiom. To produce a Danish translation like the earlier version, which, however faithfully it adhered to the original, was unintelligible or strange to the Danish reader, seemed to him a fatal mistake. Petersen's translation was published at Antwerp in 1529, for he had followed the deposed King to the Netherlands. It was warmly welcomed by his countrymen, and a second edition was soon called for. Even if it cannot compare with the translation of Luther, it exerted an important influence in fixing the national language and forming a literary standard.

The fortunes of the Roman Church had sunk to a low ebb by the close of 1529, but in the following year they sank lower still. It was on the Monastic Orders, especially on the Mendicants, that the full weight of their Church's unpopularity fell. Many were compelled to surrender their monasteries for want of money. Others were driven out by angry mobs who refused to tolerate them any longer. In some cases the monastic buildings were appropriated for hospitals or parish churches. The Minorites of Copenhagen in the spring of 1530 wrote a public letter in which they pathetically observed that, as the populace would not put up with them any longer, and as they were forbidden to ask for alms, they voluntarily

surrendered their buildings to the Magistrates, Council,
and burghers of the capital. The Minorites of Aalborg
were treated with unscrupulous violence; first one part of
their buildings and then another was seized, their provisions were taken from them, the clappers of their bells
were removed, and at length they were driven out in a
body. In some towns the monastic property was made
over to the burghers as soon as the monks had quitted the
monasteries : in others a compact was made ; the property
should be surrendered to the burghers, but any monks
who wished to remain should be maintained until their
death at the public expense. Nowhere did any monasteries find defenders ; the nobles laid hands on all they
could get ; and even bishops pressed forward to join in the
general pillage.

Two satires in rhyme which were published at this
period throw a strong side-light upon the currents of
popular feeling. "The Sick Mass" is an adaptation of
one of the most widely-circulated satires against the
Church of Rome which appeared in the sixteenth century.
Originally written in prose by a priest of Berne, it was
reproduced with modifications in High German, Low
German, and Dutch, as well as in Danish. It is interesting as a proof of the bitterness with which the Medieval
Mass was regarded by the Reformers in all countries to
which the new doctrines had penetrated. It is interesting
also as a mark of the religious fellowship and literary intercourse which bound together lands lying as far apart as
Switzerland in the South, Holland in the West, and
Denmark in the North, and which formed one of the
strongest bulwarks of the Reformed Churches in the early
years of their existence. The Danish translation opens
with a dialogue between the Pope and his Cardinal. The
latter has received the startling and mournful tidings that
the Mass is sick unto death. When the Pope asks in
astonishment what the reason of this sickness is, the
Cardinal replies that the Mass has gained the repute of

being the grossest idolatry and a mere means for extorting
money.   What else can be expected when men confront
the Mass with the true Eucharist, when all can read the
Bible, and when they ransack the Prophets, the Acts of
the Apostles, and St. Paul for arguments and proofs?
Then the scene changes; a conclave of wise men assembles
to prescribe for the dying patient; there is a German
theologian, a Canon of Lund, a Precentor, and a Chaplain.
All remedies are unavailing, but the Canon suggests at
last that they shall roar, bawl, and screech till the heavens
are ready to fall.   Surely the sound of her mother's voice
will wake the dead.   The theologian shakes his head:
they may shout till they are hoarse and dumb before the
dead comes to life again.   Then other plans are proposed:
the Mass shall be carried into Purgatory to warm its legs,
but Purgatory is closed; it shall go on a pilgrimage to
St. Anne's image at Aabenraa, but the sacrilegious
peasants have dashed the image to pieces.   The drama
closes with a picture of the wise men leaving the house in
alarm to say that they were out of town when the patient
died, and that the guilt of its death must be laid at
Luther's door.

   " Peter Smith and Adser Peasant " is of purely Danish
origin.   The scene is laid in an inn where the two wayfarers meet.   Adser Peasant is going on a pilgrimage to
Our Lady of Karup, one of the most famous resorts for
pilgrims in Denmark.   Peter Smith, who holds Lutheran
opinions, though he disclaims the name of Lutheran,
dissuades him, and induces him to change his mind.   A
priest and a monk who are in the guest chamber join in
the conversation; and this leads Peter Smith to impeach
the whole Medieval system, adoration of Saints, pilgrimages, and monastic holiness, all pure inventions and
deceptions to wheedle money out of simple folk.   Even
tithes do not escape his searching criticism : God, it is true,
commanded them to be paid under the Old Dispensation,
but Christ in the New Testament does not say a word

about them.   The monk, who is travelling to collect alms
for his monastery, at last confesses that he is convinced :
he allows that Peter speaks the truth, that his system is a
worthless imposture, and that monks are wholly useless.
Peter Smith concludes with a summary of his creed : " If I
believe in God with a firm faith, I love Him with a perfect
love : if I love Him with all my heart, I gladly keep His
commandments at all times ; and if I fulfil His Law, I love
my neighbour as myself."

At this crisis in the religious affairs of his kingdom,
during the summer of 1530, at the very time when the
famous Diet of Augsburg was riveting the attention of
the German Empire, Frederick summoned the Romanist
prelates and the Lutheran preachers to the Diet of Copenhagen, "in order to attain to a Christian reform in religion
and to unity of doctrine." The Roman Church was represented by ten prelates who had seats in the State Council,
by the Provincial of the Dominicans, by Eliesen, and by
five Canons.   So conscious were they of the weakness of
their party that they sent to Cologne for theological
advocates to defend their cause.   The Lutherans were
represented by twenty-one Preachers, of whom Tausen
was the best known.   They drew up a " Confession of
Faith " in forty-three Articles, and at the end of a week
handed it to the King.   Not satisfied with this, they
determined to let the people know what doctrines they
held and why they held them.   Accordingly they agreed
to divide the Articles between them, and to preach two
sermons a day in defence and explanation of the Evangelical truths which they contained.   The Bishops angrily
protested, and called upon the King to silence the audacious heretics.   Frederick prohibited the sermons, and for
two days the preachers held their peace.   Then they
began again with renewed energy, preaching four sermons
daily and twelve on Sundays.   The Bishops' protest
had exhausted their resources ; they could do nothing
more.   Had it been a question of defending their secular

privileges, of improving and enlarging their ample estates, or of wringing an extra tithe out of the unhappy peasantry, they would have risen to the height of their great opportunity. But the religious questions which the heretics had raised lay beyond their ken; they did not profess to teach or to preach; and they took no shame to themselves for the avowal.

There is a marked difference between the Confession of Copenhagen and the Confession of Augsburg. The theological accuracy, the systematic arrangement, the balance, the compression, and the restraint which characterize the latter are almost entirely wanting in the former. Melanchthon's masterly Confession is pre-eminently scientific; the Confession of the Danish preachers is pre-eminently popular: Melanchthon's Confession is throughout conciliatory; the Confession of the Danish preachers is throughout polemical. The real significance and importance of the Danish Articles lie in the fact that, more than any other formal and official document of the sixteenth century, they give expression to the vehement indignation and the passionate antipathy which the errors and abuses of the Medieval Church had excited in the hearts of thousands in almost every country of Western Christendom. The studied moderation of Melanchthon's language is replaced by a fiery stream of virulent and abusive words and phrases. He who teaches any other doctrine than Scripture is blind, a fool, and an infidel. The words, the teaching, the high-sounding titles, and the fair-sounding names of human masters are treated with contempt. To teach any other righteousness or satisfaction than Christ's is to be a blasphemer and a heretic. Ceremonies which have no foundation in God's Word are a stumbling-block to the simple. The false Church curses those whom God blesses, denounces as heretics those who teach the truth, decks itself out with the figment of its own holiness, and walks after its own devices and laws. The blessings and the Indulgences of the ungodly and the hypocrites are execrable and accursed in God's sight, and their excommunication is worthless. To forbid marriage on the false plea of chastity, and to make a distinction of meats and days, are the doctrines of the devil. Monasteries, the monastic life, and monastic vows are an offence to God, and an open violation of Scripture. The true worship of God has nothing to do with canticles, masses, vigils for the dead, ornaments, churches, cowls, tonsures, and anointings, as is taught by an ignorant clergy and believed by a foolish people. The Mass offered for the living and the dead is blasphemy. Men's wisdom, holiness, pretended good works, and merits are worthless, and cannot save them, as many foolish and shameless Mass priests and monks teach at the present day. True Bishops are the preachers and ministers of God's Word, which they are bound to distribute and proclaim to the people on pain of their souls' destruction; they have no right to meddle with worldly business and worldly pomp, with military service, with lawsuits, or with courts of justice. To deny that all men ought to be subject to civil rulers and magistrates is an unchristian doctrine. Such Articles were a plain declaration of war to the death against the Medieval system.

It was arranged that there should be a public disputation on these Articles. But two difficulties arose. The Bishops demanded that the disputation should be held in Latin: the preachers refused to use any language except their own mother tongue. The preachers demanded that the Bible should be taken as the sole authority, and that the King, the State Council, and the people should decide which doctrine harmonized best with Scripture: the Bishops absolutely rejected such judges. This bold appeal from the sentence of the Popes, General Councils, and Bishops, to the enlightened judgment of thoughtful and earnest laymen, who were described in the Article of the Confession as Priests of God, in the highest and truest sense of the word, did not fail of its effect. Frederick, with the assent and approval of the Council of State, decreed that, as the Bishops had declined the disputation, the Lutherans should continue to preach God's Word until a General Council met ; in the meantime he would take both religions under his protection.

Though the Diet of Copenhagen had led to no decisive results, the actions and demeanour of the Bishops prejudiced the minds of the people still more against them. On the other hand, the trumpet of the Reformers had given forth no uncertain sound. Their boldness, their decided and outspoken opinions, the unsparing energy with which they had laid bare hypocrisy, falsehood, and ignorance, and the contempt with which they had struck at the crests of the proudest prelates, increased the admiration with which they were already regarded. While the Lutherans (thus men argued) overflowed with argument and exposition, the Bishops were unable to preach a single sermon or to deliver a single address, and could only endeavour to stifle free discussion by muzzling their opponents. When the Lutherans presented a perspicuous statement of their faith and a terrible indictment of their opponents' errors, the Bishops could only hand in a long list of the preachers' heretical tenets, as though the assertion of heresy were the proof of heresy. When the Lutherans challenged their opponents to a disputation, and offered conditions which commended themselves to all men as perfectly fair, the Bishops could only appeal to a Pope who knew nothing and to a General Council which never met.

After the Diet of Copenhagen Frederick took no more active measures in behalf of the Reformers. He had ensured them a fair field of action, he had disarmed the active hostility of their enemies, and, having done thus much, he left them to their own resources. There can be no doubt that in taking this course he was influenced by political reasons. The deposed King had never ceased spinning a web of diplomatic intrigues in order to secure

his restoration to the Danish throne. He appealed to
Frederick the Wise, Elector of Saxony, who was his
maternal uncle, to the Elector of Brandenburg, who was
his brother-in-law, and to Charles the Fifth, with whom
he was united by the closest ties through his marriage
with the Infanta Isabella. But the sympathy which he
received was purely platonic. No sovereign was inclined
to risk anything for the sake of a Prince who had only been
rewarded according to his deserts. Not before the end
of October, 1531, could he set sail from Holland with 7,000
troops and twenty-five ships, which Charles had at last
grudgingly supplied. This expedition, which Frederick
had long foreseen, filled him with alarm. It was most
important that in view of the impending danger he should
do nothing to alienate the powerful prelates or the nobles
with whom they were so closely allied by relationship and
interest. This would have been the case if he had attempted
to cast down the old Church from its dominant position,
or to organize a new Church at the expense of the
Bishops. He was rewarded for his neutrality by a complete victory over his rival. Christian the Second seems
to have lost heart when he found that the Danes would
offer a determined resistance, allowed himself to be
entrapped by an unworthy artifice, and was condemned
to imprisonment for life.

Frederick died in the next year. Though the Reformers
had not received any real assistance from him during the
last three years of his reign, the Reformation had made
steady progress. The most striking evidence of this
progress was the triumph of the Reformation in the cities
of Schonen, the increasing desertion of the monasteries,
the boldness of Tausen's controversial writings, the expulsion of the Bishop of Wiborg from his own Cathedral
by the Chapter and the Vicars with the assent of the
Town Council and the burghers, and the outburst of
Protestant passion in the capital, where the burghers
headed by the Burgomaster broke into the Church of

Our Lady, tore to pieces the missals, destroyed the ornaments, and overthrew the images of the Saints.

The death of Frederick gave the Bishops the opportunity of retrieving their fortunes for which they yearned. Frederick's eldest son, Christian, unlike his father, was a man of strong character and marked ability. Unlike his father, he held definite religious views, and was not inclined to drift with the stream or to let events shape themselves. The Bishops naturally regarded his accession to power with consternation, and foresaw that, if he became their King, his little finger would be thicker than his father's loins. But they might avert the evil day. Denmark was still, in practice as well as in theory, an elective monarchy, as Wolsey had reminded Christian the Second when he applied to the English Court for help after his deposition. The prelates were the most important members of the Council of State : they had strong supporters among the temporal members. If they could postpone indefinitely the election of a King, if in the meantime they could gather the reins of government into their own hands, if they could regain their lost privileges and obliterate the memory of their recent defeats, if by force or fraud they could sap the power of their victorious enemies, the tide might still turn in their favour, and the half-finished work of Frederick and the religious innovators might still be undone.

Nothing could have been more fatally short-sighted than such a policy. By adopting it the Bishops signed the death-warrant of the Roman Church in Denmark. It fully justified the profound insight of the Reformers who had declared that the meddling of ecclesiastics with affairs of State could only be fraught with mischief to the Church as well as the State. For the moment, it is true, they were completely successful. The Council of State adopted their resolution. In vain were warning voices raised in protest, in vain were they reminded that their selfish greed and intemperate revenge would be fruitful of serious evils.

Blind with arrogance, blind with passion, blind with hatred, they pressed recklessly forward, and plunged their country into the horrors of a civil war. For three years the struggle raged. Christian had on his side the two Duchies, Jutland, and Sweden. He proved himself more than a match for his enemies in capacity and resources. He humbled the proud Hanse city of Lubeck, won a great victory which made him master of the island of Funen, in union with the Swedish fleet gained another great victory at sea, laid siege to the rebellious capital, forced it to surrender after a prolonged blockade, and at the beginning of August, 1536, saw all Denmark at his feet.

The victorious King did not lose a moment before striking the decisive blow. A meeting of the State Council was held at which only the temporal Lords were present. It was resolved that the Bishops should be deprived of all spiritual and temporal power, and that their property should fall to the Crown. In order that the episcopal enemies of the King and the people might be taken off their guard, this agreement was signed under an oath of secrecy. When the Archbishop and one of the Bishops came to congratulate the King on the success of his arms, they were placed under arrest, and the others shortly after shared the same fate. This daring measure heralded the final downfall of the Medieval system in Denmark. After six centuries of unimpaired supremacy the ecclesiastical power was overthrown, and the spell which it had cast over the kingdoms of the north was broken for ever.

Two months later a Diet was held at Copenhagen, and Christian came forward with a formal impeachment of the Bishops. Though he allowed that all Orders had in some measure been partakers of the Bishops' sins, the great guilt of the civil war lay upon the Bishops alone. They had inflicted a deadly wrong on the kingdom by postponing the election of a King; they had made the laws of the country null and void by their decrees; they had usurped the right of sovereignty in their own dioceses.   In addition to this, they had resisted the Reformation, had persecuted the preachers of the Gospel, had not lived like Bishops but like knights and warriors, and had refused to assist their country with their wealth; they were all worthless, their pride was intolerable, and their rule was pernicious.   The Diet unanimously voted that the Bishops should be deposed, that the episcopal office in the Medieval sense should be abolished, that the vast episcopal property should be devoted to lightening the fiscal burdens, and that they would have in future " true Christian Bishops."   Then the Bishops were asked if they would undertake to remain quiet, to resign their share in the government of the State, to make no efforts to regain their former position, and to offer no opposition to the Reformation.   With one exception they agreed to these terms.

After the old system had been swept away, the King was anxious to organize the new Church.   One man was marked out by general consent as pre-eminently fitted to undertake this important task.   Bugenhagen, who. ranks among the most distinguished of Luther's converts and disciples, had made a great name for himself in North Germany by the ability with which he had organized the Churches of Hamburg, Lubeck, Brunswick, and Pomerania. His learning, his judgment, his moderation, his zeal, and his experience were recognized by Christian as gifts which would prove of inestimable value to the young Church of Denmark, and the Elector of Saxony allowed Bugenhagen to accept the invitation of the Danish King.   He arrived in 1537, and stayed till the spring of 1539.

The "Ordering of the Church of Denmark " may be taken as an admirable example of the Lutheran system. It begins with explaining why it is of no avail to wait for a General Council, which is always promised and never meets, gives a list of the errors and corruptions in the religious system of the Middle Ages, declares that Faith is the foundation of the spiritual life, and that the law of love is the only law of the Christian's life ; specifies the chief heads of doctrine, states the chief subjects on which the Christian preacher should dwell, and warns him against rashly dealing with mysterious questions which are far beyond the comprehension of man. Private Masses shall be abolished; only the public Mass for communicants on Sunday shall be retained, and shall be celebrated in the usual vestments, with a covered altar and the customary vessels and lights. The communicants shall come to the altar, the men on the right and the women on the left ; the Minister shall, if he thinks fit, elevate the consecrated elements with a moderate elevation, and at the same moment the cymbals shall sound ; the elements shall be administered in perfect silence, except that during the administration a chant shall be sung. The preacher shall not preach for more than an hour ; he shall not indulge in his own fancies, shall abstain from all invectives and calumnies, and shall not denounce the Romanists in an odious manner. Special festivals are marked by appropriate subjects for special sermons : on Saint Stephen's Day the care for the poor, on Saint John the Evangelist's Day the importance of the Christian's calling, " that he may not desert it and seek after another," on Saint John the Baptist's Day the ministry of the Word, and on All Saints' Day the faith and imitation of the Saints.

A special section is devoted to Absolution and Confession. The city clergy shall be in their churches on Saturday evening, and the country clergy on Sundays, to hear the confession of communicants. But no enumeration of separate sins must be required; only a general confession, or a confession of the sins of his calling, or of any special sins which trouble him. " And the Minister shall absolve him with the laying on of hands." No one may be admitted to the Eucharist if he has not given in his name to the Minister, or cannot give a reason for his faith, or lives a life which contradicts his profession.

The rules concerning the Ministry are of special importance.   The election of Bishops rests with the city clergy,
who are ordered to commission four of their number to
select a suitable candidate, and to present him to the
Bishop of the neighbouring diocese.   If he approves of
their choice, the Bishop-elect shall be sent to the King for
his confirmation.   The wealth of the deposed Bishops and
the evil which resulted from it led Bugenhagen to specify
in the minutest manner the limits of the Lutheran
Bishop's expenditure.   He might not have more than two
maid-servants, a secretary, a groom, a coachman, and a
valet.   As a true Bishop of the Church, he is not now
called " to canonical repose but to mighty toils ": his
duty is to study the Bible and to teach it to others, to
preach God's Word to the people throughout his diocese,
to promote peace and obedience among the King's subjects by impressing among them the duty of submission to
the powers that be, and to see that all preachers teach
Christ's Gospel in sincerity and harmony.   They shall
visit the schools in every city to which they come, and in
union with the King's Governors see that they are rightly
administered, and shall carefully enquire what provision is
made for the poor.   Every Bishop, after consultation with
the King's Governor, the Provost, the Elders, and the
Councillors of each city, shall appoint men who love God's
Word to be Deacons of the poor.   He shall hold a visitation in his diocese once every year, unless he sees reason
to hold it more frequently.   Seeing that the Bishops are
called to these mighty labours and cares for the Church's
sake, and may not demand the most trifling payment in
return, the King undertakes to make fitting provision for
their wants.

The supreme importance of the episcopal office made it
necessary to guard jealously against any misuse of it by
unworthy Bishops.   It was, therefore, enacted that, if a
Bishop neglected his office, or suffered himself to be
corrupted by gifts, or had been guilty of vice or heresy,

his case should be tried by the King, and his defence
should be heard before two or three Bishops.   If he did
not repent of his vice or error, he should be punished by
deposition.

A Provost shall be appointed for each Province or Pre-
fecture, all the Presbyters meeting together to elect one of
their number to the office.   If a living falls vacant, the
chief men of the parish, after consultation with the
Provost, shall appoint a suitable incumbent: they shall
send him to the Bishop with a testimonial of good conversation and character, and the Bishop shall examine
him.   In cities or towns the Town Council and the Magistrates shall have the right of nomination.   The new
pastor shall be publicly ordained to his office by the laying
on of the hands of the Bishop and the presbyters in the
church to which he is appointed, the Bishop having first
charged the candidate to preach the Gospel in sincerity
and to administer the sacraments duly, to teach aright
concerning repentance, obedience to rulers, and good
works, to oppose all errors by sound doctrine, to study
the Bible carefully, and to be constant in prayer.   Owing
to the smallness of the population and the poverty of some
parishes, it is impossible to provide an adequate stipend
for the minister ; it is, therefore, the duty of the Bishop
and Provost to provide, where it is needful, for the union
of parishes, taking care that no minister has more than he
can conveniently serve with the ministry of the Word
and Sacraments, with teaching the catechism, and with
visiting.   No parish priests may be involved in civil business, nor carry on any trade (except in such articles as they
themselves produce), much less the calling of an innkeeper.
The country clergy shall be free from all civil and spiritual
burdens and payments, and shall always wear becoming
garments which befit their sacred calling.

Excommunication is the Church's last resource for the
control of vice, and must therefore be firmly retained.   All
open sinners, whose conduct is a scandal to the Church,

and who will not reform their lives in spite of repeated admonitions, must be regarded as heathen men, and may not be admitted to the Eucharist until they repent. They must be warned not to despise the judgment pronounced by the ministers in the Church's name, lest they "turn the scourge of Mother Church into their eternal condemnation. For whatever the preachers decree in accordance with God's Word, God will ratify." Everything else must be left to the magistrate, for "the sword owes the Church its assistance thus far, that by its means the Church may act in peace."

The duty of supporting and maintaining schools is strongly pressed upon the Church. The training of the young is vitally important, whether we have regard to the defence and confirmation of religion or to the preservation of the civil government. Accordingly there shall be Latin schools in all cities and towns, directed by competent teachers. The ministers shall everywhere remind their people that they owe their children this education, and that God requires it at their hands, in order that the heritage of godliness may be handed down to posterity, and that provision may be made for the welfare of the State as well as the Church. To impress this more upon the people, the Bishop and the King's Governor, when they hold a Visitation, are bound to promote the prosperity of schools by their advice and help, and to urge and commend all subjects in the King's name to discharge this duty.

With the publication of the Ordering of the Church and the appointment of the new Bishops the Reformation was definitely established in Denmark. Here, as elsewhere, the early years of the Reformed Church were beset with difficulties. Education, instead of advancing, seemed at first to fall back: the University of Copenhagen sank to a low ebb, partly in consequence of the disastrous effect of the civil war and the siege of the capital. It was difficult to obtain an adequate supply of clergy who attained to the high standard which the Reformers had set up. The legacy of superstition and vice which the old system had bequeathed to the new called for sleepless vigilance and constant efforts. Yet in spite of all these drawbacks Bugenhagen could bestow upon the Danish Church this high praise : " I have never been anywhere where sermons are listened to so constantly and so gladly as in Denmark, even on work-days, even in winter, even before daybreak, and on holy days throughout the day ; and they pray constantly."

The history of the Reformation in Sweden was more eventful and more peculiar than in any other country of Europe. In no other country was it so completely the work of a single man. In no other country was the soil so little prepared by the previous labours of advocates or teachers of the new doctrines. Nowhere else did political, patriotic, and personal motives exert a greater influence. Nowhere else did the whole fabric of the Medieval Church fall so suddenly and with so great a fall beneath a single impulse from without. What is even more deserving of notice, in Sweden alone the heads of the Medieval Church took a decisive part in the overthrow of their own power.

Gustavus Vasa is the dramatic figure in whom the whole interest of the Swedish Reformation centres. Born in 1496, and allied by blood and sympathy with the leaders of the Liberal and National party in Sweden, he came prominently forward when still quite a young man, after Christian the Second of Denmark had by the massacre of Stockholm effectually scotched, as he thought, the snake of disaffection. The father of Gustavus was one of the victims of the massacre, and he himself was sent to Denmark as a hostage for the good conduct of his fellow-countrymen. Making his escape from the Danish prison he fled to Lubeck, and from Lubeck to Sweden. No other monarch of ancient or modern times, not even Alfred the Great, or William the Conqueror, or Robert Bruce, had a more romantic career. Landing at Stenso in the spring of 1520, he found the Danes triumphant. Wandering about from place to place, he strove to rouse the national feeling among the peasantry. At first his efforts were unavailing : there was a general desire for peace, and the lower classes were gratified by Christian the Second's democratic sentiments. Gustavus went about in fear for his life; the Governor tried to seize him; he had more than one hairbreadth escape, was compelled to resort to different disguises, and on one occasion hired himself as a farm servant and wielded the threshing flail.

But before long the temper of the people changed, as Christian revealed himself in his true colours. The hatred of the union revived, the peasants sent for Gustavus and elected him as their chief, and soon the greater part of Dalecarlia fell away from Christian. Then Gustavus displayed his natural ability, organized his forces, defeated the Danish troops, and drove them back upon Westeras. Yet his difficulties were very great. The Swedish peasants were badly armed ; they had no cavalry and no firearms ; Gustavus exerted himself to get better arrows for them ; he lengthened their pikes to enable them to resist the charge of cavalry ; he extemporized a new coinage. With an army of 15,000 he marched to Westmonland, and fought a pitched battle in which he was completely victorious, foiling the cavalry with the new lances, and seizing the enemy's artillery. One success led to another : the result of the victory was that the national insurrection spread : the carelessness of the Danish Governor enabled Gustavus to get possession of the archiepiscopal city of Upsala : the Archbishop marched out of Stockholm to regain his city, was worsted by the troops of Gustavus, was forced to retreat to the capital, and was besieged by the victorious army.

Here, however, Gustavus was checked. He had no ships, the Danes had command of the sea, and his financial difficulties increased. Fortunately Brask, Bishop of Linkoping, the most powerful prelate of the Swedish

Church after the Archbishop, took his side, and brought over with him the chief of the Swedish nobles, his friend Jonson of Westgothland. An Assembly met at Wadstena which was anxious to elect Gustavus King. But he wisely held back ; he would not, he said, accept any higher dignity for the present than the title of Governor of the Kingdom. In spite of the capture of towns and castles, Stockholm, girt round by the waters of the lake, still defied him ; and the garrison made such desperate sallies that at one time the siege was practically raised for four weeks.

It was the intervention of Lubeck which decided the war in favour of the Swedes. The great Hanse town, alarmed at the prospect of a formidable naval power arising in the united kingdoms of Denmark, Sweden, and Norway, determined to support Gustavus with ships, guns, powder, and other munitions of war. In this manner it was possible to blockade Stockholm effectively. At the same time Christian was deposed from the Danish throne, and there was no probability of Denmark reinforcing the capital. The war was clearly drawing to a close, and a Diet was held at Strengnas in June, 1523. The Cathedral Provost addressed the Diet in a set speech, declaring that the welfare of the country demanded the election of a national King ; the Governor had been the saviour of Sweden, and had delivered it out of the hands of its oppressors ; no one could doubt that he was the man best fitted to wear the crown. The nobles gave their consent, the burghers and peasants hailed the proposal with joyful acclamations, and Gustavus saw his devoted and heroic efforts to secure his nation's liberty rewarded with the throne which no man could have more fully deserved.

Up to this time little had been heard in Sweden of the new religious doctrines. Only one active preacher of them had as yet appeared. Olaus Petri had matriculated in 1516 at Leipzig, but had soon moved to the sister University of Wittenberg. He was in residence on the memorable All Saints' Eve of 1517, took the degree of Master of Arts and philosophy in the following year, in 1520 was ordained Deacon by the Bishop of Strengnas, and was appointed to a post in the Cathedral. How far he was a Lutheran at this time is uncertain. But he began to read portions of the Old and New Testament with young preachers and with the choir boys who belonged to the Cathedral school, declared in the Cathedral pulpit that the sermon was the most important part of the service, and that the reading of masses had not much significance; urged the importance of confessing sins to God and not to the priest, and bade men put their trust in God alone and not in the Virgin or the Saints. These new and startling doctrines were strongly opposed by the Dean and Chapter of Strengnas and by Bishop Brask, who sent to all his clergy copies of the Papal Breve against Luther, and nailed on all the church doors a missive to forbid the reading of Lutheran books.

Before long Gustavus brought Petri to Stockholm, and took him under his protection. The capital was the only city in Sweden where a large number of foreigners had settled. The German element was strong, and when Petri preached in the great parish church he found a favourable audience. In all his sermons he appealed to Scripture as the one infallible rule of faith: he would admit no doctrine which could not be proved from the Bible. The preaching of Lutheran doctrine was followed by the sale of Lutheran books. Brask called upon the King to stop it; but Gustavus replied that Luther had as yet been condemned by his enemies alone, and not by any impartial body of men; he could not, therefore, hold him guilty. This scandal, however, was trifling compared with the scandal which Petri caused by his marriage. Brask again appealed to the King; by this enormity, committed under the King's eye in his capital, the preacher was *ipso facto* excommunicated. Gustavus bluntly answered that the Papal laws tolerated clerical immorality, which God condemned; he only tolerated clerical marriage, which God sanctioned.

The King's leaning towards the new doctrines could not be any longer questioned. Secretly and indirectly he furthered their spread in monasteries, in nunneries, and among the nobles in the Provinces; and in every part of the kingdom opponents of the Medieval system arose. He pressed on the translation of the Bible as an even more effectual means of promoting the cause of Evangelical truth, and before the end of 1526 the translation of the New Testament was published. But it was not only the pure love of truth which animated him. As a statesman he realized the financial difficulties by which the newly-founded religion was beset; he looked with jealous eyes upon the unbounded wealth of the Church; he saw that the political importance of the ecclesiastical Order was in great measure dependent upon their vast possessions. Yet he would not startle the nation and the Church by a premature declaration of his intentions. With wary caution he disguised his real purpose under a fair-sounding name; he did not breathe the word taxation, he would only speak of loans. The Diet of Strengnas empowered him to raise a loan on ecclesiastical property. He had scarcely entered Stockholm, in 1523, before a royal letter was despatched to all parts of the kingdom. "We are compelled to borrow from churches or monasteries; you must, therefore, send us without delay your jewels, pyxes, chalices, or whatever you have, as well as your hard cash." Encouraged by the success of this attempt, he repeated it in the following year on the occasion of an expedition to Gothland. The response which his demand met with was enthusiastic. The Archbishop and the Bishops of Strengnas, Abo, Linkoping, and Skara pledged their word that they would spare neither their own property nor the Church's to supply his need. When the expedition was ended, his resources were again exhausted: once more he appealed to the Church, and the Archbishop, the Bishop of Westeras, and the Bishop of Strengnas granted him the ecclesiastical tithes for the year, only deducting what was absolutely necessary for the administration of the sacraments. When he applied to the Bishop of Linkoping, Brask remonstrated, but in vain. "Necessity," such was the King's haughty answer, "is justified in breaking not only man's law but God's." At the beginning of 1526 another Assembly met at Wadstena, and the Church was forced to sacrifice two-thirds of its tithes to the King. Seven months later he increased his demands with the same result: two-thirds of the tithes were granted him, a loan of 15,000 marks, and a number of horsemen which the prelates supplied in proportion to the value of their crown fiefs. Not content with this, Gustavus quartered his troops upon Bishops and monasteries. Brask again came forward as the spokesman of clerical discontent. "The King's actions disturbed the service of God." Gustavus had no tenderness for such scruples. "The best way of serving God," was his ready answer, "is by caring for the common weal."

The troubles of the newly-elected monarch were not yet at an end. The prolonged hostilities had caused great want in the country, and the great want had bred disaffection, especially among the lower orders. The high place to which Gustavus had been raised, though it was not an extravagant reward for the priceless services rendered to his country, naturally excited the envy of rivals, to whom he seemed no better and no worthier than one of themselves. His evident bias against the Medieval Church moved the deep suspicion and mistrust of all who from noble or ignoble motives were interested in its preservation. These representatives of a widespread discontent combined in a dangerous outbreak. The castle of Calmar, one of the strongest fortresses in the North, was held against the King, and could only be taken after a frightful carnage of his troops. The capture of the castle greatly discouraged the peasantry. Gustavus practised a praiseworthy and politic clemency, and the revolt gradually died out.

This rebellion increased the King's dislike of the Clergy, and he determined to continue his attacks upon the property of the Church. At the end of 1525 he demanded the restoration of monastic property which had been given by his father, on the ground that it had been bestowed under compulsion, and the Diet confirmed his claim. In May, 1526, he went to Upsala, and addressed a crowded Assembly, setting forth that the regular and secular clergy had degenerated so far as to make them unfit for the administration of ecclesiastical property; he proposed that the worthless members should be driven out, and that the pious and learned should have stipends assigned to them sufficient for their decent maintenance; the ecclesiastical property and buildings should be utilized for schools, hospitals, and almshouses. This time, however, Gustavus outstripped the conservative instincts of his audience. So far from adopting his proposals they brought forward their religious grievances—the prohibition of the Latin Mass and the discountenancing of the old religion. Gustavus quickly drew his own conclusion from these speeches: the clergy of the diocese were secretly poisoning the minds of the people against him, and the Metropolitan of Sweden was egging them on. With the promptitude of a great statesman and warrior he girded himself for the inevitable struggle which he saw looming in the near future.

Only a year later Gustavus summoned a Diet at Westeras. It was attended by 129 nobles, 32 burghers as representatives of the commercial cities, 12 miners as representatives of the mining centres, 105 peasants drawn in a fixed proportion from the judicial circuits, the four Bishops of Westeras, Linkoping, Skara, and Strengnas, deputies from the Cathedral Chapters, and twelve members of the Council of State. Of the leading men of the country only the Archbishop of Upsala was absent.

Gustavus had secured himself against his opposition by sending him on an embassy to the King of Poland.

At the beginning of the session the Chancellor read the King's proposals to the Assembly. He began by a statement of the debt which was still owing to Lubeck, the enormous expenses of the King and the insufficiency of his income, the decline of the important Order of Knights because they had given up so much of their property to the Church; he enlarged upon the prevailing restlessness and confusion owing to the reports which were sedulously spread that the King intended to introduce a new form of religion. The King was perfectly prepared to prove that the only preaching which he had sanctioned was the preaching of the pure Word of God: as for the financial difficulties of the State, in his opinion there was only one way in which they could be met, by utilizing the vast possessions of the Church. After this statement the Chancellor, instead of asking the opinion of the spiritual members of the Diet, according to precedent, turned to the nobles, and called upon Jonson as their chief to say what he thought of the King's proposals. Jonson shrank from the grave responsibility, asked for a few minutes' delay, and suggested that Brask should speak first. The Bishop at once acknowledged that he had promised to be faithful to the King, but on the important condition that nothing should be required of him which clashed with his obedience to the Pope. He could not consent to a change in the doctrine of the Church, nor to a change in her material condition, unless the Pope approved them. After this speech the Chancellor turned again to the nobles, and Jonson in their name endorsed the opinions of Brask.

Then the King rose and spoke in a strain of impassioned eloquence. He complained of the injustice with which he was treated. Every calamity, every disaster, whether it were the work of God or man, was laid to his charge, pestilence and famine, rain and drought; he would be

King no longer; his position was intolerable; any priest
might set himself over his head and dictate to him : if he
had accepted the crown, it was from no ambitious motive
but because he had the welfare of his unhappy people at
heart. For this cause he had sacrificed his own property ;
let this property be restored to him. " Then," he added,
while his voice trembled with emotion, " I will go into a
foreign land, and spend the rest of my days there, without
setting eyes on my blind and thankless country again."
With these words he left the room ; and the meeting,
dumbfounded by the passionate indignation and resolution
which had inspired his words, broke up in consternation
and perplexity.

On the following day the representatives of the peasants
and the miners pressed for a decision, and threatened to
take the matter into their own hands : they were joined
by the representatives of the cities, the deputies from the
capital declaring that they would hold it for three years
in the King's name. At last the Bishop of Strengnas
spoke. He thanked Jonson for his defence of the Church.
But it would be madness to choose any other King than
Gustavus, and the alternative, therefore, was a simple one:
should the Church make sacrifices, or should Sweden
perish ? These words naturally produced a great effect :
here was one of the heads of the Church advocating the
very course which the King proposed. The adherents of
the new doctrines instantly raised their voices to impugn
the old system, and the hours passed away in a religious
dispute. On the third day the burghers and peasants
attended the Diet in a mood which would brook no opposition. The Chancellor and Olaus Petri were sent to beg
the King to change his resolution. But the King was
inexorable. A second deputation proved equally unavailing. A third attempt was made, and Gustavus, satisfied
with having humbled his opponents to the dust, and with
having tested his undisputed empire over the hearts of his
subjects, at last gave way.

This extraordinary scene revealed the weakness of the Church and the strength of the King's position. The labours, the anxieties, the sacrifices, and the sufferings of seven years had not been in vain. Gustavus had become indispensable to his people, and in the hour of trial they learnt to recognize the fact. Mysterious power, immemorial prescription, the reverence of ages, and the mighty claims of an ancient faith weighed as dust in the balance against the assurance of national independence and domestic peace. There had not been in Sweden as in Denmark any widespread dissatisfaction with the religious system and its representatives. There were no eager questionings, no serious doubts about accepted beliefs, no fervent admiration of preachers who had touched new chords in men's hearts and awakened new sympathies. Those who had listened favourably to the Reformed doctrines must have been an insignificant minority. But when Gustavus decided that the Reformation was a political even more than a religious necessity, when he appealed to the nation to accept his decision, and when he staked his very crown on the success of his appeal, all Swedes who dreaded anarchy more than heresy, and cared more for the welfare of their country than of their Church, had no choice but to sacrifice their religious prejudices to their national interests.

On June 27th, 1527, the Decree of Westeras was drawn up. It gave the King the right to seize the Bishops' castles for the security of the realm, to dispose as he pleased of the revenues of Bishops, Chapters, and Canons, to give over the administration of the monasteries to nobles, and to use the monastic buildings and the monastic revenues for the benefit of the State. On certain specified conditions the nobles were allowed to recover property which had been given to the Church. " God's pure Word and Gospel " should be preached in the kingdom, and all who spoke evil of it should be punished. The order in which these clauses stand is significant and instructive.

A few days later the Ordinances of Westeras were issued. None but duly qualified candidates might be ordained priests. No livings might be bestowed by Bishops without the King's confirmation : if he chose he might exercise the right of nomination : he had the right to deprive unworthy or incapable incumbents of their benefices. In all temporal matters the clergy should be subject to the decision of civil tribunals. A valid marriage according to the laws of the State should be regarded as "a true marriage in God's sight," even though the Church had not blessed it. No monarch in any country claimed and exercised more extensive ecclesiastical prerogatives.

A national Synod met at Orebro in February, 1529. The Chancellor presided as the King's representative. Three Bishops were present, Skara, Strengnas, and Westeras, and representatives of the Chapters and Clergy of all the Swedish dioceses. No account of the proceedings has been preserved : but it was resolved that the representatives of the Clergy were bound to proclaim and to spread God's Word, to preach it in all its purity in all churches, to organize daily Bible readings with profitable interpretations in all Cathedrals for the benefit of the country clergy, to see that in the Cathedral schools the choral Vicars gave instruction in Holy Writ, and to make provision in the cities for learned preachers who might advise all in the country round. Not a single writer in Sweden came forward to attack the Reformed doctrines. The defence of the Medieval Church was left to the Danish writer, Eliesen, whose efforts were crowned with even less success than in his own country.

A desperate attempt was made by the adherents of the old system in April, 1529, to undo the work of preceding years. Jonson, the leading noble in Sweden, headed a revolt against Gustavus, and was joined by the Bishop of Skara. In a public letter they recapitulated the King's crimes and misdemeanours. He had introduced an unchristian government, had pulled down and pillaged

monasteries, had plundered without cause and reason
what Christian had spared, had suppressed and dishonoured
the sacraments, had crushed the people with oppressive
taxes, had expelled bishops and prelates, monks and
priests, and had set up as pastors heretics and runaway
monks.   In another letter Gustavus was charged with the
abolition of fasts, images, confession, and the Latin Mass.

Gustavus met this danger with his usual confidence.
He wrote an answer to the insurgents' letter, reminding
his people that he had done nothing without the consent
of the Diet, and that the doctrines which he authorized,
so far from being unchristian, were in strict accordance
with the Word of God; if any other doctrines had been
preached, it was without his consent and approval.
Beyond the sphere of Jonson's personal influence the
revolt had no vitality.   The conviction that Gustavus was
the only possible King, and that therefore his policy was
the only possible policy, rapidly gained ground.   The
leading rebels recognized the hopelessness of their cause,
and fled to Denmark.   A Diet was held at Strengnas ·in
June, 1529, and the question was asked whether it would
ratify the Decree of Westeras.   The answer was in the
affirmative, and from that day, in spite of the attempts of
Christian and the ill-will and discontent which still
smouldered in parts of the country, the throne of Gustavus
and the Reformed Church of Sweden were never in
real danger.

CHAPTER VI.

THE REFORMATION IN GENEVA AND FRANCE.

THE city of Geneva occupies an unique position in the history of the sixteenth century. Other cities became famous through commercial enterprise, political greatness, strategical importance, intellectual development, or literary pre-eminence. Geneva rose to a foremost place through the religious reformation alone, and was enabled to vie in reputation and influence with the capitals of mighty monarchies. The rise of the city forcibly illustrates the effect of political combinations in furthering the cause of the Evangelical Church. It illustrates with no less force the important truth that in every country of Europe to which the Reformation penetrated the fall of the Medieval Church was in large measure due to the advocates and supporters of the old system, to their ignorance, their lax morality, their blindness to the signs of the times, and their readiness to sacrifice everything, even the commonest instincts of patriotism, to the preservation of their privileges and revenues.

For three hundred years before the Reformation the Counts and Dukes of Savoy had cast covetous glances upon the royal and episcopal city lying at the extremity of Lake Leman on the borders of France, Germany and Italy. From the middle of the thirteenth century their restless ambition had never ceased plotting to gain the costly prize by force or fraud. About the middle of the fifteenth century their efforts seemed to be crowned with success. They had extended their conquests along both sides of the lake, had bought up the ancient rights and possessions of the Counts of Geneva, and had secured the bishopric as an appanage of their House to the lasting detriment of the city's religious life. These encroachments met with a fitful resistance from the burghers, who, like so many of their contemporaries in the episcopal cities of the Middle Ages, had, towards the close of the fourteenth century, wrested from their Bishop a charter of emancipation. But at the beginning of the sixteenth century matters came to a crisis. In 1519 the Duke of Savoy attempted to surprise the city; and the attempt only failed through his indecision and the arrival of troops from the friendly city of Freiburg. Six years later war broke out in Italy between Charles the Fifth and Francis the First, and the Duke, absorbed in the vicissitudes of the European struggle, finally gave up his personal share in the attacks upon Geneva.

The great perils from which they had barely escaped opened the eyes of the Genevese to the dangers of their position. At the beginning of 1526 they formed an alliance with the powerful city of Berne, the signs of the supremacy of Savoy were obliterated, the city was fortified, and the Duke's avowed adherents within its walls were sternly suppressed. But the Duke did not abandon his schemes: his agents were busy in exciting prejudice against Geneva among the burghers of the confederate cities; the nobles of Savoy in the neighbourhood of the lake were eagerly watching for favourable opportunities; and the Bishop of Geneva, a slothful and self-indulgent prelate, who fleeted away the time, as in the golden age of episcopal worldliness and luxury, among his castles and abbeys in feasting upon fat capons and choice wines, saw his abbeys seized by the Savoyard nobles, was excommunicated by his Metropolitan, the Archbishop of Vienne, was offered dazzling bribes by the wily Duke, and committed the fatal error of casting in his lot with the avowed enemies of his episcopal city. He issued a manifesto, stigmatized his spiritual children as rebels, called upon the Savoyard nobles to protect his cause, and gave Berne the desired pretext for effectual interference on behalf of the city. A powerful army set out for Geneva in October, 1530, laying waste the territory of Savoy and burning the nobles' castles on its march, and practically established the city's independence.

As a natural consequence of these events the cause of civic independence became indissolubly bound up with the cause of religious reform. The Duke and Bishop had sowed the wind, and they reaped the whirlwind. By posing as the champions of the Romanist faith and as the champions of arbitrary government at the same time, they irretrievably ruined the cause of the Church of Rome in Geneva. The Bernese threw themselves with missionary ardour into the task of converting their new allies, flung down images, crucifixes, and altars, and placed a Reformed preacher in the pulpit of Saint Peter's Cathedral to thunder against idolatry. Pope Clement the Seventh, not to be outdone in folly by his allies the Duke and the Bishop, proclaimed a Jubilee Indulgence in Geneva; and at the same time a new preacher of the Reformation appeared to deal a final blow at the tottering Church.

William Farel was a native of Gap, in the Dauphinois, and in early life had come under the religious influence of the early Reformers in France. From one of the most ardent and devoted sons of the Medieval Church he had, by a not unnatural reaction, become one of the most fiery, the most daring, and the most uncompromising preachers of the new doctrines. Such was his fervour that, in spite of his ignorance of German, he went through German Switzerland, preaching and arguing alternately in French and Latin. When through the influence of Berne the Reformed doctrines began to make way in French-speaking Switzerland, Farel rushed at once into the forefront of the battle, boldly entered Geneva, undauntedly repelled the charge of blasphemy on which he was brought before the

Council, and persuaded a friend to continue his work after he was forced to give it up. Through the mediation of Freiburg, which was strongly Romanist, the Bishop once more reappeared, marred his cause anew by his incompetence and cowardice, and incensed the Evangelicals to the utmost by forbidding any one to speak of the Bible and to preach the Gospel without episcopal license. They were still more incensed by the Advent sermons of a Dominican, who was put up to advocate the Romanist cause in the Cathedral, and who compared them to the soldiers beneath the Cross dividing the seamless robe of Christ. An appeal was made to Berne, and Berne sent a formal message complaining of the treatment of Farel and his successor, of the persecution of the truth, and of the lies and blasphemies of the Dominican. The Council of Geneva were forced to comply with the demands of their confederates, to arrest, condemn, and imprison the monk, and to allow the Evangelical preachers to take one of the Churches for their services.

All this was sufficiently humiliating for the members of the old Church. But in the lowest depth they found a lower deep. Their religious processions were mobbed; some of the regular and secular clergy joined the Reformation and married; the Bishop again intervened by taking the side of Savoy; his adherents made a futile attempt to surprise the city by night, and the citizens in bitter indignation renounced their allegiance to him. After this, the triumph of the Reformation could not long be delayed. A religious disputation ended in the easy overthrow of the Romanists; the destruction of the symbols of Romanist worship recommenced; one Church after another was seized by the Evangelical party; Farel took upon himself to preach in the Cathedral, and at last, appearing before the Council, boldly demanded that Popery should be abolished in Geneva. The Council, reluctant to take extreme measures, gave the Romanists another chance by calling upon them to justify images, masses, and the adoration of saints.   None of them were willing to accept the challenge: the regular clergy pleaded that they had not the needful learning for the task, the secular clergy that the Bishop had forbidden them to engage in discussions with the heretics.   Judgment went against them by default, and Geneva ceased to be, in name as well as in reality, a Romanist city.

Once more the Duke and the Bishop attempted to regain the position which they had lost, and the Genevese, reduced to sore straits by prolonged hostilities, appealed, and not in vain, to their allies in Berne.   War was declared against Savoy.   A force of six thousand Bernese entered Geneva early in 1536, drove the Romanist population with fire and sword out of the surrounding villages, marched along the south bank of the lake conquering as they went, and then, returning on their steps, made themselves masters of the north bank.   With this campaign the power of Savoy on Lake Leman was effectively broken, and the independence of Geneva was secured against the ducal House.   Yet Farel's religious difficulties were not at an end.   Though the public profession of the Romanist religion had been forbidden, there were many secret Romanists.   The priests who still remained in the city held services in private houses and fostered religious discontent.   A large section of the inhabitants had been animated by a love of political liberty, not by any love of the Reformation, and their sympathies were still with the Medieval Church.   The Protestants were far from irreproachable in life and faith.   The views of the Council on many points differed from the Reformer's.   Farel became conscious that the work was only half done, and that the hardest part of his task still lay before him. The qualities which he lacked were the precise qualities which at this moment were urgently required—genius for organization, breadth of mind, a statesmanlike temper, a comprehensive glance, profound learning, argumentative power, the gift of adapting means to ends, the ability to

moùld the characters of men. In the midst of his perplexity the news was brought to him that Calvin had
arrived in Geneva, and he recognized at once that Calvin
was the very man whom the Church of Geneva needed.

John Calvin was born at Noyon, an episcopal city of
Picardy, in 1509. His father held office under the Bishop,
and the boy's gifts naturally marked him out for the
priesthood. Indeed, at an early age, in accordance with
the corrupt system which prevailed at that time in the
Church of France, he was nominated to a chaplaincy.
But his father soon changed his views and determined
that the boy should study law. In this point Calvin
differed from all the other leading Reformers, and the
effects of his legal training may be traced throughout his
life in his writings, his character, and his work. Of the
religious opinions of his early life, nothing is known:
there is no record even of the inward and outward
influences to which his conversion was due. He only
alludes to the deep yearning for an assurance of salvation,
which was satisfied by the Evangelical doctrine of Justification by Faith, and to the profound conviction which he
gained from discussions with his Evangelical friends, that
in purifying the Church from abuses he was not separating
from its communion, but was ministering to its edification. During these early years he resided in turn at
Orleans, Bourges, Angoulême, Nerac, and Paris. Everywhere he left the same impression on all with whom he
came in contact of the loftiness of his moral character
and the pre-eminence of his intellectual abilities. In
1534 he left Paris, and from that day never again set
foot on French soil. During the thirty most important
years of his life the greatest Frenchman of the sixteenth
century was an exile from his native country.

From Paris Calvin went to Basle, famous as the home
of Erasmus' later life, and as one of the intellectual centres
of Europe. Here he resumed his former life, devoted
himself to intense study, and at an age when most men of

ability have just left off competing for prize essays, wrote a work which in a few years was read and admired all over Europe, which has been translated into almost every European language, which has passed through countless editions, which in its French form has stamped Calvin as the first consummate master of French prose, which has moulded the faith of millions on both sides of the Atlantic, and which for originality of conception, breadth of treatment, masculine disregard of scholastic subtleties or theological quibbles, religious depth, dialectical power, and stately eloquence has had no rival in Christian literature since the days of Saint Augustine. Calvin's " Christian Institution " is the more remarkable because at the time when he wrote it the earlier leaders of the Reformation might seem to have exhausted the great religious questions which had engrossed men's minds for more than twenty years. Yet such was the force of Calvin's genius that there was not a single Evangelical doctrine which he did not set in a new light, strengthen by original arguments, and enrich by fresh illustrations ; and that he elaborated a system of Church government and Church discipline which, even if it had been partially anticipated by earlier workers in the same field, received its perfect form from his master mind, and in this form vitally influenced countries differing as widely from one another in national character, political government, intellectual development, and historical antecedents as Switzerland, France, Germany, Scotland, England, and the Low Countries. If Calvin cannot compare with Luther in geniality of temperament, in natural and unstudied eloquence, in imaginative vision, in tenderness, humour, and pathos, in the indefinable grace which adorns all that it touches, in the intense humanity which soars with every soul to the sunlit heights of hope and joy and pierces to the darkest depths of doubt and despair, in the passion which thrills the reader's heart and kindles the flame of sympathy within it, it may be confidently affirmed that no single work of Luther can be set by the side of Calvin's masterpiece, and that the systematic arrangement and sustained power of the "Institution" were altogether beyond Luther's reach.

The "Christian Institution," taken alone, would give a very imperfect idea of the strength and weakness of Calvin's character, or of the nature of his life, aims, and methods. Fortunately his correspondence, singularly wide and varied like Luther's and Melanchthon's, completes the picture. The loving friend, the tender pastor of souls, the director of troubled consciences, the consummate theologian, the great ecclesiastical statesman, the apostle of the French-speaking peoples, the sickly and laborious teacher beset with human infirmities, stands revealed in page after page of simple, pathetic, indignant, austere, and incisive eloquence. Every tone of sympathy, of consolation, of warning, of rebuke, of encouragement, of lofty expostulation, of wise counsel, of suggestive criticism, flowed from that untiring pen through the letters of many years. The young were reminded of the corruption of the age, of the allurements of the world and the false charms with which it enticed the unwary, of their need of the single aim of self-surrender to the obedience of Christ, of the danger lest the precious seed should be choked or marred, of the duty of rousing themselves from their torpor, of goading themselves on, of taking themselves constantly to task. The suffering were consoled by the thought that it was expedient for trials to befall them for the testing of the firmness and constancy of their faith, that there was a danger lest their eyes should be dazzled by a trust in men, that the battle under their Saviour's Cross was better than all the triumphs of the world, that the reliance which God bade them place on His grace and His power would be ever an unconquerable fortress. The prisoners of Jesus Christ were bidden to reflect how God willed to seal His truth with their blood, how they were mortified in order to be offered as sacrifices to Him, how the glorious Victor

was an infallible pledge of their triumph, how He had
granted them the privilege of awakening those whom He
had resolved to edify by their death.   The faint-hearted
were admonished that man cannot always have everything
as he wishes, that, while we are in this world, we must be
like birds on the branch, that every place where God is
worshipped in purity is better than our native land, that
no one, great or small, ought to be exempted from suffering in the cause of his Divine King, and that it cannot be
worth while to preserve this frail and transitory life at the
cost of our allegiance to Christ.   The great and the noble,
Kings, Princes, and Lords, were addressed in a strain to
which they had long been strangers.   Two letters to the
weak and licentious King of Navarre, the unworthy
husband of the noble and heroic Joan d'Albret, are
admirable examples of Calvin's exhortations to the mighty
ones of the earth.   He prays the King to reflect deeply on
the opening which God has given him for advancing the
pure truth of His Gospel.   God is drawing him by the
hand, demanding that he should serve as His witness.
The high position which he holds does not exempt him from
the law and rule which is common to all believers.   As he is
exalted above the rest, he is all the more bound to exert
himself in showing the way to this great people.   He who
takes the lead in honour and rank ought to be the
standard-bearer of virtue, and to testify to God's Word
before Kings, even though they be unwilling to hear it.
Knowing, then, that God has put him at this hour to the
test, let him rest upon His power, hide under His protection, offer himself and the authority which has been given
him as a sacrifice to the Most High, so that the confession
which he makes shall serve as a buckler to an infinite
number of poor believers.   It is a pity that these noble
words were wasted, as a second letter proves that they
were, upon such a sordid and ignoble soul.

Some of the most remarkable and significant pages of
the correspondence deal with questions of the day, and

show unmistakably how Calvin's greatness enabled him
to rise above the narrowness of mind which disfigured so
many of his contemporaries. A correspondent asked him
whether it was lawful under any circumstances to accept
of baptism in the Church of Rome. Calvin unhesitatingly
replied in the affirmative: deeply as he detested the
Church of Rome, strongly as he disapproved of its superstitious rites, it could not be denied that it was part of
the Church of Christ, and that the baptism which it
administered was valid; to reject baptism altogether
would, therefore, in his judgment be a greater scandal
than to accept it under these adverse conditions; for his
part he would be willing to receive baptism from a sceptic
like Lucian, or from the devil himself, rather than go
without it altogether. He pronounced ceremonies to be
indifferent matters, unless they were plainly repugnant to
God's Word; men who were ready to quit the Church on
account of a difference about ceremonies ill understood in
what the true unity of Christians consisted, and how each
member ought to conform to the Church in which he
lived; no one should refuse to partake of the Eucharist
from dislike of lights or chasubles; an absence of uniformity in ceremonies was a positive advantage, because
it proved that the essence of faith and the unity of the
Church were absolutely independent of them. The Church
of Geneva had rejected the observance of the great festivals
and the administration of the Eucharist to the sick: but
Calvin did not attempt to conceal that he was in favour
of them, though he acquiesced in the judgment of his
Church and refrained for the sake of peace from pressing
for any change. He was strongly of opinion that no
Church in which the Eucharist was not administered
every Sunday had attained to the Christian ideal; but he
frankly allowed that this was not always feasible nor
desirable, and refused to insist on any hard-and-fast rules.
His judgment even on questions which were in his eyes of
supreme importance was marked by the same liberality

and moderation : he considered the right of excommunication absolutely essential for the preservation of the Church's
purity, and declared that he would die rather than surrender it ; but he unreservedly acknowledged that many
wise and godly men thought otherwise : he would not
condemn their view, and asked that they should not
condemn his.   In the same spirit he reproved in the
strongest terms the violent iconoclasm of the Huguenots :
" God has given no orders to cast down idols, except to
each one in his own house, and in public to those whom
He arms with authority."   To desire the extermination
of idols was well, but obedience was better than sacrifice.
In the same spirit he unsparingly condemned the intolerance of the ultra-Lutherans.   They were fighting, he
vehemently declared, for the shadow and not for the
substance ; they cursed and execrated Melanchthon, the
light and glory of the German Reformation ; instead of
seeking the things which made for peace, they were rend-
ing the Church in twain, not for any vital doctrine but for
mere metaphysical quibbles.   The judgment which he
passed upon Luther himself is eminently characteristic.
Luther's faults, his rashness, his unreasoning vehemence,
his headstrong wilfulness, his blindness to his own defects,
his unsparing condemnation of all who differed from him,
did not escape the keen penetration of Calvin ; but he
urged those who grew impatient with Luther to remember
his rare gifts, his fortitude and constancy of soul, the skill
and power with which he had laboured for the truth and
had served God's Church ; men might well bear with his
defects in consideration of his splendid qualities and of
the vast debt which they all owed to one of the foremost
ministers of Christ : " Even if he were to call me a
devil," Calvin added, " I should still recognize him as a
distinguished servant of God."

Calvin's first stay in Geneva did not last long.   He was
still young and inexperienced ; his views were partial ; his
judgment was not matured ; and the Council and people

of Geneva had not yet learnt to value their great teacher at his true worth. A short and sharp struggle ended in Calvin's banishment. Possibly he did not regret the termination of his connection with the city. He declared afterwards that not a day had passed during his first residence when he had not wished himself dead ten times over. In his retirement at Basle he looked forward with delight to the renewal of the studies which had given him such happiness and peace of mind in the past, and to which he purposed to devote himself in the future. But this was not to be. Bucer, one of Calvin's greatest admirers, would not rest until he had induced him to come to Strasburg, persuading him that it would be a sin to hide his great talents in a napkin, and convincing him that his bitterest enemies would be silenced and put to shame if they saw him an honoured worker in the church of the free and imperial city, whose influence on the German Reformation had been so decisive. There can be no doubt that Bucer judged rightly. In that ampler air Calvin breathed more freely; his zeal was tempered and his genius was braced; his connection with the religion and politics of the Empire gave him a wider outlook and broader interests; he formed a warm and life-long friendship with Melanchthon, and softened the asperities of his own character by communion with that sweet and gentle soul; and when in the autumn of 1541 he yielded to the earnest solicitations of the repentant Genevese, he returned to the city a greater and a wiser man.

Calvin's return was marked by the attempt to establish in Geneva the ideal of Church discipline and Church government which he deemed indispensable for the religious and moral well-being of the community, and which is known under the name of Presbyterian. The consideration of his system of Church government may be fitly postponed to a later chapter; for it was in Scotland that it received its fullest development, and has borne its richest fruits. But the system of Church discipline, as it was conceived by Calvin and carried out under his own eyes, was not a whit less characteristic of him, and may be best studied on the narrow arena within the walls of Geneva.

It was a favourite taunt of Roman controversialists in the era of the Reformation that the Reformed doctrines had been specially devised to give liberty to the flesh, and that, wherever these doctrines had prevailed, the bonds of morality had been fatally relaxed, and a contempt for Christian holiness had inevitably followed. Calvin's system was with justice adduced by himself and his followers as a triumphant answer to this charge. It aimed at realizing, as far as the purely external action of the Church and the unavoidable imperfections of human nature admitted, the Christian conception of a holy people having neither spot nor wrinkle nor any such thing. To suppose that this aim could be satisfied by the laws of the State, which were primarily intended to safeguard the persons and property of the citizens, was in Calvin's eyes a complete misconception : it was a misconception no less grave to suppose that it could be satisfied by the penances imposed by the priest in the confessional. Offences against God's Law must be condemned by the voice, and punished with the assent, of the whole community ; and where the power or the will to do this was wanting, the true Church, in the highest sense of the words, could not be said to exist, for no real attempt had been made to fulfil the commandment of the Most High, " Be ye holy, even as I am holy." The organ of the community appointed by Calvin for the maintenance of Church discipline was the Consistory. It was composed in Geneva of six clergymen and twelve laymen : the laymen were taken from the three Councils which formed the representative assemblies of the city. If offenders refused to listen to the admonitions of the Church officers, they were summoned before the Consistory and publicly rebuked : if this had no effect, they were excommunicated and excluded from participation in the Eucharist, until they had given proofs of their repentance. The number and variety of cases with which the Consistory dealt was surprising. They ranged from adultery and blasphemy to extravagance in dress and luxury in food. At one time a contest raged over the burning question of "slashed breeches"; not, as Calvin observed, that any special iniquity clave to this particular article of dress, but because, as straws show which way the wind blows, the moral corruption of the age was veiled under this form.

According to Calvin, the right of excommunication was the core of the Church's disciplinary power; and it was precisely at this point that the resistance of his enemies was most bitter and most determined. They endeavoured to persuade the Council that the Church's claim was a sheer usurpation, and that it was derogatory to the dignity of the temporal power to submit to it. One of the leading citizens was excommunicated by the Consistory; he appealed to the Council against the sentence; and the Council, declaring that the right to pronounce such a sentence was vested in themselves alone, decreed that he should be admitted to the Eucharist. Calvin arose at once to do battle for the independence of the Church. He would rather die a hundred deaths than submit to such intolerable tyranny; he would not stay a day longer in Geneva if he were forced to profane the sacred mystery by admitting a single unworthy communicant. The uncompromising firmness and imperious tone of the spiritual Dictator completely broke down the resistance of his opponents; the rights of the Church were conspicuously vindicated; and Calvin's victory gave the signal to his followers all over Europe to tread in his steps.

About the success with which his efforts were crowned there can certainly be no question. The change which his system wrought in the character of his adopted city was marvellous. One witness after another bears testimony to the transformation of Geneva within the space of twenty years from one of the most licentious and pleasure-loving cities of Europe into a city distinguished from all others by the deep religious fervour and the high moral standard of its burghers. Few great men have left behind them a more striking memorial of the abiding and irresistible force of personal character.

Calvin's life, like the life of the other great Reformers, was beset with incessant anxieties, difficulties, and labours. His lectures, his sermons, his immense correspondence, his attendance at the meetings of the Consistory, his patient attention to all who consulted him, his employment by the Council for every kind of business, from the drawing up of civil laws to examining a new patent stove, so completely absorbed his time that for weeks he could not secure two consecutive hours without interruption, nor go outside the city gates for necessary relaxation. At times he was unable to eat or to drink for forty-eight hours together. It is difficult to understand how the frail and sickly frame held out so long against these exhausting toils, or how the fiery spirit did not sooner fret the puny body to decay. Within and without the city the malice and hatred of open or secret enemies, and the infidelity or treachery of lukewarm friends, left him no peace. One day Philip the Second clamoured for a holy league against Geneva as the pestilent hotbed of heresy, godlessness, and irreligion. Another day Charles the Ninth accused it of goading on his subjects to rebellion, and threatened it not obscurely with the vengeance of the Most Christian King. At one time Calvin's life was embittered by the dissensions and the perjury of his colleagues, at another by the unjust accusations of the Protestant ministers of Berne. No charge was too absurd for his enemies to bring against him. " I am accused of avarice," exclaimed Calvin with justifiable indignation, " of investing my money in the purchase of rich farms, of wheedling legacies out of my unwary victims, of piling up sacks of crown pieces in my cellars, of robbing the poor of their alms—I, who never possessed a square foot of ground, who cannot call the bed on which I sleep, and the board from which I eat, my own, who have steadfastly refused to receive what has been bequeathed to me by will, who have persistently declined the handsome presents which the Council of Geneva have pressed upon my acceptance!"

From the year 1548 Calvin's influence throughout Europe steadily increased. Nowhere was this influence greater than in the country of his birth. Frenchmen who were driven from their homes by religious persecution no longer took refuge in the Reformed cities of Germany; they naturally turned to the Romance city on the shores of Lake Leman, where their great countryman was the presiding genius of the place. In 1548 the number of Frenchmen who settled in Geneva was 172; three years later the number had risen to 285; in the year ending February, 1557, 347 new residents settled in Geneva, including the famous printer, Robert Stephanus; in the following twelve months 836 more were admitted, and 809 in the last ten months of 1558. A little later the numbers had swelled to nearly 1,700 in the course of a single year. The effect of this immigration was very great. The new residents were almost without exception men who had left all and sacrificed all from the highest motives; they brought to their new home the spirit of religious earnestness and ready self-surrender which had animated them in their native land; they found in Calvin a temper which was perfectly in harmony with their own. As eye-witnesses of the courage, the devotion, and the genius of the great leader and pastor of the Genevese Church, they learnt to venerate him more than ever, and, by spreading his fame far and wide, they riveted the allegiance which countless hearts had already rendered him.

The foundation of the Academy of Geneva enhanced even the great reputation of Calvin. Like the other leaders of the Reformation, he set the highest value on education. As early as the year 1541 he had sketched the outline of the new institution, but it was not till fifteen years later that it assumed a definite form. Even then its progress was hampered by lack of funds. At last, in 1559, it was opened. The expenses were largely defrayed from legacies, Stephanus having bequeathed more than 300 florins, and another printer nearly 500. Three Professors were appointed, in Hebrew, Greek, and Latin. The object of the Academy was avowedly to show gratitude to God for His unspeakable gifts by training learned men to be the ministers of His Holy Word in all parts of the world. Students crowded to it from almost every country of Europe, John Knox being among the number. Twenty-seven lectures were delivered weekly, three in theology, eight in Hebrew, seven in the Greek poets and orators, five in dialectic and rhetoric, and three in physics and mathematics. The success of the new seat of learning surpassed the expectations of its founders. It gave the same intellectual stamp to the Reformation of Calvin as Wittenberg had given to the Reformation of Luther. It spread his doctrines in the most effective manner by sending forth a host of devoted missionaries who had drawn their inspiration from the fountain-head of his teaching.

France holds a peculiar position in the history of the Reformation. It is the only Romance country in which the new religious movement won a great victory, and numbered its adherents by hundreds of thousands. It is the only country in which the Protestants successfully defied for many years the whole power of the Government supported by a hostile majority, and eventually gained a formal recognition from their Romanist opponents. It is the only country in which during the sixteenth century a great Church sprang up and was organized in complete independence of the civil power. In France alone the Chief of the Protestants became the Chief of the Romanists and effected a reconciliation between them. In France alone during the epoch of the Reformation a powerful party arose, which held aloof from both religious parties, which maintained that there was no reason why they should not live together in peace, enjoying the same rights and privileges under the same civil government, and which thus set a striking example for the political advocates of toleration in a future age.

The beginning of the French Reformation dates from the year 1512. James Lefevre, of Etaples, who was nearly thirty years older than Luther, had become a Doctor of Sorbonne, the great theological School of France, and one of the most conservative Romanist bodies at the beginning of the sixteenth century. He published in 1512 a Latin commentary on the Epistle of Saint Paul, and ten years later another on the Gospels. He declared in language almost as strong as Luther's that Christ was all in all, that the Word of God was all in all, that everything else was vain and worthless, that if men trusted to anything else save Jesus Christ for their salvation they were still encompassed with thick darkness, and that the time would come when the Gospel of Christ should be purified from the traditions of men. To his pupil, Farel, he more than once uttered the remarkable prophecy : " God will renovate the world, and you will live to see it."

Through the influence of Lefevre the new doctrines spread to Meaux, where one of his pupils was Bishop. Here a small knot of Reformers collected, who preached in the diocese as itinerant Evangelists. Here Lefevre published a French translation of the New Testament, in 1523. It had a large sale, and during the two following years was reprinted several times. But in February, 1526, a decree of the Parliament of Paris, the chief judicial and legislative Court of the kingdom, was published at all the cross-roads in Paris, forbidding any one to possess or to sell the Epistles of Saint Paul, the Apocalypse, " and other books translated into French." Yet in spite of this prohibition the French New Testament was still printed

at Basle, and pedlars continued to smuggle copies of it
into the kingdom in large numbers.   Meanwhile the
authorities had taken the alarm; at public meetings of
the magistrates and clergy graphic pictures were drawn of
the baneful progress which heresy was making in the land;
a special court was appointed to deal with the heretics;
provincial synods solemnly condemned the new teaching;
and even the Queen of Navarre, sister of Francis the First,
did not escape the attacks of the orthodox Romanists.
She had appointed one of the heretics as her chaplain, and
she had written a book in which the saints and meritorious
works had been passed over in silence, the Blood of Jesus
Christ was declared to be the only Purgatory, and the
hymn to the Virgin, known as the " Salve Regina," was
transferred to her Son.   She was represented in a comedy
as a Fury of Hell; the Sorbonne in an excess of religious
fervour condemned her book; Francis the First was
compelled to intervene; and at his instigation the
University of Paris disavowed the action of its theological
faculty.

Meantime the blood of the martyrs, which was to be the
seed of the new Church, was shed in different parts of
France.   The religious excitement increased.   An image of
the Virgin, credited with the power of working miracles,
was found thrown down and broken to pieces in the streets
of Paris.   Placards, couched in the most violent language,
and denouncing the enormity and impiety of the Mass,
were printed in spite of the protests of the wiser and more
temperate Huguenots, were posted in the squares and
streets of the capital and other cities, and were even
affixed to the door of the King's chamber.   Francis was
so provoked by this audacious act that he ordered the
arrest of all suspected Lutherans, and, in order to manifest
to the world his irreproachable orthodoxy, held a grand
religious procession at the end of January, 1535.   It was
headed by the Monastic Orders and the representatives of
the Parisian parishes with their reliquaries, the shrine of

Saint Genevieve, the patron Saint of Paris, followed, escorted by the University and the Archbishops and Bishops of France, with the Bishop of Paris under a baldachin, bearing the pyx; the King and his three sons took part in the ceremony, walking bareheaded and carrying lighted torches; the Queen and her ladies-in-waiting, mounted on horseback, Princes, nobles, and senators of the Parliament closed the long line. An immense concourse crowded the streets to gaze on the gorgeous spectacle, and by the King's orders six heretics, one of them a schoolmistress, were burnt at the same time over a slow fire as a holocaust to his outraged piety.

Yet, in spite of the orthodox fervour of Francis, his Romanist principles were at times hardly less open to question than Henry the Eighth's. He had dealings with the mortal foe of Christendom, the Ottoman Turk: he uttered speeches of ambiguous import on the subject of the prevalent abuses in the Church of Rome; he selected the notorious Lefevre to, be his son's tutor; he twice interposed to save an even more notorious heretic from his just punishment; he invited the arch-heretic Melanchthon to his Court to advise him on religious questions; he was repeatedly making proposals of offering concessions to the German Protestants. In this point his son, Henry the Second, resembled him. He too, like his father, allowed political interests to outweigh religious prejudices, and cared more for the overthrow of his rival, Charles the Fifth, than for the union of Romanist sovereigns against their ubiquitous and impalpable foe. But Henry was a far bitterer and more consistent persecutor than his father. He even stooped to browbeat one of his unhappy victims, and to feast his eyes upon the martyr's dying agonies. The alarm which he felt at the progress of heresy was in truth amply justified. In spite of the appointment of a special Inquisitor for France, "a man of great learning and excellent zeal," nominated by Paul the Third, in spite of twenty-six articles of faith drawn up by the learned and orthodox Sorbonne, which were to serve, like Ithuriel's spear, as the touchstone for the detection of falsehood and error, in spite of the list of prohibited books, which shows how numerous and important they were, and how the never-slackening zeal and activity of the colporteurs during these years of trial and danger scattered Bibles, New Testaments, catechisms, controversial pamphlets, and edifying works over the face of the whole land, the rising waters of heresy did not abate. The terms of the Edict of Chateaubriand in 1551 give evidence, all the more remarkable because it is impartial, of the strides which the new teaching had made. It lamented that all previous measures had proved ineffectual; from day to day and hour to hour error waxed stronger and stronger; it had become a general plague, so contagious that in many large towns and other places it had infected the majority of the inhabitants, men and women of all classes, and even little children who were fed with this poison; the pro- hibition of ungodly books had been a dead letter, for they were to be found in every place; uneducated persons'were forbidden to discuss or talk about controversial subjects; no one might correspond with exiles in Geneva nor send them money; all bearers of heretical letters from Geneva incurred the penalties of heresy. To whet the zeal of the informers a third part of the property of the condemned Huguenots was made over to them; and the royal favourite, Diana of Poictiers, Duchess of Valentinois, the infamous and incestuous mistress of the father and the son, battened upon the spoils of men the hem of whose garments she was unworthy to touch. The fires of persecution were kindled with renewed ardour in every part of France, at Rouen, Angers, Agen, Lyons, Nismes, Toulouse, Chartres, Evreux, Dijon, Montpelier, Nevers, Limoges, Autun, Chambery, Blois, Bordeaux, and Paris, which, in the indignant language of the Huguenot historian, was the "murderous and sanguinary city above all others." The victims belonged to every class, priests

and monks, lawyers and merchants, men of letters and
men-at-arms, students and colporteurs, wool-carders and
tailors. A single anecdote will serve to illustrate the
temper in which the sufferers faced their death. A
gentleman, Louis de Mersac, because he had followed the
profession of arms, was exempted by the Judge's sentence
from the indignity of going to the place of execution, like
the rest of the Huguenots, with a halter round his neck.
He protested to the magistrate against this distinction.
"Are my companions," he asked, "better than I am? Why,
then, do you not honour me also with the same collar, and
create me the Knight of so illustrious an Order?"

Side by side with these important and significant
measures for the suppression of heresy Henry the Second
resolved to take energetic action against the most eminent
and independent Court of his kingdom, the Parliament
of Paris. It is not surprising that the professors of the
Evangelical doctrines should have met with sympathy
among the distinguished men who composed this Court.
As early as the year 1555 its members had addressed a
remonstrance to the King which might well excite his
gravest suspicions. They pointed to the practice of the
early Church, which did not establish and propagate
religion by fire and sword but by pure doctrine and the
exemplary lives of its Bishops. They urged the King to
preserve religion by the same means which had ensured
its triumph in earlier days, to force the Bishops to tend
their flocks and guide them in person, to provide for the
preaching of God's Word by capable priests, to enforce
the holy living of ecclesiastics, and to present no one to
benefices who was unable to teach the people. That
this remonstrance, which savoured so strongly of Luther
and Calvin, was distasteful to Henry may be easily
imagined. But in 1559 the influential minority who
opposed the persecutions, and who wished to remit all
penalties for heresy until a General Council had settled
the religious disputes with fairness and impartiality, had

become so powerful that the ardent Romanists persuaded
Henry the Second to attend a sitting of the Parliament,
and to judge for himself of the orthodoxy of his Councillors.   Accordingly, on June 15th, 1559, he went to the
Parliament   in   state,   accompanied   by   the   Bourbon
Princes,   Duke   Francis   of   Guise,   the   Constable   of
France, and the Cardinals of Lorraine and Guise.   But
the Parliament contained men who would not suffer themselves to be intimidated by the presence of the King, or to
be debarred from their lawful rights and privileges by the
fear of his displeasure.   One speaker declaimed against
the immoralities of the Roman Curia, the abuses which it
had introduced into the Church, and the sects to which it
had given rise.   Another suggested that, when the Church
was rent by a religious schism, the momentous question
was with whom the responsibility for the schism lay, lest
they should be constrained to make the same answer as
Elijah made to Ahab, " It is thou that troublest Israel."
Another pointed to the contrast between the immunity
enjoyed by notorious sinners of the worst type and the
cruelty with which men were daily punished for exposing
the faults of Rome.   At this plain speaking the King's
despotic temper flamed into wrath.   The daring speakers
were arrested and thrown into prison.   The Parliament
of Paris, purged after this drastic fashion of its noblest
and most learned members, sank into the servile, short-
sighted and intolerant instrument of tyrannical power or
factious violence.

A few weeks later the sudden death of Henry the
Second changed the aspect of the French Court.   Francis
the Second, a sickly and feeble youth, succeeded his
father.   He had just been married to Mary of Scotland,
the daughter of Mary of Guise; and with her husband's
accession to the throne the House of Guise rose to the
foremost place in French politics, and acquired an importance which it did not lose until the close of the century.
At this time Duke Francis of Guise and his brother, the

Cardinal of Lorraine, were the leading members of their House. The Duke, one of the most brilliant captains of the sixteenth century, had already rendered signal services to the French crown by his capture of Calais from the English and his masterly defence of the fortress of Metz against the powerful army led by Charles the Fifth. He had increased the popularity which his martial qualities and his chivalrous bearing had gained for him, by his unsullied orthodoxy and his ardent zeal in defence of the Romanist Church. His enemies hastened to retort that this zeal was not according to knowledge, and with bitter scorn told the tale how, when a French translation of the Bible fell into his hands, he firmly believed that it was an original work composed within the last twenty years for the express purpose of foisting the errors of the heretics upon an ignorant public. The Cardinal possessed qualities scarcely less valuable than his brother's, eloquence, diplomatic skill, courtly manners and an engaging address. But he was at the same time one of the most unprincipled and unscrupulous ecclesiastics of his day, believing that in the warfare with heretics force and fraud were equally legitimate and equally serviceable weapons.

The position which Catherine de Medici obtained as Queen-Mother after Henry's death, and which she held under three of her sons in succession, enabled her to wield an influence even greater than the Guises' over the course of the French Reformation. It is difficult to speak of her in language which does not sound exaggerated. For the worst sovereigns of modern times in comparison with her wear the semblance of dignity, unselfishness, veracity, and uprightness. The Medusa of heathen mythology, the Semiramis of Eastern legend, and the Duessa of the English poet's allegory are humane, virtuous, and amiable figures compared with this heartless, vicious, unprincipled woman, without faith or honour, without purity or modesty, without pity or remorse, the tempter and seducer of all who entered the poisoned atmosphere of her Court.

It must be conceded in mitigation of this severe judgment that Catherine was sinned against as well as sinning. A niece of Pope Clement the Seventh, she was born and brought up in a country proverbial in the sixteenth century for the terrible laxity of its morals—a country which, within a few years, produced a Pope like Alexander the Sixth, a Prince like Cæsar Borgia, and a political leader like Machiavelli. Her marriage had been lightened by few gleams of happiness ; and a father-in-law like Francis the First, a husband like Henry the Second, and a spiritual adviser like the Cardinal of Lorraine were not fitted to mould heroic characters or to foster elevated virtue.

The supremacy of the Guises at the French Court was the signal for renewed persecutions. They plied against the Huguenots the unscrupulous devices with which they had consolidated their temporal power. Informers were hired to spy out the Huguenot meetings. Worthless members, who had been excluded from the fellowship of the Reformed Church, took their revenge by betraying their brethren, and received ample rewards from the confiscated property. The Romanist clergy threatened with the terrors of excommunication all who did not denounce the heretics. The horrible calumnies by which the populace had been goaded on against the early Christians were made to serve the same turn against the Huguenots : they were charged with making their nightly meetings a cloak to cover incest, promiscuous debauchery, and cannibal feasts. The mob were egged on to tear the condemned heretics out of the hands of their executioners, that they might put them to death with tortures even more cruel than the cruel laws permitted. Images of the Virgin were set up at all the street corners for the express purpose of detecting from the gestures and demeanour of the passers-by whether it would be possible to denounce them on a charge of constructive heresy. In short, to quote the energetic language of the Huguenot historian,

what Christ said to His disciples of the coming tribu-
lation might be said of this persecution which lasted only
seventeen months that, if the days had not been shortened
for the elects' sake, none could have been saved.

At this critical point in the history of the French
Reformation a general survey may fitly be taken of the
character and number of the Huguenots, of the progress
which they had made, and of the causes which contributed
to their success.

The manner in which the Reformed doctrines spread in
the most important centres of France may be illustrated
by two typical examples, Dieppe in the North, and Nismes
in the South.   If a contemporary account may be believed,
the craving for a purer form of religion had already made
itself felt in Dieppe during the first half of the sixteenth
century; for the Romanist preachers could only instruct
their hearers in the stories and fables of the "Golden
Legend," of miracles of bleeding Hosts, of sweating,
winking, and nodding images, of apparitions of departed
spirits, and of souls returning from Purgatory.   But the
first sower of the good seed was a colporteur of humble
station, named Venable, who, at the end of August, 1557,
brought from Geneva a small store of well-selected books.
Through his efforts some dozen inquirers after truth
formed the nucleus of a small Church, assembling secretly
in private houses, reading the Scriptures, and offering up
prayers together.   After a short time Venable began to
catechize and deliver addresses; and before the end of the
year he communicated with La Jonchée, the Genevese
minister at Rouen, eagerly urging him to visit Dieppe,
where the harvest was plenteous but the labourers were
few.   This appeal led to a visit from La Jonchée, who
delivered several sermons, ordained Elders, and left
Venable in charge of the congregation until they should
be able to obtain Pastors.

The Ministers of Geneva, having received the welcome
news, sent as Pastor the scion of a good family in Provence,

who, from his arrival at the beginning of 1558 till his premature death in the following June, in spite of the presence and opposition of the Duke of Bouillon, the Lieutenant-General of Normandy, laboured assiduously in the infant Church, preaching every night in private houses, and largely increasing the number of the faithful. His successor arrived in the following November, but at the beginning of 1559 received the powerful aid of John Knox, who stayed in the city for six weeks on his journey from Geneva, by his inspiring eloquence swelled the ranks of the Huguenots, encouraged them to hold their meetings in broad daylight, and witnessed the admission of several men and women of note in the province to membership in the Reformed Church. The effects of the religious discipline which accompanied the new faith were soon evident, especially among the seafaring folk: oaths and blasphemies were no longer heard, taverns and houses of ill-fame were deserted, and public masquerades and gambling were abjured.

The progress of the Reformed Church led to the intervention of the Cardinal of Bourbon, Archbishop of Rouen, who sent his Grand Vicar at the end of May, 1559, to restore the falling fortunes of the old Church. He organized a great procession in which the Host was solemnly carried round: but the Huguenots retaliated by assembling to the number of 500 in the late evening, marching to and fro before the Vicar's house, and singing defiantly the Huguenot psalms which had become the war-cry of the new faith. This demonstration so effectually intimidated the Romanist champion that he quitted the city early in the following day. He was succeeded by the Marquis of Elbœuf, the violent and licentious uncle of Mary Stuart, who was detained at Dieppe for two months by contrary winds on his journey to Scotland. After his departure the Reformed Church made a fresh start, the meetings were more frequent and more numerously attended than ever, and the services were held by day as well as by night, in the country as well as in the city. In April, 1560, a second Minister was appointed. On May 6th, five days after the Cardinal of Bourbon had personally organized a grand procession in which the Host was carried through the streets, the Eucharist was celebrated for the first time according to the Reformed rites; of the 1,700 members who composed the Church nearly half communicated. A month later it was resolved by the Huguenots to bury their dead in the daytime and in the presence of the members of their Church. As many as 700 or 800 attended the funerals, and in 1561 the coffin was taken to the grave with singing of psalms. At last, in July, the sermons were preached openly by day, and two large places were hired in which the Reformed services could be held.

The course of the Reformation in Nismes was more chequered and more troubled than in Dieppe. It is significant that as late as the year 1539 the Canons of Nismes, who had lived under the rule of Saint Augustine for centuries, prayed their Bishop that, in consequence of the laxity and dissoluteness which had crept in among them, they might be secularized; and their petition, supported by the powerful advocacy of Francis the First, was granted by the Pope. Only four years later the Parliament of Toulouse issued stringent orders for the suppression of heresy in Nismes and its neighbourhood. In 1552 the influence of Geneva began to make itself felt; meetings were held outside the city; the Parliament of Toulouse ordered a strict search to be made for the offenders; and when they escaped into Switzerland, commanded them to be burnt in effigy. Yet so ineffectual were these measures that in 1554 a preacher, who had for some time taught in secret, began to preach in public, was arrested, tried, condemned, and hanged; his dead body was burnt, and the ashes scattered to the winds. The Prior of the Jacobins, who had been sent to turn him from the error of his ways, became a convert to the Reformed doctrines, escaped secretly to Geneva, and there made public profession of his faith.

On September 29th, 1559, the first regular Minister entered Nismes, and preached in the daytime in a private house. The Eucharist was administered on the following Easter to a large number of communicants, who came in fully armed from the surrounding villages. Two months later churches were seized in Nismes and the neighbourhood in which Huguenot services were held; and in the autumn the City Council wrote to the Constable confessing that they were powerless to prevent the meetings. The importation of heretical books issued by the Geneva press powerfully aided the cause of the Reformers in Nismes as in Dieppe. How great the number of these books was may be judged from the fact that two or three loads were burnt by the Governor of the province at Beaucaire alone.

A few months later the Huguenots gained a fresh vantage ground. Just before Lady Day, 1561, a Consistory was established in Nismes, which met every Saturday and enforced the discipline of Calvin; the city was divided into ten parts, and a superintendent was set over each; in each division four women were appointed to collect alms for the poor; and the organization of the Church was completed by the establishment of a temporary school for the training of young ministers. At the end of May the Eucharist was administered in a large garden to an immense number of communicants.

By this time the Huguenots of the province had become fully conscious of their strength, and at Sauve and the villages around they had violently entered churches, had driven out the priests, and had thrown down crosses, images, and altars. This lawless spirit spread to Nismes, where the Huguenots already numbered more than 5,000; and in spite of the admonitions of the Consistory and the Minister, who urged them to obey the magistrates in all lawful matters, they seized a large monastic church outside the city gates, giving the monks the option of continuing the Romanist services at such times as the church was not required by the Protestants. The arrival of Peter Viret at Nismes as second Minister confirmed the supremacy of the new doctrines. His personal character, his theological ability, his wide experience, and the power and eloquence of his sermons, exercised a decisive influence. Towards the close of the year 1561 the monks, alarmed at the growing power of the heretics, began to desert their monasteries and churches. A general meeting of the Council was held, and was attended by the Bishop of Nismes, the King's Procurator, the Judges, the royal officers, and the civic officers. So threatening was the aspect of the populace that it was reluctantly decided to give up the formal possession of two more churches to the Huguenots. Yet even this concession failed to satisfy them. A few days later, though the Consistory solemnly protested against acts of violence, a mob numbering 2,000 broke into the Cathedral, destroyed all the symbols of Romanist worship, treated the other churches of Nismes in the same manner, compelled the Bishop to flee to Arles, drove the monks and nuns out of the city, and, spreading themselves over the country, made havoc in every church that they entered, and forcibly suppressed all "idolatrous services."

From this time the Romanists practically disappeared in Nismes and the neighbourhood. The Prior of Milhaud and the Abbess of Tarascon, with other monks and nuns, joined the Reformed Church. At the beginning of 1562 the Eucharist was celebrated in the Cathedral at five in the morning and again at eight, and each celebration was attended by more than 7,000 communicants. A few weeks later, in compliance with the orders of the King, the Huguenots, moved by the earnest exhortations of Viret, restored the churches which they had taken, and the Romanist worship was again celebrated in the Cathedral and the Church of the Carmelites. But this was scarcely

more than a form.   Nismes had become a Reformed city ;
and the fact was emphasized by the meeting of a provincial
synod of the Protestant Churches within its walls.

By the year 1560 the Reformed Church had spread all
over France, from Picardy in the north to Provence in the
south.   The evidence of its enemies is conclusive on this
point.   One French Cardinal complained that villages,
boroughs, and cities echoed with the din of the Huguenot
meetings, that all the world ran to hear their sermons,
that there was no more zeal or affection for the ancient
worship, and that the populace were deserting the Romanist
Church for the new religion.   Another Cardinal declared
in his private correspondence with a brother Cardinal that
the French kingdom was half Huguenot, that it was completely and hopelessly undermined by heresy, and that the
head and the members were alike affected.   The Protestants of Normandy presented a petition to the King, and
assured him that, if he desired it, they could obtain more
than 50,000 signatures from their province alone.   The
number of Huguenot Churches was authoritatively stated
to be more than 2,100.   How large a membership these
Churches represented it is impossible to determine with
any approach to accuracy.   Probably the estimate of the
eminent historian, De Thou, who had exceptional sources
of information, and whose impartiality makes his evidence
specially valuable, may be accepted without much demur.
He reckons the Huguenots at two millions ; and even if
we reduce this estimate by one-half, it would still represent
a dissentient body of the most formidable dimensions.
But it was not their numbers alone which made the
Huguenots formidable.   They had drawn into their ranks
the flower of the French gentry and the flower of the
French middle class and artizans.   The fervour and
earnestness of their preachers had commended the truth
of their religious doctrines, and the high moral standard
which they enforced proved singularly attractive to their
hearers.   Impartial accounts produced from the civic records

bear evidence to the marvellous change which had come over towns where the inhabitants had been converted to the Huguenot Church, how brawling, lawlessness, and a dissolute life had given place as if by magic to a sober, temperate, and God-fearing spirit. Gaspard de Coligny, Admiral of France, whose remarkable political and military ability, combined with his unsullied purity, spotless honour, transparent truthfulness, ardent patriotism, lofty morality, and deep religious convictions, made him one of the noblest heroes of the sixteenth century, was the leader and type of a band of men fertile, like himself, of the highest virtues which adorn and enrich a State, the very salt of the society in which they moved. To these representatives of the Huguenot Church the words in which a contemporary Romanist historian has described the early Huguenots might be applied without qualification : " Men who could not believe that such a Christian life as theirs appeared to be was compatible with false doctrine were shaken in their ancient faith, and ran after these people who breathed nothing but sanctity. On every occasion the name of the Lord and of Christ was on their lips ; and ' certainly ' or ' truly ' was their usual oath. They were the avowed foes of luxury, of the public excesses and worldly jests which are only too common among the Romanists. At their assemblies and feasts, instead of dances and musical instruments, there was reading in the Bible, which was laid on the table, and religious songs, especially Psalms."

The singing of Psalms mentioned in this passage was so distinctive a mark, so unfailing a resource, so supreme a consolation, and so attractive a feature of the Churches which arose under the influence of Calvin, that it merits a detailed notice. In France, in Switzerland, in Germany, in the Low Countries, in England, and in Scotland the singing of a metrical version of the Psalms became an indispensable part of the public worship and of the private devotions of these Churches. The first verse translation was one of the latest works of Marot, the leading French poet of Francis the First's reign. At the suggestion and with the help of Vatable, Professor of Hebrew at the new Royal College, Marot translated thirty of the Psalms. These were the first fifteen, and fifteen others selected from different parts of the Psalter, including some which in all ages have been specially endeared to Christians by their spiritual depth and artistic beauty, such as the 19th, the 51st, the 103rd, and the 104th. The poet dedicated his translation to Francis the First, was ordered by the King to present them to Charles the Fifth on his visit to Paris in 1540, received the Emperor's gracious commendations, and was rewarded by him with a present of two hundred doubloons. The reward which he received from the Sorbonne and the Parliament of Paris was very different; the former condemned the heretical book, the latter ordered the arrest of the author; and Marot, to escape from his persecutors, was compelled to flee to Geneva. Here he translated nineteen more Psalms and the Song of Simeon. These "Fifty Psalms," as they were called, he published in 1543 with a poetical preface, in which he prophetically anticipated the day when the labourer at his plough, the waggoner in the street, the workman in his shop, and the shepherd in the woods should lighten their toils by the singing of Psalm or Canticle; and a Romanist Bishop a century later testified to the literal fulfilment of this prediction.

It was only after an interval of some years that an addition was made to the "Fifty Psalms." In 1548 Beza heard for the first time in the service of the Genevese Church Marot's version of the 91st Psalm. It made a life-long impression upon him; and when Calvin urged him to consecrate his poetical gifts to God's service by completing the version of the whole Psalter, he gladly acceded to the request. In 1552 thirty-four of Beza's Psalms were printed with Marot's; in the editions of 1554 and 1559 seven more were added; in 1562 the 150 had been finished, Charles the Ninth had granted his royal "privilege" for the printing, and they were published in the same year at Lyons. The success of the version was extraordinary. Even in the corrupt and dissolute French Court Henry the Second, Catherine de Medici, and the notorious Diana of Poictiers had each a favourite Psalm. The Sorbonne thundered in vain against it; the Parliament of Bordeaux in vain denounced the severest penalties against all who in churches, streets, and houses should sing the Psalms of David " translated into French in mockery of the Christian religion and to the great scandal of it."

Three eminent citizens of the Netherlands produced three separate versions suggested by the French; the contagion spread to Germany, England, and Scotland; other versions appeared in Italian, Gascon, Spanish, Polish, and Czech; and the French poets reached the zenith of their popularity when an ingenious Hebrew Professor retranslated their Psalms into Hebrew according to the original words and metres of the French version! On the scaffold and at the stake, in the executioner's cart and while the faggots were piled around them, the French martyrs gave expression to their joy and hope, their unwavering confidence and jealousy for God's honour, in the singing of Beza's Psalms. At the setting and relieving guard, on the eve of battle and in the hour of a great deliverance, the familiar melodies rose to the Huguenots' lips. Children sang them on sitting down to meals; exiles beguiled the sad and toilsome journey into a far country with their home-like strains. During the thirty years preceding the Massacre of Saint Bartholomew as many as eighty-eight editions were published.

The death of Francis the Second at once altered the aspect of the French Court, and weakened the power of the Guises. The " foreigners " were momentarily thrown into the background, and the Bourbon Princes, Navarre and Condé, resumed their rightful position at the side of the throne, and countenanced the Huguenot cause. But the Guises were too influential, too ambitious, too

unscrupulous, and too able to suffer more than a temporary
check. The Duke of Guise united with the Constable of
France and the Marshal of St. André, a prodigal and
licentious voluptuary, who had amassed an immense
fortune with unclean hands ; the Duchess of Valentinois
fitly acted as the mediator of the alliance : one of the
Guises married the daughter of the royal harlot, and
another the daughter of St. André. In this way the
" Triumvirate " were still able to hold their own against
the Bourbons and the Colignys. Yet the progress which
the Reformation was making became more apparent than
ever after the accession of Charles the Ninth. At the
meeting of the States General in December, 1560, the
speaker of the nobles condemned the greed of the clergy
and their interference in civil matters, prayed that ecclesiastics might be compelled to reside on their cures, and
asked that no benefices might be bestowed on unworthy
incumbents. The speaker of the Third Estate used
stronger language ; the three vices of the clergy, ignorance, avarice, and luxury, were so notorious and so
universal that it was waste of time to dwell upon them.
The speaker of the Clergy, although he poured forth
invectives against the heretics, was forced to admit that
the faults of the Clergy were glaring and enormous. It
was a further sign of the times that the Queen-Mother
began to veer round to the side of the Huguenots.
The Bishop of Valence, an open adherent of the Protestant Church, was invited to preach in the King's castle,
and Charles and the courtiers attended the sermons, to
the unconcealed disgust of the Triumvirate. It was less
surprising that the Cardinal of Chatillon, brother of the
Admiral, and one of the highest ecclesiastics in France,
celebrated the Eucharist according to the Reformed rite,
and communicated in both kinds, at Easter, 1561.

The result of all these changes was the Edict of July,
1561, in which the Court attempted to settle the religious
question by making concessions to both parties. To

please the Romanists it was enacted that the Huguenots should not hold meetings, nor celebrate the Sacraments except according to the rites of the Church of Rome : to please the Huguenots it was decreed that neither party should attack the other, and that banishment should be the severest punishment which could be inflicted on heretics. Naturally the Edict satisfied neither party : the Huguenots were indignant that their right of meeting was not recognized : the Romanists were indignant that heresy had been indirectly sanctioned, and that the time-honoured punishments of the Inquisition had been replaced by a brand-new punishment which it was morally and physically impossible to inflict. Their indignation was heightened by Catherine's next step. She proposed that representatives of both parties should meet and discuss the religious questions at issue in presence of the King and the Court. The proposal was hailed with acclamation by the Huguenots. There was nothing for which they longed more than the opportunity of publicly refuting their opponents' calumnies by giving, in the most solemn and impressive manner, a reason for the faith that was in them. They had everything to gain and nothing to lose by such a discussion : it would, they hoped, disarm the malignity of their enemies, arrest the attention of the indifferent, and confirm the faith of their friends. The vehement Romanists, on the other hand, entered an energetic protest. To set the Huguenot ministers on an equality with Romanist prelates ! To express even indirectly any toleration of heresies which Pope after Pope and Council after Council had condemned ! To treat as open questions the most sacred doctrines of the Church ! What an unutterable scandal ! But the Cardinal of Lorraine sided with Catherine, and his influence carried the day.

The Colloquy of Poissy, like the other religious conferences of the sixteenth century, led to no practical result. The discussion was confined to two subjects, the Church

and the Eucharist; and the speeches on both sides only
served the purpose of emphasizing the irreconcileable
differences between the two Confessions. But indirectly
the discussion furthered the cause of the French Reformation. Beza, whose wit, poetical imagination, literary
enthusiasm, and winning address had made him in his
youth a favourite of Parisian society, startled and impressed
his courtly audience by appearing in the novel character
of a Huguenot minister. He was supported by the gentle
and persuasive Peter Martyr, the tried theologian of a
hundred battles, who had already left his mark on three
countries. The Huguenots observed with pride and joy
that these champions were able to hold their own in
eloquence, learning, and argumentative skill against the
Cardinal of Lorraine and Lainez, the celebrated and
vesatile General of the Society of Jesus. The Conference
had scarcely broken up before the Huguenots held their
meetings everywhere in larger numbers and with increasing
boldness. In Paris, where the persecution of the Huguenots had been most bitter and most prolonged, 6,000,
8,000, and even more, assembled at a single service.
When Beza visited the capital, he was pressed to preach
daily sermons, and at each sermon he had an audience of
thousands. In Lyons there were 20,000 communicants
at a single celebration of the Eucharist, in Orleans
22,000, in Rouen an even larger number. In parts of
France where a few months ago one Minister was sufficient
ten were now required. In comparatively insignificant
places where the Huguenots had recently numbered ten,
thirty, or fifty, they suddenly increased to 100, 300, and 500.
In Gascony it was possible to travel for scores of miles
without finding a single Romanist priest. It was openly
asserted that, if 1,000 duly qualified ministers could be
sent into France at once, the number would be insufficient
to supply the communities who were clamouring for
pastors. The differences between the two Churches were
freely and publicly discussed in every society. The nobles

in great numbers joined the Reformed Church. The Papal Legate, the Cardinal of Ferrara, who had the misfortune to be the grandson of Pope Alexander the Sixth and the son of Lucretia Borgia, suffered the humiliation of seeing his grandfather and his mother mercilessly satirized and caricatured. Under these circumstances a meeting of the chief members of all the Parliaments in the kingdom was summoned by the Government. The Chancellor, the celebrated L'Hospital, delivered a speech in which he clearly stated the principles of the " political " party, that laws are useless, and worse than useless, if they cannot be enforced, that religious differences are a far less evil than civil war, that men may separate from the Church and yet be good citizens, and that it is possible for two religious parties to live in peace, even though they do not observe the same ceremonies and the same usages. After a long discussion the Edict of January was drawn up to take the place of the Edict of July. By the terms of the Edict it was enacted that all churches which the Huguenots had taken from the Romanists should be restored, and that no outrages should be committed in Romanist places of worship. Both parties were forbidden to revile and pro-voke one another, and were urged to live in mutual peace and amity. Religious meetings of the Huguenots within the walls of cities were prohibited, but they were allowed to hold services and preach sermons outside the civic boundaries; and if they observed these con-ditions, no Judges or Government officials might interfere with them.

The Edict of January is important because it contained the first formal recognition of the great principle for which the Chancellor and the " political " party con-tended, and which finally triumphed nearly forty years later. But it is easy to see that the conditions which it assumed, and which were absolutely necessary to ensure its observance, had no existence except in theory. The Government did not possess the resolute will and the strong hand to suppress all resistance to it. The Parliament of Paris loudly maintained that it violated the fundamental law of the constitution. The Triumvirate openly endeavoured to make it of none effect. All the influence of Philip the Second, who could now plead at the French Court with increased authority as the brother-in-law of Charles the Ninth, was exerted on the side of intolerance. The vast majority of the Romanist clergy, and a considerable proportion of the Huguenot, eyed it with unconcealed repugnance, did not even affect to regard it as a just and wise decree, and had neither the spirit of compromise and concession, nor the mutual goodwill, which alone could have made it an effectual measure. The rank and file of the Romanist majority and a large number of the Huguenots, blinded by fanaticism and bigotry, embittered by the religious hostility of years, and exasperated by real or fancied wrongs, could not be expected to show more forbearance and moderation than their leaders. Whether in the heated state of men's minds any power could have averted the civil war may be reasonably doubted; but in the face of these adverse conditions the chances of peace dwindled to a vanishing point.

The Massacre of Vassy, which changed in a moment the whole face of the country, which estranged Huguenots and Romanists more completely than the persecutions and the fires of forty years, and which ushered in the long train of civil and religious wars, was unquestionably due to the action of the Romanist leader. The Duke of Guise, returning from an elaborate comedy of perfidy and hypocrisy which he and his brother the Cardinal had been acting at the expense of the Lutherans of Wurtemberg, passed through Vassy, a little town of 3,000 inhabitants, belonging to his principality of Joinville. His unwarranted interruption of the Huguenot service was resented by the alarmed worshippers, who attempted to exclude the intruders. The armed force which the Duke

had brought with him, composed of vassals as bigoted
and unscrupulous as their lord, forced their way into the
barn with sanguinary cries, cut down the defenceless
Huguenots, men and women, young and old, indiscrimi-
nately, killed more than fifty and wounded more than two
hundred.   The Duke attempted afterwards to clear himself from all responsibility for the guilt of this wanton
outrage; but it is evident from his own words that he
regarded this heretical rabble as scandalous, arrogant,
disloyal, seditious, disobedient, and undutiful people, who
refused to cringe at the feet of the lordly House of Guise,
who had actually been guilty not long before of refuting
and covering with confusion the Bishop of Chalons, who
were at that moment rebels in disguise, " possessed of
arquebuses, pistols, and other weapons," and who in their
insolence refuse' :o listen to the " gracious and honest
admonition," with which he proposed to address them.
Not unnaturally, the Huguenots, knowing from long
experience the character of Guise and the undisguised
hatred with which he had always regarded them, refused
to accept his defence, maintained that he had provoked
the quarrel and had not stopped the massacre, and felt
that henceforward nothing but the sword could decide
between him and them.

The religious wars profoundly affected the course of
the French Reformation.   The religious question was in
a great measure obscured and overlaid by the rivalry
between the Guises and the Bourbons, the ambitious
intrigues of the Queen-Mother, the ecclesiastical and
political schemes of Philip the Second, the selfish and
vacillating policy of Elizabeth, the half-hearted interference of the Protestant Princes of Germany, the shifting
fortunes of the war in the Low Countries, the plots of
Mary Stuart's adherents in England, the dynastic rights
of Henry the Fourth, the rise of a new democracy in the
French capital, and the extravagant claims of the
Romanist priesthood.   That the cause of the Huguenots

should have suffered far more than the cause of the Romanists from this prolonged and barbarous contest, waged with a ferocity, a refinement of cruelty, and a disregard of the elementary laws of civilisation, which would have disgraced Marius or Sulla, was inevitable. The attractive power of the Huguenots, by the common consent of friends and foes, had lain in the endeavour to realize, alike in the public life of their Church and in the private life of its individual members, the ideal standard of Christian holiness. When, therefore, according to the highest authority, the civil wars produced a million Epicureans and Libertines, made the most part of the French nation so wild, cruel, and savage, that instead of sheep they had become tigers, and established a new kingdom of impiety, injustice, and wickedness, these stains showed darkest upon the brightest background. When the Huguenot morality had been sapped by the fatal demoralisation which overspread France, when Huguenot soldiers and Huguenot ministers committed or condoned atrocities from which the worshippers of Diana of the Ephesians might have shrunk back aghast, impartial or cynical onlookers naturally applied to them the poet's maxim,

" Lilies that fester smell far worse than weeds."

Where (men asked ironically) is the Christian steadfastness which was proof against all temptations, the Christian love which could bear all things, and endure all things, the Christian sanctity which took for its motto, " Lex Dei suprema salus " ? The pithy verdict of the Huguenot historian that the Huguenots waged the first civil war like angels, the second like men, and the third like devils incarnate, illustrates this truth with painful force. The fine gold had become dim, and the silver had become dross.

The Huguenot cause was further weakened by two important changes in the policy of their Romanist opponents which decisively altered the religious future of France. The admirable organisation of the Huguenot Church had unquestionably been one of the chief causes of its success. By the Consistories, or governing bodies of the several Churches, by the Colloquies, which united a group of neighbouring Consistories, by the Synods, or deliberative and executive bodies of the sixteen Provinces into which France had been provisionally divided, and by the General Assemblies or National Synods, which constituted the supreme legislative body and Court of Appeal for the whole Church, the ecclesiastical system of the Huguenots had acquired an elasticity and power, a combination of local government and centralized administration which left the government of the Romanist Church far behind. But after the religious wars had begun, the Romanist leaders were wise enough to confront the Huguenot organisation with an organisation of equal efficiency by skilfully blending religion and politics and enrolling the Romanist population in Leagues, called Confraternities of the Holy Spirit, which should unite all the faithful children of Mother Church in their resistance to heresy, and should make their allegiance to the Sovereign dependent on his unwavering defence of the Romanist religion. These Leagues originated in Burgundy, and established their head-quarters in the important city of Dijon. Men of all classes joined them. Consistories were formed to support and strengthen the good cause. By degrees they absorbed the authority and power of the King and the royal Governors, enlisted soldiers, raised money, took action against the Huguenots, whom they far outnumbered, extolled Philip the Second to the skies while they decried their own monarch, and held up the crusading orthodoxy of Spain as a model for the imitation of all right-minded Frenchmen.

It may, however, be doubted whether these Leagues would have met with such unqualified success if they had not been aided by the whole strength of the Society

of Jesus. The history of this Order in the kingdom of
France is curious and instructive. As early as 1550 Henry
the Second, in accordance with the Pope's Breve, had
given the Society leave to settle in the kingdom, to receive
alms, and to build a College and Chapel in Paris and other
important cities. Four years later the Parliament laid the
King's letter and the Pope's Breve before the Bishop of
Paris and the Theological Faculty. Nothing could be
more unfavourable than the opinion of this important
body. Their severe judgment seems to have quelled the
spirit of the Fathers for a time. But on the accession of
Francis the Second, in reliance upon the favour of the
Guises, they made a fresh appeal to the Bishop of Paris.
His denunciation of the Order was as strongly worded as
the preceding. Then the King, at the suggestion of the
Cardinal of Lorraine, referred the question to the Parliament, and the Parliament in turn referred it to the General
Assembly of the Gallican Church. The French Prelates
signified their approval of the Order if it would accept
certain definite conditions ; and the College of Clermont
was accordingly opened by the Jesuits in Paris. Instantly
the University raised a protest against this invasion of
their privileges. But by this time the Parliament, alarmed
at the steady progress of the Reformed doctrines, were
eager to avail themselves of any auxiliaries who could aid
them in the coming struggle, and decided in their favour.
The importance of this decision can hardly be exaggerated.
For the first time since the beginning of the French
Reformation the Huguenots were pitted against opponents
as fervent, as pious, as learned, as indifferent to wealth
and worldly honours as themselves. Men of the world were
charmed by their manners. Enthusiasts were delighted
with their enthusiasm. Devotees recognized in them a
spirit of devotion as exalted and fantastic as their own.
Anxious parents found in them the most inspiring and
self-sacrificing of educators. The clergy were eclipsed by
their allies in zeal for the Church and its prerogatives.

The monastic Orders were half aroused from their lethargy by the stimulating rivalry of the new Order. But in addition to these valuable qualities they possessed another more valuable than all at a time of religious crisis. For the Jesuits were nothing if not intolerant of heresy. The hatred with which the Huguenots had up to this time inspired the French clergy seemed pale and colourless by the side of theirs. Even in their daily life they breathed the atmosphere of the Spanish Inquisition. To tolerate heretics was a sin; to unite with heretics was a still darker sin; to imagine that faith need be kept with heretics was an unhallowed delusion; to feel scruples about breaking a solemn oath taken to heretics was a criminal weakness; the extermination of heretics was a godly work, which, like the Apostle's charity, covered a multitude of sins. What was lacking in the doctrine of the Jesuits on the subject of heresy was amply supplied by the teaching of Pope Pius the Fifth, who has received from the Church of Rome the doubtful honour of canonisation. The scriptural precedents which the Jesuits had quoted, Moses ordering the worshippers of the Golden Calf to be cut down, and Jehu treacherously massacring the worshippers of Baal, did not satisfy this implacable Pontiff, who had served his apprenticeship in the school of the Inquisition. The only Biblical parallel which, in his opinion, met the requirements of the case was the extermination of the Amalekites by Saul, who did not spare even the unconscious infant at the breast.

In this way everything was prepared for the most gigantic political crime of the sixteenth century, the Massacre of Saint Bartholomew. The full truth about the massacre will probably never be known. But there can be no doubt that throughout Europe it was regarded as a blow dealt at the Huguenots in their religious character, that it was greeted with shouts of triumph by the Romanist clergy in France, Italy, and Spain, that it was extolled to the skies by the leading agents and supporters of Rome in all the Romanist Courts, and that it was applauded to the echo by the fanatical populace of Paris, who could only see the most sublime piety and the highest patriotism in the deeds and words of the Queen-Mother and her infamous sons—deeds and words so treacherous, so dastardly, so foul, and so revolting that the annals of history may be ransacked in vain for a parallel.   Whether the victims numbered 5,000 or 10,000, or 20,000, matters little.   They included men whose death weakened the Huguenot cause more than the loss of fifty battles, and with whom the heroic age of French Protestantism passed away for ever.   Henceforth their places were filled by men of a lower and a coarser type, who deemed that Paris was well worth a Mass, who looked upon religion as a stepping-stone to worldly dignities and honours, or whose piety was darkened by a repulsive narrowness of soul.

It was not the least important result of the Massacre of Saint Bartholomew that it led to a searching examination of the origin, the conditions, and the limits of the royal power in France.   Two Frenchmen, both of them Pro-testants, both enjoying European reputations, both perfectly familiar with the events of the last forty years, both eye-witnesses of the massacre, in which they ran the greatest personal risk, subjected Charles the Ninth and his regal claims to the scalpel of their pitiless criticism. Their writings anticipated by a hundred years some of the most important principles on which the English Parliament acted, and by two hundred years the still more radical doctrines of the French Encyclopædists.

Hotman, in his " Franco-Gallia," maintains that the French monarchy, like the German, Danish, Swedish, and Polish, is in principle elective.   Not only have the French people the right of electing their Kings ; they have also the right of deposing them, and as a matter of fact have repeatedly deposed them, for adultery and licen-tiousness, for pride and cruelty, for sloth and cowardice. But apart from the exercise of these exceptional powers

they have permanently limited the kingly prerogatives by
the yearly meeting of the great Council of the nation, or
the Parliament of the Three Estates. This assembling of
the National Council has enforced three principles of
supreme importance: it has shown that what concerns
the whole people must be approved by the whole people :
it has reminded the royal ministers that for the powers
and privileges with which they are entrusted by the King
they are responsible to the nation : it has demonstrated
the infinite superiority of a popular Council to the Privy
Council of the monarch; for the former studies the
welfare of the kingdom, the latter is composed of men
who only minister to the royal caprices and further the
selfish interests of their master.

The divinity which hedges round a King is treated by
the distinguished jurist with contemptuous scorn. The
King may be a fool or a madman, may lose his balance of
mind through the indulgence of unlawful desires, may
suffer from infirmities, or age, or levity, may be misled by
covetous and rapacious Councillors, may be seduced or
depraved by the debauched youths of high birth with
whom he associates, or may be infatuated by a silly
mistress and fling the reins of power into her hands.
History teems with such examples of misused sovereignty.
Finally, as the pupil does not exist for the sake of the
tutor, nor the guardian for the sake of the ward, nor the
ship for the sake of the pilot, the people do not exist for
the sake of the King; they would prosper under an aristocratic or democratic form of government every whit as
well as under a monarchical.

To prove that the power of the French King is neither
absolute, nor unlimited, nor arbitrary, Hotman quotes the
famous historian of the fifteenth century, Philip de
Comines, who asserts that no King, least of all a French
King, can venture to raise taxes, even to the value of one
farthing, without the people's consent. How comes it,
then, that the power of the French monarchy has risen to

its present inordinate height? The chief cause may be found in the jealousy with which during many years the French Kings have eyed the vast and undisputed prerogatives of the States General, and in the assiduity with which they have laboured to undermine and curtail them. This perfidious policy has culminated in the substitution of spurious and counterfeit Parliaments for the lawful and genuine Parliament of the nation. These Parliaments, which have sprung up in the chief cities, Paris, Toulouse, Rouen, Bordeaux, and others, usurp the august name of the National Council, are filled with subservient creatures of the King, expressly nominated by himself, and have been invested by him with three momentous privileges to which they have not the shadow of a right: none of the King's decrees are valid unless they have been approved and ratified by these Parliaments; every magistrate and officer in France, whether civil or military, must be confirmed in his appointment by the Parliament; there can be no appeal against their judgment, but all their decrees are absolutely valid. In short, all the authority and power which for many years have been vested in the great Council of the nation are now transferred to the sham Parliament. Such are the words with which Hotman, looking back upon the earlier history of the nation, remembering the arbitrary proceedings of Henry the Second, and recalling to mind the servile applause with which the shameless Parliament of Paris greeted the Saint Bartholomew, closes his indictment of the unconstitutional government of France.

Languet, who published his " Vindiciæ contra tyrannos " under the suggestive pseudonym of " Junius Brutus," took a very different line from Hotman, laid down principles more abstract and more comprehensive, and arrived at conclusions even more sweeping. Hotman writes throughout as a great constitutional lawyer, Languet as a political philosopher. Hotman nowhere alludes to the religious question, Languet places it in the forefront of his treatise.

Hotman has in view the French monarchy alone, Languet monarchy in general. Hotman illustrates every page of his pamphlet with examples from French history; Languet carefully avoids any allusion to France, and it is only by reading between the lines that the student can detect the fatal effect with which his keen dagger stabs the worthless character and the lawless policy of Charles the Ninth.

Starting from the doctrines that God alone possesses absolute and unlimited power, and that Kings like all other men are only His delegates and vassals, Languet draws the conclusion that, if God commands one thing and the King commands another, we are bound to keep the commandments of God and to disregard the orders of the King. What is true of the individual subject is true of the people as a whole. If the King attempts to draw them after strange gods, to abolish God's Law, and to overthrow His service and His Church, the people are bound to resist him, even to the taking up of arms, if he uses the sword to compel and to persecute them. For the people have made two covenants and taken two oaths, one to be God's people, the other to obey the King as the governor and leader of God's people. Even the Turks may teach us a lesson. Though they forcibly introduce the impious doctrine of Mahomet into the countries which they subdue, yet they constrain no man's conscience. But he who is a greater adversary of Christ and His Gospel, in union with all Kings whom he has enchanted, constrains men to become idolaters by fire and the rack, maintaining his laws by perfidious disloyalty and his traditions by continual treachery.

Like Hotman, Languet insists that the King's office is elective, that the nation has the right to depose him for intemperance and inefficiency, that the yearly meeting of the States General was designed to curb and check the regal power, and that the only duty of Kings is to provide for the people's good, to administer impartial justice to their subjects, and to repel the invasion of foreign foes.

What, then, can be said of the minions of the Court, who proclaim as undeniable maxims that Princes have an absolute power of life and death over their subjects, that they are Gods whose sayings must be received as oracles, and that nothing is just or equitable in itself, but derives all its justice and equity from the Prince's ordinance? The simple truth is that the King is bound to obey the laws which are made in the National Assembly just as much as the humblest of his subjects, and that his promise to govern the people justly is an absolute promise, but the people's promise to obey him if he rules uprightly is a conditional promise. If, therefore, the Prince devotes himself to his private profit and pleasure, despises and perverts all laws, treats his subjects more cruelly than the most barbarous enemy would treat them, purposely ruins the Commonwealth and lays waste the State, resists all legal proceedings and lawful rights, and cares not a jot for faith, covenants, justice, or piety, he may be fitly described as a malefactor, a violator of law and equity, and a tyrant, in other words, an enemy of God and man. But tyranny is the greatest of vices. A tyrant subverts the State, pillages the people, lays ambuscades to take away their lives, breaks promise with all, scoffs at the sacred obligation of a solemn oath, and is viler than the vilest of ordinary malefactors in proportion as offences committed against a community deserve greater punishment than those which only affect private individuals. More than this, as the King receives his royal authority from the people, and the people are, therefore, above the King and greater than the King, it necessarily follows that a tyrant is guilty of rebellion against the majesty of the people, and may be deposed by those who are his lords, or justly punished according to the ancient law which condemns the offenders against the public weal : or, if all other means fail, the inferior magistrates who have been appointed by the people, may call the people to arms, may enrol troops, may put forth all their power, and may employ all the advantages and stratagems of war against him as the enemy of the Commonwealth and the disturber of the public peace.*

The twenty-five years which followed the Massacre of Saint Bartholomew are one of the most melancholy periods of French history. They are marked by a definite lowering of the spiritual, moral, and political life of the nation, by the rise of the " Politicians," who strove to merge the religious in the political question, by the wild schemes of the " foreign" Guises for obtaining the crown of France, by the efforts of Philip the Second to make France a province of Spain and to anticipate Louis the Fourteenth's boast that the Pyrenees existed no longer, by the consolidation of the fierce democracy of the League, who were ready with blind and unprofitable consistency to sacrifice patriotism to the imaginary interests of religion, and whose leaders unblushingly proclaimed the need of a fresh " Saint Bartholomew bleeding," revived the most extravagant doctrines of the Middle Ages, declared that the Pope could change the laws and constitutions of States at his pleasure, and assumed as a self-evident axiom the power of the Church to make peace or war, to unsheath the sword in defence of the faith, to give the people the signal for rebellion, and to depose Kings. Two political events of primary importance brought this period to a close, the defeat of Philip the Second's schemes against France, and the reception of Henry of Navarre into the Church of Rome, which made him the real as well as the titular King of France. The first event led to the complete overthrow of the League and the extreme Romanist party, to the expulsion of the Jesuits, and to the tardy repentance of that powerful Order for their political sins ;

* It is interesting to observe that two editions of a translation of Languet's work were published in England bearing the date of two critical years in English history, 1648 and 1649. It would be still more interesting to know what circulation they had among the opponents and enemies of Charles the First.

the second set the crown on the policy of toleration which the " Politicians " had advocated for nearly forty years, and forced even the Pope to a grudging acceptance of the new system.   These two events made it possible for Henry the Fourth to end the long series of civil and religious wars by passing the celebrated Edict of Nantes.

The Edict, if all the circumstances are taken into account, must be recognized as one of the most important and remarkable results of the Reformation. The Religious Peace of Augsburg had indeed established the toleration of both Confessions in Germany: but Germany was united only in name, and toleration within the limits of the Empire meant very much less than toleration in a homogeneous kingdom with a centralized government like France. The victory of the new principle was for this reason far more significant and complete in France than in Germany and the Low Countries.   It proclaimed with an emphasis not to be mistaken that the Medieval fabric of Church and State had crumbled to pieces, and that every reaction which attempted to make the shadow go back on the dial of history, however great its success might be for a time, was doomed to failure.

The Edict of Nantes made three great concessions to the Huguenots.   It granted them not only liberty of conscience but also freedom of public worship, with two limitations: the Huguenots were forbidden to hold services in the capital and its neighbourhood, or in the cities which were archiepiscopal or episcopal Sees.   At the same time special regulations were made to protect their graves; and the horrible practice, which had prevailed widely under the influence of the League, of disinterring those who had died in the Reformed faith was decisively checked.   In the second place, the Huguenot ministers were subsidized from the royal chest.   " If " (they argued) " we contribute by the payment of tithes to the maintenance of the Romanist worship, which we cannot in our consciences approve, is it not fair that we should be indemnified for this sacrifice?" Henry recognized the justice of their appeal, and for the first time in European history the principle of concurrent endowment was formally acknowledged. Forty-five thousand crowns were assigned for the payment of ministers' stipends, and for the maintenance of two Huguenot Universities at Saumur and Montauban. In the third place, the admission of the Huguenots to public offices was made legal, in spite of the fierce resistance of their opponents. The Chancellor of France, L'Hospital's successor, maintained that this question was a thousand times more important than the question of permitting the public worship of the Reformed Church. Even Henry wavered for a time: at last he yielded; and to the close of his reign distinguished Protestants, like Sully and Turenne, filled the highest offices in the State. Unhappily for the Huguenots, the Edict came too late to restore their broken fortunes. War and exile, treachery and massacre, the renewed strength of their enemies and the desertion of renegade friends, had fatally thinned their ranks; and of the 2,100 churches of forty years before, little more than a third survived to witness the establishment of the Religious Peace.

CHAPTER VII.

THE REFORMATION IN THE LOW COUNTRIES.

THE Low Countries during the course of the sixteenth century became one of the most important parts of the vast Spanish monarchy. From no part of Charles the Fifth's widespread dominions did a more ceaseless stream of gold flow into his exchequer than from the provinces which, favoured by natural advantages, and still more by the skill, the industry, and the enterprise of their inhabitants, had placed themselves in the very van of the commercial life of Europe. The wealth and intelligence of their citizens, the size and population of their towns, their countless ships, their crowded marts, and their splendid buildings, moved the envy of the citizens of ruder States. It was natural that among such a people the new doctrines of the Reformation should find a ready admission and an eager acceptance. In the North and South alike, in Flanders and Brabant, as well as in Groningen and Friesland, the heretical teachers found crowds of listeners. As soon as the Reformed doctrines had gained a footing in Germany, they spread to the Low Countries. In August, 1525, Erasmus wrote that the majority of the population in Holland, Zeeland, and Flanders were acquainted with Luther's doctrine, and were filled with the deadliest hatred of the monks. Charles's Governor, Margaret of Austria, who had ruled the Netherlands since 1507, wrote to her Deputy-Governor in Holland that she had enquired into the causes of the spread of Lutheranism, and found that it might be traced to the abuses which prevailed in the Church, such as illegal censures, pecuniary exactions, the sale of sacraments, the permission to marry at forbidden seasons, and the dispensation from banns; and adherents were gained for Lutheranism by the exposure and criticism of these ecclesiastical abuses. In 1525 she sent orders to all the magistrates in Holland to keep a watchful eye upon the schoolmasters within their domain, to observe whether they were in evil repute on account of the Lutheran sect and other godless ideas, and whether they taught any books which the Emperor had forbidden.

The Augustinian monastery of Dort was one of the most richly endowed in the Northern Netherlands. The Prior, Henry of Zutphen, had studied at Wittenberg, and had become an intimate friend of Luther. The monastery soon became a hotbed of heresy. The monks took up the new doctrines and taught them in their daily conversation, in the confessional, and from the pulpit. The Provincial of the monastery was called in, but could not or would not do anything but give evasive answers. To counteract the evil influence of these heretics, a Dominican preacher, described by Erasmus as unmatched for his folly, stupidity, ignorance, lying, and shamelessness, appeared in Dort. But his sermons produced so little effect that the people set upon him in a fury, and he only fled in time to escape a death by stoning. At Utrecht, the episcopal city of the most important See in the Northern Netherlands, the general attention was arrested by Walter, who received from the people the nickname of the " Lutheran monk." Forced to fly from Utrecht, he had wandered from city to city till he had settled in Delft. An Indulgence had been preached in Delft on behalf of Saint Lorenzo's Church in Rotterdam, and large numbers of the burghers of Delft had been persuaded to buy the Indulgence. Walter preached against this abuse in the strongest terms: if the forgiveness of sins could be bought with money, why should God have given His Son to die on the Cross? Even more important for the progress of the Reformation in Delft and the Hague was the influence of Hoen, an advocate and a man of the highest character, whose study of the writings of Wessel, the Medieval Reformer, led him to reject the doctrine of transubstantiation and to adopt a new view of the Eucharist. At Antwerp, Propst, another friend of Luther, and student of the University of Wittenberg, was at the head of the Augustinian monastery, and preached with increasing fervour against Indulgences and the intercession of Saints. Among his adherents were the city clerk and the master of the chief school. The Reformation had soon gained so much ground in the city that it was resolved to hold open-air services because no building was large enough to contain the crowds who pressed to hear the new preachers, in defiance of the Emperor's edicts, of the authority of the Governor, and of the commands of the magistrates. In Leyden the Evangelicals were equally active, and gained adherents among men of learning and position. In May, 1522, the magistrates complained that the burghers only obeyed the Emperor's edicts with the greatest reluctance, persisted in keeping Luther's books in their possession, and were anxious to argue openly in defence of them.

It was impossible that Charles the Fifth, who was actively engaged in the effort to suppress heresy in the German provinces of the Empire, could contemplate with equanimity the spread of heretical doctrines in his hereditary dominions. In 1521 the Edict of Worms was published in Louvain, Antwerp, and other important cities. In 1522 a fresh Edict was published in Holland and Zeeland, and Van der Hulst was appointed Inquisitor with full power to adopt the severest measures. After a short term of grace he was to proceed against all heretics, especially against those who read, gave, lent, sold, or bought heretical books. It was easy to understand the reason for this arbitrary proceeding. In the Low Countries, as elsewhere, the wealth and privileges of the clergy, their immunity from taxation, and their greed of power, had excited the deep jealousy of the temporal authorities. Even a staunch Catholic like Charles lost patience when he was checked and thwarted at every step by an overbearing priesthood. To deliver the heretics for trial in the ecclesiastical Courts would increase the very evil which he longed to crush. But, the appointment of secular judges, who were completely independent of spiritual Courts, and who could pay the confiscated property into the Emperor's exchequer without suffering it to swell the overgrown estates of the Clergy, would deal a severe blow at that powerful Order.

Unfortunately Charles encountered obstinate resistance from an unexpected quarter. The Hollanders and Zeelanders watched over their rights with as keen a jealousy as any people in Europe. A foreign Inquisitor, armed with full power to arrest without further notice any citizen, no matter what his rank or station might be, to confiscate his goods, and to try him without even the show of impartiality or the chance of an appeal, might, they thought, suit the Spaniards well enough, who, having been trampled under foot for centuries by Moorish despots, probably regarded even the Inquisition as a pledge of national liberty. But the freemen of Holland had been reared under a different system: it was a fundamental axiom of their constitution that every inhabitant of Holland and Zeeland could only be summoned by the magistrates of the district in which he dwelt, and might refuse any other summons, however august the personage or however powerful the Court by whom it was issued. Was it not sheer madness to suppose that they could passively permit a poor man, who was inadvertently holding an heretical book in his hand or was discussing Indulgences over his dinner, to be subjected to the most cruel punishments by an immoral, passionate, and unscrupulous bigot like Van der Hulst?

The matter was soon brought to an issue. In February, 1523, by the orders of Van der Hulst, in defiance of the native Court of Justice and of the country's privileges,

Hoen was arrested in his house at the Hague and flung into the common prison at Gertruydenberg. The States with one voice appealed to Margaret to defend their rights; and Margaret, foreseeing the approaching storm, at once sided with them, disavowed the Inquisitor's action, and had Hoen brought back to the Hague. A few months later another actor intervened. Pope Adrian the Sixth, "of his own motion and by virtue of his apostolic power," appointed Van der Hulst Universal and General Inquisitor with plenary authority in the Duchy of Brabant, the Counties of Flanders, Holland, and Zeeland, and all other dominions of Charles the Fifth in the Low Countries. This appointment made the Inquisitor's jurisdiction absolute: no one, lay or cleric, could refuse it or appeal against it.

Again the States of Holland entered a forcible protest, and were strongly supported by the Clergy, who clung to their own power with even more tenacity than to the persecution of heresy. They openly defied Charles, snapped their fingers in Margaret's face, quashed the sentences of her judges, forcibly carried away her prisoners to be tried in their own Courts, and in answer to all remonstrances calmly replied, "We have taken cognisance of the case: all further judicial proceedings belong to us." Even the intervention of the Pope proved unavailing. Though Margaret implored Clement the Seventh to give her Inquisitors ample powers, and though he gave them powers ampler than she had dared to ask, powers sufficient to overrule the jurisdiction of all Bishops and other spiritual persons, the Clergy of the Netherlands proved that the virtue of holy obstinacy was at least equal to the virtue of holy obedience, and, quietly ignoring the Pope and his commands, viewed even the threat of excommunication with unshaken self-confidence.

Thus the powerful Emperor repeatedly found himself almost as powerless as Gulliver beneath the countless threads of his Liliputian antagonists. A typical case of the year 1527 will make this clear.   By the Edict of 1525, the publication and sale of heretical books were to be punished with a loss of the third of the bookseller's property and perpetual banishment from the town where he resided : the holding of meetings and the reading of forbidden books in private houses involved a fine of twenty dollars.   A bookseller and a lady were brought up before the Court of Justice in Amsterdam, charged with these two offences.   The bookseller was condemned to two months' imprisonment and a fine of twelve dollars ; the lady was fined three dollars.   Charles's Procurator-General instantly called upon the Supreme Court to quash the sentence and to imprison the bookseller at the Hague. But the Sheriffs refused to give way, denied that the sale of heretical books was heresy, and appealed to the famous privilege "De non evocando."

To these difficulties which Charles encountered in his own dominions, other difficulties were before long added. Though his possessions in Spain and Italy were guarded by the mighty barriers of the Alps and the Pyrenees, heresy had penetrated even into them from the outer world.   But his possessions in the Low Countries bordered upon States whose constant influence for good or for evil it was impossible to exclude.   The Duke of Cleves, after a short period of hesitation and wavering, threw in his lot with the Reformation.   In 1525 he published an Ordering of the Church, in which he complained of the intolerable abuses and errors of the Medieval clergy and the Medieval doctrines, bade all preachers preach the pure Word of God and administer the Sacraments gratuitously, limited the Masses for the dead, the processional use of images, and the taking of monastic vows, ordered all the Mendicant friars to leave the country, and forbade the appointment of beneficed priests unless they were pious and learned. Count Edzard of East Friesland was hardly less open in his support of the Reformation.   In 1518 he appointed the leader of the Evangelicals in his country to the post of tutor to his sons, and a little later encouraged him to preach in his capital, Emden. When the opposition of the Clergy grew too hot, the Count allowed him to deliver his sermons in the open country before the city gates, till the disciples whom he had gained far outnumbered his enemies, and carried him back triumphantly to the Church from which he had been expelled. From Emden the Evangelical doctrines spread to other towns of East Friesland : " Without any orders from the authorities," writes the historian, " the form of religion changed through the power of the divine Word, and the old superstition slunk away into private houses or into monasteries and nunneries."

Thus two converging streams of heresy flowed into the Emperor's provinces from the neighbouring lands ; two havens of refuge stood almost at the doors of his heretical subjects ; and Charles, like other sovereigns before and since, verified the truth of the great poet's words—

> " Hard thou know'st it to exclude
> Spiritual substance with corporeal bar."

At the same time two towns in Germany powerfully aided the Evangelical cause in the Netherlands. Bremen had been invaded by the Evangelical doctrines, and as early as the spring of 1524, the converts to the Reformation had got possession of all the churches except one, and had been joined by four active Reformed teachers from the Low Countries. Wittenberg was the cynosure of numerous students in the Netherlands, who flocked to the University from Dort, Zieriksee, Gertruydenberg, Breda, Amsterdam, Deventer, Koevorden, Meppel, Leeuwarden, Groningen, and Bolsward, and returned deeply attached to their religious and intellectual mother, and to the teaching of Luther and Melanchthon. Yet Charles was not daunted : he pressed on with dogged perseverance in spite of the impediments which blocked his path : with a profound and touching faith in the efficacy of his Edicts he poured out one after another with ludicrous iteration in 1521, 1522, 1524, 1525, 1527, 1529, and 1531. After this date they appeared every·six months with the unfailing regularity of the spring cabbages and the summer roses.

The influence of the Reformers' literary activity was perhaps even more widely spread and more powerful than the influence of their public sermons or their private teaching. The education and intellectual development of the Netherlands rendered them peculiarly susceptible to literary influences. The close connection between the language of Germany and the language of a large portion of the Low Countries made it easy for the Dutch-speaking Netherlanders to assimilate the works which issued from the printing-presses of Germany. This was especially true of books printed in Low German, the dialect which at the beginning of the sixteenth century was almost exclusively spoken and read in the German provinces which bordered upon the Baltic. Under these circumstances the pamphlets of Luther were more generally read in the Netherlands than in any part of Europe outside Germany. In 1518 two letters were written, one by Erasmus, the other by Nesenus, a member of the noble company of the Humanists, testifying to the ease with which Luther's books could be procured in the Low Countries, and to the eagerness with which they were studied by ardent enquirers after truth. Nor must it be imagined that the perusal of these books was confined to the learned : they permeated into all ranks of society. Men who were acquainted with the German language were busily engaged in translating them into their own tongue. In this way Luther's treatise on the Ten Commandments, his Tessera-decas, and his exposition of the seven Penitential Psalms, appeared in Dutch shortly after their publication in Germany. It is not surprising that Charles, the temporal authorities, and the clergy should have made search for these books with frenzied zeal. In Antwerp, where the booksellers sold Luther's works without scruple in 1518, and where the celebrated artist, Albert Durer, read the famous treatise on the Babylonian captivity of the Church in 1521, the books of the great heretic were openly burnt twice in the space of ten months. In Utrecht recourse was had to the same measure at the same time in presence of a crowd so great that the police were ordered out for fear of a popular disturbance. How unavailing this precaution was is proved by the fact that, as each new book appeared from Luther's restless pen, it was eagerly called for and devoured by his numerous admirers in Charles's dominions.

It was not the least of the imperishable services which the illustrious Reformer rendered to the Christian faith that his translation of the New Testament in 1522 gave the first impulse to the publication of a Dutch version. The Dutch Bible which had been printed as early as 1477 contained nothing but the Old Testament and the Apocrypha. The only portions of the New Testament which had been published were the Gospels and Epistles appointed to be read by the Medieval Church during the course of the Christian year. But in December, 1523, the first Dutch translation was issued. Charles the Fifth, three months later, ordered all the copies to be destroyed. Yet, undeterred by the rigid censorship of the press which the system of repression had inaugurated, two more versions were put forth in the course of a few months. Accordingly, before the close of the year 1524, there was one Dutch version based upon Luther's translation, a second based upon the Vulgate, and a third upon the Latin version of Erasmus. Of these translations the first appeared in three different editions. From this time the New Testament became the people's book. All the terrors of the Edict could not quench the thirst for it. The publishers could hardly keep pace with the popular demand. Sometimes the watchfulness of the Inquisitors was lulled by the device of representing an original version as a translation of the Vulgate. More frequently the publishers scorned any such device, and boldly ran the risk of bringing it out in its true colours, trusting in the sympathy of their fellow-citizens, in the connivance of the local authorities, and in the feuds which divided their enemies. Eight years had not passed before twenty-eight editions of the New Testament had been issued, not reckoning four different versions of the whole Bible.

The translations of the New Testament, of the complete Bible, and of Luther's works were followed by original works of Dutch authors. Among the earliest of these were the sermons of a monk named Pieters. They emphasized the free forgiveness of sins for Christ's sake, without any works or merits of man : in Christ alone is all the Christian's blessedness and the Christian's hope. It is false to assert that Christ has atoned for original sin alone, and that for actual sins we must ourselves make atonement. We need no intercession with Christ, for Christ loves us more deeply than any creature or Saint can love us, and the Saints would be the first to disclaim the reverence which is paid them, and to urge us to bestow on the poor the money with which we deck their images or go on pilgrimage to their shrines. It is the work of the devil to run from the Creator to the creature, as though the Creator were too weak or too indifferent to help His servants.

Another book dealt with the chief doctrines of the Christian faith "which are comfortable, useful, and needful for a man to know." It contained chapters with such titles as "Works justify no man, and justification comes from faith alone," "Against outward service or ceremonies," "Christ alone is our Mediator," "Can the righteousness or faith of another justify any man ? " A number of texts were collected in proof of these doctrines, and were accompanied by a running commentary : "There is nothing in the Gospels which all Christians cannot well understand " : "Christ's people do all things, not because they are commanded, nor from hope of reward, nor from

fear of punishment, but only to honour God and to show
their gratitude to Him ": " Works give evidence of our
faith, and assure us that our faith is a right faith."

Another book attained a far wider circulation. It was
translated into Italian, French, and English, and probably
was much read in England, because it appears in the
English list of prohibited books under the title of " The
Sum of Scripture." The first edition came out in 1523,
and a second in 1524; two editions appeared in 1526.
The book professed to teach and instruct all men " what
is the Law of Christ whereby we are all saved." The
author declared that in it he had briefly comprehended the
foundation and sum of Holy Writ. Faith, from which
spring hope and love, is the foundation of the Bible and
the foundation of Christianity. The power of baptism
does not lie in the baptismal water, but in our faith.
Saving faith consists above all in the conviction that we
are God's children. He alone possesses true faith who
seeks all his hope, his trust, his consolation, his salvation,
and his refuge in God, without relying upon his own
merits and good works. We must always perform our
good works from love and for the benefit of our fellow-
men, not in order to obtain salvation by them. The
writer expresses an ardent wish for the diffusion of education to ensure the full knowledge of God's Word : would
that the children of the poor were sent to school at the
expense of the community, or that the money were devoted
to this purpose which is now so lavishly spent on the
adorning of images of Saints, on the purchase of gold
vessels, or on the founding of monasteries and vicarages ;
for there are many old men who cannot even say their
Paternoster and Creed.

It is impossible to gauge with any accuracy the extent
of this literary activity. Many of the books which were
published at this time consisted, like modern tracts, of a
few pages only, and disappeared when they had served
their purpose. Many were published for greater security

without the publisher's name, or the date of publication, or the place where they were printed. In consequence of the multiplied edicts they were hunted down with such unsleeping pertinacity by the agents of the Inquisition that not a single copy can now be found. This explains the fact that works which are mentioned in the judicial records of the time are unknown even to the bibliophile.

About the year 1530 the Reformation in the Low Countries entered upon a new phase. In most of the provinces the Lutherans were thrown into the background by the Anabaptists. The rise of Anabaptism is one of the most remarkable events of the sixteenth century. Switzerland, South Germany, North Germany, and the Low Countries were the chief centres of Anabaptist activity, though there was scarcely a country to which some of these strange missionaries did not sooner or later penetrate. No religious movement is more difficult to explain, because it assumed the most diverse forms, adopted the most contradictory tenets, and rested upon the most visionary truths. In some points the Anabaptists resembled the Gnostics, in others the Montanists, in others the Donatists, in others the Monastic Orders of the Medieval Church. For it would be an error to imagine that the adherents of the new sect had a definite creed which was common to the whole body. Almost every shade and variety of opinion was found in that motley host. Observers counted as many as forty different sects, which were included under the general name of Enthusiasts, Fanatics, or Anabaptists, applied to them indifferently by their opponents. Even the repudiation of Infant Baptism, though it was the tenet on which all were agreed, was regarded by some as the chief doctrine, by others as a doctrine of altogether subordinate importance.

The vein of mystical enthusiasm which ran through the teaching of the Anabaptists, the passionate eagerness with which they pursued their ideal, the vision of supernatural holiness on which they fixed their gaze, the contempt for

the world, its pursuits, its pleasures, its aims, and its
methods, which they constantly professed, the joyful
readiness with which they endured suffering and death
rather than sacrifice one jot or tittle of the truths which
they held, account in great measure for the extraordinary
popularity which they enjoyed. That popularity was
nowhere more marked than in the Low Countries; and
between the years 1530 and 1559 they were by far the
most numerous victims of the fires of persecution.

The dislike with which the Reformers regarded the new
visionaries is perfectly intelligible. They recognized in
them the counterparts of the Medieval monks, the men
who described monasticism as a second baptism; who
regarded the monastic life as the counsel of Evangelical perfection, and who looked upon the world and all that was in
the world as common and unclean. The arrogant assumption of superior holiness, which led the Anabaptists to look
down with unconcealed contempt on all other Churches
as lying in Egyptian darkness, was regarded with abhorrence by religious teachers who had absolutely discarded
the Pharisaical standards of the Middle Ages. But in
addition to this, they had special and grave reasons for
regarding the Anabaptist teaching with profound repugnance. It seemed to them to cut at the very roots of
religious, moral, political, and social life. The Anabaptists
rejected the teaching of the universal Church on the subject of Christ's Person, explained away the Incarnation,
denied the Atonement, and maintained that the Founder
of the Church had only left mankind the pattern of His
active and passive obedience. From this depreciation of
Christ's work and Person they went on to the assertion
of doctrines which the Reformers not unjustly stigmatized
as blasphemous. One Anabaptist called himself "our
God," another described himself as "the indwelling
life of God," and a third styled himself "the deified
man," and pretended that he was greater than Moses
and Christ.

Of a similar character was their attack upon the Bible. There was no text which they had more constantly upon their lips than Saint Paul's words, " The letter killeth, but the spirit giveth life." By "the letter," they understood the canonical books of the Old and New Testament ; by "the spirit," the secret promptings, the wild fancies and the extravagant conceptions of their own mind and heart. They called the Bible childish and imperfect, a children's alphabet, good enough for the world in its youth, but now antiquated, and replaced by the teaching of the Spirit. The Bible was not God's Word, but a shadow of the Word, a mere manger of Christ, a closed book, an eternal allegory, which had a hidden meaning completely contrary to the letter. This contempt for the Bible was the more offensive to the Reformers because the Anabaptists laid no claim to solid learning, to exegetical ability, or to knowledge of Church history ; indeed, they put aside these earthly qualifications with profound scorn. They quoted Saint John's words, " The Spirit bloweth where it listeth," and believed that the humblest and most ignorant Anabaptist might have more true knowledge of the mysteries of God, not only than Luther and Melanchthon, but even than Saint Peter and Saint Paul.

The political teaching of the Anabaptists was in the Reformers' eyes as dangerous as their religious teaching. They reverted to the Medieval conception of the State as something too impure and unholy for the elect children of God to meddle with. They contended that Christians ought not to hold the office of a magistrate or to bear the sword ; that they ought to have no rulers except the ministers of the Gospel ; and that they were not bound to take oaths at the bidding of the civil power. They denied that the marriages which were sanctioned by the temporal government had of necessity any binding force on true Christians ; they scandalized the Reformers by maintaining that the union between believers and unbelievers was null and void in God's sight ; and they refused to receive into their Church any convert who did not without more ado abandon his unconverted wife.

There was one more vital point of difference between the Reformed Church and the Anabaptists. The former held strongly that excommunication was the last resource of the Church in dealing with notorious, impenitent, and incorrigible sinners, and that so terrible a punishment ought never to be used lightly or unadvisedly. The latter used it so recklessly that, had Saint Paul acted upon their principles, he would have excommunicated not a single offender but the collective Corinthian Church. This practice proved their bane ; they split up into sects which excommunicated each other as well as their several members with increasing bitterness. After thirty years Anabaptism had spent its force ; its emissaries had lost their missionary fervour and persuasive eloquence ; its Churches had lost their creative energy ; and the great movement which at one time threatened to flood Christendom had run into the sands, or had been merged in the vaster stream of the Reformation.

In 1555 Charles the Fifth, prematurely worn out by the exhausting labours of twenty-five years, weakened by prolonged ill-health, and overshadowed by the morbid melancholy which he had inherited from his unhappy mother, resigned his dominions in the Old and New Worlds, and bequeathed to his son the greatest, the richest, and the most powerful of European monarchies. From that year Philip the Second became the central figure of the religious and political history of the Low Countries, and for this reason he deserves more than a passing notice.

The differences between Philip and his father were great and marked. Charles possessed in a large measure the military, political, and administrative talents which befit the ruler of a composite monarchy. In no part of his dominions, except perhaps in Germany, was he unpopular with his subjects. In the Netherlands he was regarded with peculiar affection ; for they remembered with justifiable pride that he had been born amongst them, and the title, "Charles of Ghent," which his enemies applied to him in scorn, was in their eyes a title of honour. The Council, which included representatives from all parts of his kingdoms, was a testimony to the statesmanlike liberality which characterized his government. When Philip came to the throne he managed the affairs of his immense empire as if he were managing the affairs of a metropolitan vestry. He had fully determined in his own mind that Spaniards alone possessed political and administrative gifts, that Spaniards alone were inflexibly loyal to his crown, that Spaniards alone could inaugurate the reign of peace, virtue, and true religion ; and, in spite of the evidence of his own senses, he persisted in believing that Spanish governors and Spanish soldiers were the indispensable conditions of national prosperity in all his subject States. He revealed the essential littleness of his mind by forming the vastest and most comprehensive schemes without the slightest misgiving, without the faintest distrust of his own powers. He would incorporate Portugal in the Spanish Kingdom, he would be lord of Germany, he would lay all Italy at his feet, he would be master of France, he would conquer England, he would dispose at his pleasure of the crown of Scotland ; and to the execution of these schemes, which would have taxed the military and political resources of a Julius Cæsar or a Charlemagne, he brought abilities just respectable enough to make him a capable Mayor of a provincial town.

His truculent bigotry, his impenetrable stupidity, and his ludicrous incompetence gave him a sinister pre-eminence among all the sovereigns of the sixteenth century. When the Emperor wrote to expostulate with him on his treatment of the heretics in the Low Countries, he indignantly repudiated the charge. He cruel ! he pitiless ! His only fault was, he confessed it with sorrow, that he had been too forbearing, too tender-hearted, too full to overflowing of the milk of human kindness for these damnable heretics.

When the rapid spread of heresy might have made a prudent sovereign pause, he fancied that he had devised a master stroke of policy by inducing the Spanish Inquisition to condemn the whole population of the Netherlands, with a few insignificant exceptions, to the scaffold and the gallows. When the growing disaffection in the Low Countries required the most delicate and masterly handling, he flattered himself that the mission of the brutal Alva was a veritable inspiration of genius. Alva's incapacity was, if possible, one degree greater than Philip's; for his ideas of political administration would have disgraced the worst Turkish Pasha in the worst days of the Ottoman Empire, and were summed up in the three expressive words—confiscation, hanging, and burning. The financial schemes which he and his master devised for the maintenance of the commercial prosperity of the Netherlands were justly regarded by competent judges as insane. At the very crisis of the fortunes of the Low Countries Philip reduced his viceroys to despair by leaving letters of the utmost importance unanswered for months and even years. His idea of a just and equitable government was to reject the fair demands, to flout the reasonable complaints, and to trample under foot the unquestioned rights, of his subjects. It was true that he had solemnly sworn to maintain these rights; but what was the binding force of oaths taken by a Prince such as he was to men such as they were? What were the liberties of a high-spirited people compared with the unspeakable honour of becoming the butts of a Spaniard's tyranny? When he was at last reluctantly induced to grant a pardon and amnesty, he excepted from its operation every individual of influence or importance, and his dull brain was unable to see the consummate folly of such a proceeding. Though his Spanish soldiers broke out into the most terrible mutiny because they were left unpaid for months, though his Governors were forced to melt down their plate and yet had not money enough to buy an ounce of powder, though

every hundred pounds raised for the soldiers' pay cost
him four hundred or five hundred before it left the pay-
master's hands, though Romanists and Protestants alike
cried shame on him and his Councillors, though his choicest
troops were foiled by the desperate resistance of insignificant
cities, though Alva was forced to confess that every hamlet
in the Northern Netherlands was a natural fortress, though
Philip's men-of-war were sunk and burnt by the mariners
whom he despised, nothing could induce him to abandon the
system which he had marked out. He harped incessantly
upon the same string. "Take any measure which you
think advisable, provided always that the supremacy of the
holy Catholic Church is maintained, and that my royal
authority remains unimpaired"—a decision as sensible as
if he had said, "By all means let the Nile flow seawards,
on the express condition that it does not rise, and that it
does not overflow its banks." Warning after warning was
sent him from the Netherlands by men who were thoroughly
acquainted with the temper of the people and the character
of their institutions, that the inhabitants were reduced to
despair by the excesses and the vices of the Spanish soldiery,
that hundreds of houses and estates lay unoccupied, that
the harshness with which the people were treated had no
parallel in ancient or modern times, and that it was the
wildest dream of a disordered imagination to look to
military force as the unfailing cure for these evils. But
Philip, who had not set foot in the Netherlands for years,
who could not read the Dutch language, and who knew
his Dutch subjects as little as his Mexican or Peruvian,
considered himself an infinitely better judge than any
statesman of the treatment which they required. It is
no marvel that the art of misgovernment, carried to such
a height of perfection, should have found its fitting
consummation in total and irretrievable ruin.

It was disastrous for Philip that, soon after his accession
to the sovereignty of the Low Countries, when the great
struggle on which the eyes of Europe were fixed for nearly

half a century was on the point of breaking out, he should have encountered three antagonists, each of whom was formidable separately, and whose partial union made them more than a match for him.

His sister-in-law, Elizabeth, was not indeed a deadly and irreconcilable foe. It seemed at times as though she were playing into his hands. It is possible that, if she had been free to act as she pleased, she would have maintained a strict neutrality. But she had the strongest reasons for siding with Philip's opponents. She was astute enough to see that her brother-in-law was little better than a fool, and she was even more intolerant and suspicious of fools than of knaves. She was the Queen of a Protestant nation, of a nation which had conceived a violent antipathy to Spain, an antipathy which was partly religious, partly political, and partly commercial. The emigrants and exiles from Philip's provinces swarmed in the eastern counties, and could be numbered by hundreds and thousands in London, Norwich, Canterbury, Sandwich, Maidstone, and Colchester. More than once William of Orange appealed, and not in vain, to the unity of blood and community of interest which connected the Netherlands on both sides of the sea, urged those whom God had so richly blessed in England to come to the aid of their suffering and struggling countrymen, and received from them substantial pecuniary and military help. Each of these colonies, therefore, was a centre from which hatred of Spanish tyranny and Spanish bigotry radiated far and wide among the Protestant freemen of England. Finally, Philip committed one of the most gigantic blunders of his life by taking up the cause of Mary Stuart, and estranged Elizabeth for ever by this irrefutable proof of his ignorance and prejudice.

In his treatment of William of Orange Philip blundered even more fatally than in his treatment of Elizabeth. He hated and despised Orange with all the intensity of hatred and contempt which goads little minds to madness when they are opposed and foiled by great minds. William's political ability was as remarkable as Philip's political incapacity; his power of attraction was as great as Philip's power of repulsion; he was as conspicuous for broad-minded toleration as Philip for narrow-minded bigotry. He had gifts of head and of heart which marked him out as a great leader of men; he was prudent or daring, cautious or bold, as occasion required; obloquy could not move him, adversity could not daunt him, prosperity could not warp the clearness of his judgment, flattery and favour could not seduce him from his path; he loved his oppressed country and his persecuted people with a passionate love which shrank from no sacrifices and no risks. As the aversion and distrust with which Philip was regarded deepened, the affection for William, and the confidence in his aims and ability, increased. Saint Aldegonde's famous " William Song," masterly alike in conception and execution, stamped the image of the illustrious patriot, of his aspirations and his motives, on the hearts of his people, and remains as an imperishable memorial of the fascination and charm of the great statesman, whose very faults were the faults of a noble and generous nature.

Philip's third antagonist was not an individual but a community, the new Reformed Church in the Netherlands. It is difficult to fix the exact time when the influence of Wittenberg gave way to the influence of Geneva; but from the time that the great tide of Anabaptism began to ebb, the latter influence became predominant. The presbyterian system penetrated into the Low Countries from the south and the north simultaneously. From France it found its way into the French-speaking communities of the south, from East Friesland into the northern provinces, which in language and blood were most closely allied to the Low Germans. Everywhere the ministers, the elders, and the members of the Church displayed the same energy, the same zeal, and the same dauntless faith which had won for the disciples of Calvin their victories in Scotland

and in France. The life of a minister who in those days
undertook to serve his Church in the Low Countries was
precarious in the extreme. He was compelled to change
his residence eight or ten times in the year, or even oftener,
to escape the spies and the bailiffs of the Inquisition. He
addressed small gatherings of the faithful in an upper room
lighted by the lurid glare of the martyrs' fires outside.
His enemies in secret collusion with the persecutors
feigned a warm friendship for him that they might the more
easily take him unawares. At one time he crept into the
city in a workman's disguise, at another he wandered about
the fields at nightfall, not knowing where to lay his head.
To be noted for his eloquence, for his power of exposition,
for his moving discourses, or for his contagious heroism
and faith, was to become the mark of his relentless foes.
Swept hither and thither by the restless tide of exile, he
could call no city his own city, and no land his own
country ; for he was compelled to verify to the letter the
Apostle's words, " strangers and pilgrims," " here we have
no continuing city, but we seek one to come." One year
he was in France, another in Switzerland : then he moved
to Flanders, from Flanders to Brabant, from Brabant to
England, from England to the Palatinate, from the Palatinate to North Holland. It is not the least astonishing
fact of such a life that these men should have been able
to prosecute their studies, to write books, to draw up Confessions of Faith, to edit parts of Scripture in Syriac or
Hebrew, and even to hold Professorships in Universities.
The impression which they produced was unquestionably
very great. Large classes of the population were wholly
or in part won over to the new teaching, and presbyterian
congregations, regularly organized, were formed in every
considerable town. Had Philip been shrewd enough to
take the measure of the popular forces which were mus-
tering against him, he might well have been uneasy at
this ominous combination of religious faith and political
liberty. But he was absolutely incapable of taking the

true measure of any movement or of any institution. He was fully resolved not to be cowed, as his father had been, by the childish bugbears of national rights and popular privileges; the opponents of the Romish Church and of his sovereign authority, those two causes which were equally sacred in his eyes, were doomed to a swift destruction, and should be all alike stamped out by Alva's iron heel as worthless vermin.

The new sovereign and his subjects were not long in coming to an open breach. It had been part of the policy of Charles to strengthen his government and the Roman Church at the same time by establishing a number of new bishoprics in the Netherlands. The occupants of the new Sees could be utilized to break down the clerical opposition which had often baffled him, and to make the powers of the Inquisition more formidable and more ubiquitous. But for different reasons this reorganization of the ecclesiastical system was again and again postponed, and not till 1559 was the Papal Bull obtained, which in place of the four original bishoprics established three archbishoprics and fourteen bishoprics. The laity, who had watched with growing ill-will the odious system of the Inquisition firmly planted on their free soil, were indignant at this important accession to the ranks of the persecutors. The clergy were scarcely less discontented, for the stipends of the new bishops were made up by subtracting large sums from their revenues. To the burning of heretics they had no objection; but if they were to be burnt at the expense of the existing prelates and beneficed priests, it would be far better to leave them untouched. The fact that the new bishops were men of no learning, ability, or force of character made the general dissatisfaction greater. The bishopric of Leeuwarden was established in August, 1561, and received an income of 4,500 gold ducats as well as the revenues of a provostship, an abbey, and a monastery. The clergy of the diocese rose in rebellion, and were strongly supported by the provincial Estates and the

people. The Bishop found it impossible to enter into
possession of his see, the Governor of the province could
not induce the Estates to receive him, and when the Archbishop and the Duchess of Parma, Philip's Stadtholder,
interposed, deputies were sent to plead that the founding
of the new bishopric was an infringement of their country's
laws and privileges. In the Southern Netherlands the
new Bishop of Bruges excited no less discontent. He
came forward as the close ally of the Inquisitor, required
full lists of all the parishioners that it might be known
whether they went to confession, summoned all schoolmasters before him for dismissal or confirmation, and
called upon all incumbents to certify that the recipients of
poor relief in their parishes attended confession and Mass.
The magistrates boldly opposed " this great novelty,"
because the populace thought that these measures pointed
to the introduction of the Spanish Inquisition ; they
refused to listen to the claims of the Inquisitor, and sent
petition after petition to the Duchess of Parma : the
Inquisition, which conflicted with their rights, liberties,
and customs, ought to be completely annulled and
abolished so far as it affected the laity, for it had not been
accepted by the Estates of Flanders in general nor by
Bruges in particular, and therefore could not possibly
curtail their rights. In a final petition they used still
stronger language : the Inquisitor was drawing the whole
jurisdiction of the city and district into his own hands,
overriding the local authorities, making the magistrates
mere ushers of his Court, disposing of every man's life,
person and property as he pleased, till no one, however
pious and catholic he might be, could feel secure against
the calumny and hatred of his personal enemies.

Such was the spirit which pervaded the whole country,
and which was stirred to still further indignation by
Philip's attempt to enforce the decrees of the Council of
Trent. As soon as that famous assembly had finished its
work, the most Catholic King resolved that his subjects in

the Netherlands should join with him in doing homage to the divine inspiration which had guided its proceedings. Unfortunately, there were large numbers of Romanists in Europe who had watched the meeting of the Council with misgivings, who had followed its sessions with growing alarm, and who had contemplated its decrees with feelings little short of repugnance. Accordingly, when Philip wrote to the Duchess of Parma ordering her to proclaim the decrees in the Low Countries, there was an universal outcry. Orange delivered a weighty speech against the King's misguided action ; Egmont, one of the most distinguished nobles of the Netherlands, was sent as ambassador to Spain to enlighten Philip ; all classes of the community set forth the intolerable grievances from which they were suffering ; spies and informers, false accusations and fictitious charges, were loudly denounced ; pamphlets, fly-sheets, satires, and caricatures portrayed in every tone of indignation and contempt the shameful slavery under which the freest people in Europe were groaning, and which could only be paralleled by the worst days of Nero and Diocletian. In April, 1566, the general resistance came to a head in the famous petition of the nobles, demanding the abolition of the Inquisition, which gave rise to the historic name of the " Beggars."

Philip met the rising storm with his usual unscrupulousness and blind obstinacy. He made promises, and straightway broke them; the emissaries who were sent to him from the Netherlands disappeared after a fashion which would have been considered mysterious at any other Court ; the representations of the Stadtholder and of the provincial assemblies were disregarded ; William of Orange, for the crime of speaking out his mind, of defending his countrymen's cause with consummate ability, of standing upon his unquestionable rights, and of refusing to be a partner in illegal and unconstitutional action of the most flagrant kind, became the object of the tyrant's implacable wrath. Philip, acting on his favourite maxim that the

head of a salmon is worth whole shoals of smaller fry,
endeavoured to entice Orange into his toils. But the
great statesman was too clear-sighted and too prudent to
fall into the net.

The immediate result of Philip's action was to promote
the alliance between the political and religious parties in
the Netherlands. The Reformed Church, which had
hitherto lurked unseen, teaching in secret, and satisfied
with tentative efforts at a complete organisation, saw that
its opportunity had come, and, secure in the favour and
protection of the people, ventured forth into the full light
of day. The open-air preachings which began a few weeks
after the nobles' petition had been presented, and which
had probably been suggested by the example of the
Huguenots in France, were the popular answer to Philip's
despotic measures. In the early summer of 1566 the first
meetings were held by night in the woods of Flanders,
under shelter of the sand hills on the coast, where the roar
of the waves drowned the sound of the singing. Emboldened by success, the Reformers shortly after held their
meetings in broad daylight at a distance from the city.
Before the middle of June a congregation numbering
between 400 and 500 assembled outside Antwerp. At
Oudenarde two ministers addressed an assembly of some
7,000 auditors. By July the movement had spread to
other large cities. At Zieriksee, in the island of Schowen,
400 or 500 Protestants collected about a mile outside the
city gates. At Oedelen, between Ghent and Bruges, the
preachers had many thousand hearers. Then the services
spread to Deinse, Thielt, and Ecloo. One of the best
known ministers in the Netherlands, Dathenus, delivered
his first sermon at Poperinghe, where he had formerly
been a monk, and then travelled from place to place
addressing audiences which sometimes numbered 15,000.
Near Bruges repeated services were held attended by great
crowds, sermons being preached at the same time in
Flemish and in French. In North Brabant the services

began at Hertogenbosch, and the burghers from Gorcum, Bommel, and other towns in the neighbourhood flocked to them in crowds. The sheriff appealed to the magistrate to aid him in suppressing the heretical preachers; but they only referred him to the bishop and clergy, and absolutely rejected his proposal to fine every citizen who was present when a service was held. At Tournay, Valenciennes, and Lille there were crowded meetings; children were baptised and marriages were celebrated in the open fields. In Holland sermons were preached at Haarlem, Leyden, Enkhuizen, Alkmaar, and Delft. The magistrates of Amsterdam made an energetic attempt to foil the preachers by ordering the city gates to be locked. But the enthusiastic Protestants climbed over the walls, swam across the moats and ditches, got away in boats, and with the connivance of the watch stole out of the gates when they were opened to admit the milkmaids. In places where the authorities attempted to interfere forcibly in order to put down the services, the Protestants took up arms, marched to the place of meeting in battle array, and formed a great square around which they ranged a barricade of waggons; a rude pulpit was erected in the midst, which the preacher mounted; sentries were posted to guard all the approaches and to direct newcomers; pedlars brought Bibles, Psalters, and religious books, which were disposed on extemporised bookstalls; and when all the preparations had been made, the service began.

The open-air services were not the only manifestation of the changed spirit in the Netherlands. The contagion of the King's lawlessness spread to the lawless elements of society; he had broken the laws of God and man, and they would hurl defiance at him by breaking the visible symbols of the superstition on behalf of which he had so foully played the tyrant. With a fanatical fury which was a feeble copy of Philip's, they wreaked their vengeance on the images, the decorations, and the ornaments of hundreds of churches, in spite of the efforts of the magistrates and the expostulations of the ministers. What was even stranger than this outburst of destructive rage was the passive toleration or the secret approval with which the great mass of the population looked on at these excesses. If they did not sympathise with the action, they were apparently in sympathy with the motives which prompted it.

The Duchess of Parma was so alarmed by the menacing aspect of affairs that she was prepared to consent to a compromise. But Philip and his representatives in the Low Countries had no fears. Noircarmes, one of the most detested of the adherents of Spain, was sent against Valenciennes, and easily defeated the mob of Protestants who marched to its relief; ten days later the city was taken and sacked, and the two Protestant ministers were executed. At the same time the Lord of Tholouse, who had taken up his position close to Antwerp, was attacked, his army was cut to pieces, and he himself was slain. After these two serious reverses the insurrection ended as suddenly as it had begun. Orange laid down his offices and left the country; 100,000 exiles, drawn from all classes of society, followed him; the executioners were let loose, and, according to the historian, in every place of any importance the victims could be counted by scores.

But the suppression of the insurrection did not satisfy Philip. He resolved to take an exemplary vengeance on the rebellious and heretical provinces, and Alva with a Spanish army entered Brussels in the latter half of August, 1567. The Council of disturbances, popularly known as the Council of blood, was organised, and laid down the sweeping principles that to sign or present any petition against the new bishops, the Inquisition, or the royal edicts, to assert that the Council was bound to recognise the charters and privileges of the provinces, and to deny that the King had the right to take away all those charters and privileges, if he thought fit, was a conspiracy against God and the King. The actions of the Council were in harmony with these principles. Men were hung, beheaded, and burnt by hundreds, and their carcases were suspended along the highways till the very air reeked of pestilence. The Duchess of Parma was wise enough to see the certain issue of such a policy. Before quitting the Netherlands she warned Philip that his measures would be unavailing, and could only end in civil war and widespread destruction.

At first, however, everything went against the champions of liberty. Alva was as capable a soldier as he was an incapable statesman. The Spanish army was beyond all question the finest in Europe. It was impossible that the raw militia, the hired mercenaries, and the untried officers of the Low Countries could encounter it successfully. Louis of Nassau, a brother of Orange, was defeated by Alva in the summer of 1568. A few weeks later Orange invaded the Netherlands. Alva declined to give him battle, manœuvred him out of the country, and forced him to disband his army. Alva's triumph would have been complete, had not a new danger threatened him from the sea. The armies which he had defeated were largely composed of the mercenaries hired in Germany, mere soldiers of fortune, actuated by no higher motives than the prospect of pay and the chance of plunder. The mariners known under the terrible name of the " Sea Beggars " were the daring sons of a maritime people, inured to hardships and privations, familiar with the mysteries of the great deep from their earliest childhood, fighting for their hearths, their homes, and all that made their life worth the living, content to subsist upon the gains derived from the plunder of Spanish commerce, finding secret friends in every bay, estuary, and inlet of their native shores, and inspired by the deepest personal detestation of the powerful, insolent, and cruel foes against whom they had launched their barks. In Elizabeth's harbours they had found a base of operations and a refuge. Alva insisted that the Queen should withdraw her protection from them ; Elizabeth, unwilling at that moment to risk a rupture with Spain, reluctantly gave way; they set sail for Enkhuizen, but a change of wind forced them to run into the mouth of the Maas; anchoring opposite Brill, they found that the Spanish garrison had been withdrawn, and on the memorable 1st of April, 1572, seized possession of the town.

In a moment the whole aspect of the contest had changed. The Sea Beggars, tenacious as the limpets of their native shores, clung to their country's coasts with a desperate obstinacy and fortitude against which all the efforts of Spain proved unavailing. With Enkhuizen, Flushing, and Brill, the keys to the Zuyder Zee, the Scheldt, and the Maas, in their hands, they defied the Spanish fleets, harassed Spanish commerce, and intercepted Spanish supplies and stores. The most magnificent monarchy in Europe began slowly to bleed to death on the dykes and in the rivers of Holland and Zeeland.

The work which had been begun by the Sea Beggars was completed by Alva. The ruthless cruelty with which, after the capture of a town, he put all the defenders to the sword, maddened the oppressed people, and nerved them to fight with the courage of despair. The Spaniards lost 12,000 men in a single siege, 1,000 men in a single assault. The sieges of Alkmaar and Leyden almost threw into the shade the historic sieges of Tyre, Numantia, Jerusalem, and Carthage. The Netherlanders were ready even to pierce the dykes which generations of skill and industry had raised, and to bury their fertile lands beneath the devastating waters of the sea, rather than to suffer the presence of the hated Spaniard on their soil. Everywhere the spirit of religion fought side by side with the spirit of liberty. Filled by the doctrines of Calvin with the most exalted and elevating faith, the Hollanders and Zeelanders declared that, if the Lord was on their side, they would not fear what man could do unto them. And history records few more moving scenes than the survivors of the siege of Leyden, wasted to shadows by sickness and famine, gathering together to pour out their souls in thanksgiving to God for the great deliverance which He had vouchsafed them.

At the end of 1573 Alva flung up in despair the last and greatest task of his life. At the beginning of March, 1576, his successor, Requesens, suddenly died; and the men whom Alva with brutal arrogance nicknamed the "people of butter," had become more resolute, more defiant, and more united. No one could fail to see that Philip was further than ever from the goal which he had set before him, that the breaches in his royal authority had hopelessly widened, and that the restoration of the Roman Church to undisputed supremacy in the Low Countries had faded into the land of dreams. The persecuted Protestants had grown strong enough to defy the Inquisition and its myrmidons, and were meting out to the Romanists in a lesser degree the measure with which it had been meted to them. They urged in defence of their intolerance that patriotism would not suffer them to countenance the Roman religion, for the Romanist clergy in large numbers not unnaturally sided with Spain as their only bulwark against the invading Reformation; and the Protestants, blinded by religious and political prejudice, imagined that in every priest and every monk they could detect an enemy of their country's cause. Orange, one of the wisest and most fair-minded men of the sixteenth century, would have gladly countenanced every form of Christian belief; but in spite of his immense influence and persuasive eloquence he could not induce his countrymen to adopt his views.

In November, 1576, the Pacification of Ghent was drawn up, and all the seventeen provinces were united in the resistance to Spanish tyranny and in the maintenance of their country's liberties. In April, 1577, the Spanish soldiers, after filling up the cup of national hatred against themselves by one of the most prolonged and terrible mutinies of modern times, in which they were guilty of incredible excesses and wrought incalculable destruction, were sent out of the country, and the Netherlands breathed again. In the autumn of 1578 Don John of Austria, the successor of Requesens and the ill-starred victor of Lepanto, died of a broken heart, and Alexander Farnese, Duke of Parma, one of the ablest and most distinguished men of his day, eminent alike as a statesman and a general, took his place. Had his wise and conciliatory policy been adopted twelve or fourteen years before, the course of events might have been widely different; but the injury which had been done was irreparable, and out of Philip's fair heritage in the Low Countries Farnese could only save the impoverished, devastated, and depopulated provinces of the south.

The progress which the Reformation had made in the Netherlands up to this time may be clearly seen from three examples. In Flanders the advance of the Reformed Church in the city of Bruges had been definitely checked by the arrival of Alva, and it was not till some years later that it again assumed an aggressive attitude. At the end of 1577 both parties prepared for the inevitable struggle. The Protestants, exasperated by their prolonged ill-treatment, and headed by leaders whose enthusiasm was not tempered by wisdom or moderation, had already adopted the most violent measures in Ghent. A force came from Ghent to Bruges in March, 1578, marched to the Town Hall, deposed the magistrates, appointed others hostile to Spain, and nominated a military council. Three churches were assigned to the Protestants, the clergy were compelled to pay taxes, the mendicant Orders were compelled to quit the city, the property of churches and monasteries were sold by auction. On the other hand, bands of Romanists, calling themselves " Malcontents " and " Paternoster soldiers," answered violence by violence, sacking and plundering the country up to the very gates of Bruges. A religious peace was made between the two parties, but was soon broken; and in the beginning of

1580 there was a great emigration of the Romanist clergy and laity. The celebration of the Mass ceased, and many of the monks married.

In Zeeland the progress of the Reformation was more sober, more steady, and therefore more durable, than among the excitable and passionate populace of the southern provinces. A few days after the capture of Brill, Flushing expelled the Spanish garrison, reinforcements poured in from all sides, and at the end of September, 1572, the first Dutch sermon was preached in the city. The Reformation advanced so rapidly that before long there were four ministers, and the Romanists dwindled down to an inappreciable minority. In the beginning of 1574 the important town of Middleburg was delivered into the hands of Orange, and the Reformation was introduced. This success was followed by the spread of the Reformed Church in all the towns and villages of the island of Walcheren. In August, 1572, Zieriksee surrendered to William's officers on condition that the free exercise of both creeds should be allowed. The minister, who had been driven from the city six years before, was reappointed. From Zieriksee the Reformation spread over the whole of Schowen. But in 1575 and 1576 Schowen and Duiveland were reconquered by the Spaniards, and the Reformation received its second check. The lost ground was, however, recovered when for the second time Zieriksee surrendered to Orange. Protestant schoolmasters as well as Protestant ministers were appointed. In South Beveland and Goes the progress of the Reformation was slower on account of the prolonged domination of the Spaniards. When the bailiff, burgomasters, and sheriffs gave up the city and island to Orange, it was on the express condition that he should tolerate the Roman religion, and should take all the churches and ecclesiastics under his personal protection. The Protestants of Goes, who up to this time had met in secret, now held their services openly in private houses or in fields, and shortly afterwards took violent possession of the great church. The first evangelical sermon was preached at the end of September, 1578, and the Eucharist was administered for the first time in the following April. This was followed by a remarkable change in the civil administration : the clergy were deprived of the extensive jurisdiction which they had hitherto exercised, not only in ecclesiastical but in civil cases, and an end was then put to the gravest anomaly of the Medieval system. This was the more remarkable, because for many years after the introduction of the Reformation the Protestants were in a decided minority. The island and town of Tholen surrendered to Orange in April, 1577, on condition that the Roman religion should be maintained. This condition, however, soon became a dead letter, for practically the whole population went over to the Reformed faith. The magistrates' and the guild unanimously decided that all members of the government should belong to the Reformed Church, or at least should not be hostile to it.

In the first league between Holland and Zeeland in June, 1575, the Reformation was not mentioned. But in the Union of April, 1576, the Estates definitely established the Reformed Church ; and three years later they gave as their reasons for refusing to permit the exercise of the Roman religion that their provinces were harassed by a cruel war, that nearly all the ecclesiastics and most or the Romanist laymen were secret traitors, and that they were plotting the treacherous betrayal of the strongest forts and towns to the enemy. This religious and political bitterness found expression in other regulations : students were forbidden to go to Louvain, Douay, and the Jesuit schools ; watch was kept over Anabaptists and Anabaptist publications, because that sect declined " to take the oath of fidelity to the country " ; prelacy, or the episcopal office, was abolished ; the ecclesiastical property of bishoprics, abbeys, and monasteries was sold ; and the proceeds of the sale were devoted to the maintenance of schools, churches, and ministers, in defiance of a severe decree issued by Alexander Farnese in the King's name.

The course of the Reformation in Friesland was modified by two important circumstances. Lying in the extreme north of the Low Countries, at a distance from the theatres of war and from the chief centres of religious activity, Friesland was less exposed to extraneous influences and to conflicting currents of opinion than the provinces which lay further south. At the same time the position of the Protestant East Friesland on its borders greatly strengthened the hands of the reforming party, gave them a most invaluable ally, and provided a secure retreat for them in the hour of defeat or danger.

The outburst of reforming activity in the summer of 1566 was not more marked in any part of the Netherlands than in Friesland. Leeuwarden, the capital of the province, took the lead. In September a meeting was held in the Town Hall; on the motion of the Burgomaster it was decided to clear the churches of images and ornaments; and on the following Sunday the first Evangelical sermon was preached. The monastic bells ceased ringing, and the Romanist service was only held with closed doors. A few days later four converted priests were admitted to the Evangelical ministry, and in the middle of the month the Eucharist according to the Evangelical rite was administered to a very large number of communicants. Dockum, Harlingen, Sneek, Franeker, and many villages followed the example of the capital.

This state of things lasted till the beginning of 1567, when the Governor obtained an armed force, forcibly suppressed the Protestant worship, and restored the Roman Mass. A large emigration was the result. Civic officials, Frisian nobles, a crowd of burghers, and more than a hundred Protestant ministers fled across the border to East Friesland. Two Inquisitors were appointed, attendance at Mass was made compulsory, all who died without the Roman sacraments were refused interment in consecrated ground, and offenders against the religious edicts were beheaded, hanged, or burnt. At the beginning of 1570 the new Bishop arrived, and excited general disgust by his luxury and extravagance, breaking up monasteries in order to sell the stones, and turning the churchyards into pasture lands. The few Protestant clergy who had remained to minister to the scattered communities were forced to leave the country, and the prisons were filled to overflowing.

Thus matters stood till the Pacification of Ghent. Then the exiles returned, the unpaid troops rose against the Governor, and the Bishop was placed under arrest for refusing to obey the Estates of the Province. Shortly after, the Religious Peace, granting complete toleration to both Churches, was drawn up. In Leeuwarden the Council came to an agreement with the Jacobin monks that they should have the use of the church for one part of the day and the Protestants for the other, the images, altars, and church ornaments being placed in the choir for the exclusive use of the monks. But here, as elsewhere, it was impossible for the two religious parties to live in peace side by side. The opposition to Spain had been a common meeting-ground which united all true patriots. When this uniting bond had been removed, the religious differences came to a head. The Romanists forgot their hostility to Spain in their hatred of heresy : the Protestants, conscious of a growing power, indulged in outspoken abuse of their opponents, and committed acts of violence. In Leeuwarden the burghers, indignant at the Governor's secret sympathy with the Romanists, seized the forts, commanded the Franciscans to quit the city, and ordered all the churches to be given up to the Protestants. This example was followed by other cities, and in most places was made the pretext for wanton and inexcusable acts of plundering and destruction. In the Spring of 1580 the Governor fatally injured the Romanist cause by deserting to the Spaniards, and the Frisian Estates unanimously resolved " to proceed to a thorough and Evangelical reformation in

matters of religion." The Romanist worship was absolutely
forbidden, the Romanist clergy deposed from their offices
and benefices, the property of the Medieval church devoted
to the maintenance of ministers, schools, and the poor, and
every congregation, whether in town or village, authorized
to appoint their own minister and schoolmaster. The
deposed Romanist clergy, if they had private means, or
were traitors to the national cause, received no help; if
they were well disposed and destitute, they were granted
an annuity. Many priests and monks for different reasons
embraced the Reformed faith. The Romanist laymen in
large numbers enlisted in Philip's army.

During all these years the popular literature flowed in
an unbroken stream; and we may trace in its pages the
intensity of religious conviction and the virulence of
national hatred. At one time Alva, at another the Pope,
at another the Romanist worship, at another the Spanish
army was the object of ridicule, invective, or scorn. "The
Sick Pope" summons to his bedside Bishops and Cardinals,
fat Prelates and Abbots, Mass-priests and Canons, monks,
nuns, and Jesuits. This new doctrine, he laments, is
drawing his life-blood; in every country to which it has
spread it is taking deeper root. The people are resolved to
read the Scriptures, they refuse to be subject to Babylon,
trample the Papal laws under foot, condemn the
Mass, forsake Purgatory, and abandon the Confessional.
They regard Indulgences as simple thievery, pass by the
Papal wares, and seek Christ before the Pope. The
monks are denounced as greedy folk, who do no work,
eat the bread of the poor, and rob small and great. "The
Fall of Priests" describes the downfall of the Romanist
worship; the persecuting tyrants, who forced God's
people to flee into the caves of the earth, must now flee
in their turn; they cannot sell their merits as of yore;
Complines, Vigils, and Masses, for which they have
extorted money, have fallen into decay; "your doctrine
is not in harmony with God's pure Word, therefore,

according to Scripture, it is now rooted out by main force,
and the people will not reverence it any more." In " The
Mass " the service of the Medieval church is ridiculed, the
bowing, the turning, the ducking, and the crossing of the
priest, the ringing of bells, the superstitious reverence of
the poor folk, the withholding of the cup from the laity.
Although the wares are decked out with fair words, no
one will buy them. The Englishman rejects them, the
Frenchman has half run away, the Zeelander, Hollander,
and Brabanter cast them out. " Whom will you comfort
with your Mass, poor, sick pedlars? Go with the
stench of it to Spain." " The Ten Commands of the
Earthly God " is another satire on the Pope: he is represented as calling upon Christians to pay heed to none
except himself, bidding them to make images, to run on
pilgrimages, and not to worship God alone, commanding
them to hold his name in honour on pain of fire and
sword, though to blaspheme God's name is a slight matter.
Six days are too much to work, therefore festivals have
been instituted ; father and mother may be forsaken with
impunity by all who enter the Pope's religion. Murder,
thieving, falsehood, covetousness, only bring a little money,
and you shall be absolved from all. " O men, see how
merciful my law is : whoever will guide himself by it shall
be saved, even as I am." " The Antichrist " is couched
in still more bitter terms. Christ walked on foot to
preach : the Pope's feet are so holy that the earth may
not bear him. Christ had not where to lay His Head: the
Pope is so rich that earth cannot show his like. Christ
wore a crown of thorns : the Pope wears a triple crown
of gold. He has set his doctrine above God's commands,
has made his mock at Christ's Word, has devised Indulgences, has invented the Mass, has manufactured Purgatory,
and has ordained auricular confession—all this with the
single object of extorting money. In " Alva's First
Penitential Psalm " the brutal general curses the hour
when he set foot in the Netherlands. Although he has

trodden under foot much innocent blood, has burnt and slain, throttled and hanged, has done to death many nobles and even Counts, has annihilated at one blow the privileges of the land, and has altogether despised the orders of the States General, his most fatal error has been that he was forced to touch the Netherlanders' gold; so long as he let them abide by their fleshpots, they paid no heed to the ruin of their land; but now that he forcibly touches their gold, they are resolved to drive him out of the land. In conclusion, he calls upon the Pope to pray, vow, petition, and make processions on his behalf, and to offer up 100,000 masses for his soul. The theme of "Requesens' Pardon" is the treachery and faithlessness of the Spaniards. The Governor calls upon Holland and Zeeland to support the King, to accept his pardon, to love the Pope, and to make a firm agreement to live each in his own place and in his own faith. The reply is prompt: we know what your pardon is worth, we have tested it at Zutphen, at Naerden, and at Haarlem; we have seen the terrible deception practised on the Moors, and the massacre of Saint Bartholomew, where the life even of the unborn child was taken; our reliance is on God alone. The most elaborate of these squibs, entitled "Don John," is cast into the form of a dramatic poem: the Pope addresses his Cardinals, the Duke of Alva his Catholic soldiers, the Nymph of Holland her sisters, the Prince of Orange all good patriots, Requesens the Jesuits, the Lion of Holland and Zeeland his Excellency, and Don John of Austria his followers. The Pope bewails the downfall of the Church, and glories in his two faithful sons, the Most Christian King of France and the Most Catholic King of Spain; they alone live laudable lives according to the morals of the Inquisition, they alone stand high in his paternal grace. Alva boasts that he is the faithful servant and benefactor of the Holy Father; he has proved his fidelity by the murder of Lutherans and heretics; he is the Roman angel of the new Bishops, the

guardian of Jesuits and Mendicants; through the Inquisition shall the Spaniards conquer the heretics, singing
devoutly as a song of thanksgiving, "If Saint James prays
for us, who shall overcome us?" The Nymph of Holland
appeals to her sisters to help her against the abominable
murderers—the contemptible foreign nation, who confound
all divine and imperial rights—the monsters, the hounds
of Geryon. Orange calls upon all noble barons, knights,
high lords, burghers, artisans, and merchants to be godly
and stout of heart in resisting to the death; he will maintain their ancient privileges. Requesens boasts to the
Jesuits that his unswerving obedience to the Pope's commands has raised him to his exalted station; the Inquisition has pronounced a blessing upon him for his oppression
of the heretics; "our names are written in the book of
life with the Pope at Rome; no power of the heretics
may prevail against us." The words of the Lion of
Holland and Zeeland are an answer to William's appeal:
though they seem to be a despised nation abandoned of
all men, yet God has implanted in them the stout heart
of the lion to withstand the bears and hogs of Spain; they
appeared to be overpowered, but the Lord has willed to
increase His great glory through their noble Prince of
imperial blood by baffling their foemen's tyranny; they
retain the Apostolic faith, they enjoy their ancient laws and
statutes, in spite of the Inquisition, that serpent of hell; this
is their steadfast resolve. Lastly, Don John magnifies his
faithlessness; he will forcibly introduce the Inquisition by
telling great lies, by promising wonders and not bringing
one to pass; his conscience is clear, for has he not the
absolution of the Inquisition? is he not the Pope's dearest
shield? He is following the precedents of France and
Grenada; the Roman proverb is wound on the distaff
and he must spin it: "Hereticis non esse servandan
fidem."

After 1580 events moved rapidly to a decisive issue in
the north and south. On July 26th, 1581, the assembled

representatives of the chief provinces made a solemn renun-
ciation of their allegiance to Philip, and declared him
deposed from his position as Duke, Count, and Lord in
their respective governments. At the same time Farnese,
powerfully assisted by the lawless violence and narrow-
minded extravagance of his opponents, continued his
successful career of military conquest and diplomatic
victory. Cities, where the very name of Spaniard had a
few months or a few years before been regarded with
unutterable loathing, resounded with cries of " Long live
King Philip!"; and admiring Councillors hung up his
picture in their Town Hall. Ghent, Brussels, Malines,
Bruges, and Antwerp had surrendered to Parma before
the summer of 1585 closed, and the reconquest of the
southern Netherlands was practically accomplished. But
the cost of his triumph was appalling. Vast numbers of
the population emigrated to the Northern provinces,
England, or Germany, 30,000 from Ghent alone, and
probably more than a quarter of a million from the whole
of the south. The mere numbers would have made such
an emigration a terrible loss to the country; but the great
majority were substantial burghers, the very flower of the
cities against which they shook off the dust of their feet.
The country which they quitted fell a prey to misery,
poverty, and pestilence. Whole towns were abandoned;
whole villages were left desolate. Respectable people
who had held good positions were forced by want to steal
out at dusk and beg their bread. Wild beasts multiplied,
and the tilled fields became waste lands.

Before the south had been reconquered, the north had
practically achieved its independence; and the foundations
of the new State, destined during many eventful years to
become by turns England's rival and England's ally, were
firmly laid. The new Church triumphed with the new
State. The religious energy of its members had been as
noteworthy as their political energy. In November, 1568,
the first Synod met at Wesel. The second, which was

held three years later, again assembled on foreign soil in the friendly city of Emden. Not till 1578 could they venture to summon a National Synod within the boundaries of their native land. This was followed by the Synod of Middleburg in 1581, and by the Synod of the Hague in 1586. The subjects discussed at these Synods covered a wide range: the regulation of indifferent matters in religion; the division of the ministry into four orders; the calling, election, and examination of ministers; the co-operation of godly magistrates; the voting of the whole Church; the confirmation of ministers by solemn prayers or by laying on of hands; the chief duties of ministers; the exposition of Scripture by prophets; the insisting upon faith and repentance as the two chief themes of all sermons; directions about congregational singing; the urgent need of catechizing; the momentous duties of elders; the office of deacons; the safeguards against misuse of the Eucharist; the maintenance of discipline in religion and morality; the method of dealing with different offences in laymen and ministers; the absolute equality of all Churches; the close union of the Churches; the four kinds of ecclesiastical assemblies, church councils, classes, particular synods, and national synods; the necessity of establishing schools; the conditions of church member-ship; Christian liberty in indifferent matters; the best methods of checking Anabaptism; the attendance at public dances; the quoting of the Fathers and later writers in sermons; the use of organs in churches; the abolition of holy-days; the remarriage of divorced persons; and the repression of licentiousness and irreligion.

There is one point of special interest connected with the history of the Reformation in the Netherlands which was clearly brought to light in these earlier synods of the Dutch Church. The rivalry between Church and State which had filled so large a space in the history of the Middle Ages, and had deeply affected England, France, Italy, and the Empire, could not reappear in so acute a form in the Reformed States and the Reformed Churches. The Reformers, who had so greatly magnified the office of temporal rulers and governors, could be under no temptation to dictate to the State and its representatives with the haughty and scornful dogmatism, with the calm assumption of superior holiness and of superior wisdom, of a Hildebrand, an Innocent, and a Boniface. Some of the Reformers went so far as to regard the Church as an integral part of the State, and to merge its identity in the corporate existence of the body politic. Others looked upon the Church as the nurseling and ward of the Christian State, and upon Christian rulers and governors as the best and wisest guardians of its privileges and interests. Others claimed for the Church a virtual independence, and rejected with the utmost jealousy all encroachments of the State upon its peculiar and inalienable domain. This was the case in Holland. On two important subjects there was the widest difference of opinion between the Protestant clergy and the Protestant laity. The laity claimed for the State the right to interfere in matters which concerned the government of the Church; the magistrates of every chief town should, on the advice indeed of the Church but without interference from it, select ministers for their own towns and for all other places under their jurisdiction; every minister after his election should be presented to the magistrates for their approbation; if there were any disputes about doctrine which the ministers could not compose, the question at issue should be referred to the magistrates; notice should be given to the magistrates of any misdemeanours of which the clergy had been guilty, and in the last resort the magistrates should decide upon the case; the magistrates of every place should, with the advice of the ministers, determine when and how often services should be held; and the magistrates should decide all cases relating to matrimony. In no Reformed country had the governing laity put forward more sweeping claims, and the Church vehemently demurred to all except the last. What possible value could the Church as a distinct organisation possess, if it were thus to be kept in the leading strings of the State ? Why should the magistrates have more right to appoint ministers than the ministers to appoint magistrates ? Why should the magistrates have more right to interpret doctrine than the ministers to interpret laws ? Why should the magistrates decide the hour and the frequency of the Church services if the ministers did not decide the hour and the frequency of civic meetings and sessions of law courts ?

The other disputed question was even more significant. After the establishment of the Reformed Church in the northern Netherlands there were still two large bodies who dissented from its doctrines—the Roman Catholics and the Anabaptists. What the numerical importance of these bodies was cannot be accurately ascertained ; but it is evident that they were considerable enough to cause the leaders of the Reformed Church great uneasiness. It was natural, therefore, that the Church councils should strongly advocate a policy of severe repression. But they were quite unable to convince the government of the justice or expediency of their views. The laity plainly declared that so long as the Roman Catholics were faithful to the national cause, sacredly observed the oath which they had sworn, and were willing and able to serve the State in the army and in civil employments, they would not suffer any interference with their religious belief; nay, they would gladly have permitted the public exercise of their religion, had they not recognized in the priests and friars the sworn enemies of all true patriotism. Their attitude towards the Anabaptists was even more forbearing and more tolerant. So long as the sectarians shunned all dangerous extravagance, and proved themselves to be sober, industrious, God-fearing folk, they would not persecute them on account of harmless idiosyncrasies. If it was urged that, apart from their religious doctrines, their political principles were injurious to the State, the reply was obvious, that in such a case the rulers of the State were surely the best judges of the manner in which they should be treated. Again and again the ministers returned to the attack, but every time they were foiled by the active or passive resistance of the government. Even when the Estates passed resolutions, they took no steps to enforce them ; and the condition of the Anabaptists during the seventeenth century in the United Netherlands stands out in striking and painful contrast to the condition of the Nonconformists in England under the Kings of the House of Stuart.

CHAPTER VIII.

THE REFORMATION IN ENGLAND.

By the close of the fifteenth century the traces of Lollardism in England had vanished more completely than the traces of the Hussite movement in Germany. Powerfully as its influence had been felt even so late as the reigns of Henry the Fourth and Henry the Fifth, it seems to have practically disappeared amidst the excitement and agitation of the stormy events which filled the greater part of the century. The conquest of France, the loss of France, the wars of the Roses, the final overthrow of the House of York, and the establishment of the Tudor dynasty, had thrown all religious and ecclesiastical questions into the background. When Henry the Eighth mounted the throne; when he stooped to enter the lists against Luther, and was rewarded by a grateful Pope with the stately title of " Defender of the Faith " ; when he raised Wolsey to be his chief minister and favourite; when the great statesman became Archbishop of York, Cardinal, and Papal Legate; when Erasmus, the most famous man of letters in Europe and the champion of Catholic orthodoxy, was welcomed at the King's palace and the houses of the most eminent men : the revolt of England against the authority of the Pope might have appeared as improbable as the revolt of France or Spain. No one could then imagine that the little cloud no bigger than a man's hand was gathering, which would soon cover the political and ecclesiastical heaven with blackness and tempest.

The connection, commercial and intellectual, between

England and the Continent was so close that the new
doctrines soon found their way into the country. From
the seaports of the Continent merchants and seafaring
men brought to England the tidings of the new doctrines
which they heard everywhere so eagerly discussed. From
the book-marts of the Continent volumes, written by the
foremost Reformers, were smuggled into English ports.
From the printing-presses of the Continent pamphlets,
treatises, and translations were issued by the boldest and
most active of the English Reformers. It is a matter of
deep regret that the share which these books had in laying
the foundations of the English Reformation has been so
imperfectly ascertained. That they contributed most
powerfully to spread the new doctrines admits of no doubt.
As early as the spring of 1521, Wolsey issued a proclamation ordering all Lutheran and heretical books to be given
up. Five years later, Tunstall, Bishop of London, called
in all English translations of the Scriptures, and published
a list of eighteen prohibited books by Tyndale, Roy, Luther,
Zwingli, Brenz, and Huss. Three years later Henry issued
a proclamation against eighty-five Latin books by such
authors as Œcolampadius, Zwingli, Luther, Bugenhagen,
Pellican, Bucer, Melanchthon, Brenz, and Lambert. At
the same time fifteen English books were forbidden. Nor
must it be supposed that these measures were taken against
an imaginary danger. Again and again heretics were
brought up before the Bishop's Courts, men of every station
and every calling in life from priests to serving-men, for
possessing heretical books, for studying heretical books,
for conveying them to others, for discussing them with
others. One of these, Robert Nocton, disposed of more
than fifty English New Testaments in London, Stow-
market, Bury St. Edmunds, and Norfolk. Another,
Richard Bayfield, formerly a monk, passed to and fro
between England and the Continent, where Tyndale and
Frith were superintending the printing of books. He
sold their works and the works of the German Reformers

in France as well as in England.   The list of those which
he brought over and dispersed within the space of eighteen
months comprises almost every work of importance
published by the Continental and English Reformers
during the first twelve years of the religious movement.
It was not even necessary to possess these books in order
to be acquainted with the teaching which they contained.
Companies gathered together secretly; the books were
read aloud, discussed, and explained; and the knowledge
of their contents was spread in ever-widening circles, till
London and the parts about the capital were honeycombed with heresy or with doubt of the chief Medieval
doctrines.

If anything had been needed to secure the new teachers
a favourable hearing, it would have been supplied by the
vigour of their attack and the weakness of their opponents'
defence.   At a time when great works of European
celebrity, like More's "Utopia," Erasmus' "Praise of
Folly," and Hutten's "Letters of Obscure Men," were
written in a dead language, Tyndale and his English
contemporaries in the Reformed party, like Luther in
Germany and Calvin in France, revealed to their generation the wealth of their mother tongue.   The treatises of
Tyndale are wisely modelled upon Luther's masterly
pamphlets ; whole paragraphs are almost. a translation
from the German Reformer; and the English writer's
nervous style will bear a comparison with the great
master's.   "The Supplication of Beggars," a celebrated
pamphlet by Fish, setting aside the subject-matter, would
not have done discredit to Swift for its admirable style
and effective arrangement.   On the other side, Fisher was
the only Romanist priest of any eminence who took up the
gauntlet which the Reformers had flung down.   How
ineffective his writings were may be judged from one
fact.   His answers to Luther and Œcolampadius fill
between them nearly one thousand closely printed folio
pages.   To confront the works of the Reformers with such

Titanic books was like bringing up ponderous battering rams to foil the quick parry and thrust of a Toledo rapier.

Matters stood thus, when the question of Henry's divorce suddenly changed everything. It was a just retribution that the downfall of the Papal power in England was the result of the most presumptuous and the most immoral of the rights which the Popes had exercised in the Medieval Church. The teaching of the Medieval theologians and canonists had been that the Pope had full power over all powers both in heaven and in earth, that he was the sole source of all laws, that he was all and above all, that he could do as much as Christ could do, that he could dispense with the canons and rules of Apostles and Councils, that he was not bound to observe the ordinances and laws of Christ, and that God had given him full power to bind and to loose in heaven and in earth. Of these vast powers the Popes were not slow to take advantage. God's Law forbade theft, but the Pope could allow a man to steal; God's Law commanded men to keep their vows and oaths, but the Pope could release from vows and could sanction perjury; God's Law forbade man to put asunder what He had joined together, but the Pope could allow man and wife to separate and enter monastic Orders. In no department of the moral life did the Pope make ampler and more constant use of his dispensing power than in matrimonial cases. He narrowed and enlarged the forbidden degrees of consanguinity at his pleasure; he allowed an uncle to marry his niece; he permitted a King of Portugal to marry two sisters in succession; and by virtue of the same authority he granted Henry a dispensation to marry his brother Arthur's widow. If it was objected that this dispensing power made God's Law of none effect, the answer was, "No; the Pope does not annul the Law, he only declares that it is not binding in this particular case."

The painful story of the divorce only affected the cause of the English Reformation indirectly and incidentally.

Whether Henry was consumed by a guilty passion for
Anne Boleyn, or was tortured by conscientious scruples
about his marriage with Katharine, and by pressing fears
for the succession to the crown ; whether he suspected
Wolsey of betraying his interests, and the Pope of playing
into the Cardinal's hands, or was moved by holy indignation at the violation of God's Law and by noble zeal for
his people's welfare ; whether the Pope rose to the full
height of his duty as Vicar of Christ, or was swayed by the
sordid motives of a temporal potentate ; whether Convocation and Parliament, in giving their decision according
to the King's wishes, obeyed the dictates of a tender
conscience, or servilely bowed to court the favour of their
imperious sovereign—these are questions which the
historian of the Reformation may brush aside. But there
cannot be the shadow of a doubt that the impression
which these lengthy proceedings made upon such a Prince
as Henry vitally and permanently affected the position
and the character of the English Church. His natural
force of will and strength of purpose had been deepened
and consolidated by maturity of years, by the unquestioning
obedience of his people, and by the adulation of his
ministers, nobles, and courtiers. Like his illustrious
predecessors, William the Conqueror and Henry the
Second, he would brook no opposition. Those who placed
themselves in his path or thwarted his resolve had the
choice of two alternatives only—they must bend or they
must break. Up to the last moment he was ready to offer
the Pope a fair compromise. When the offer was rejected,
he set his face as a flint. He would no longer tolerate a
divided throne in Church or State. He would show the
Pope that in his own sphere he was as mighty a magician
as Gregory the Seventh or Innocent the Third had been
in theirs, would shatter his flimsy tiara with the resistless
blows of his mailed gauntlet, would scatter his adherents
to the four winds of heaven, would divert into his own
exchequer the golden streams which had yearly flowed

into the Papal purse, and would incorporate into his own
temporal sovereignty the spiritual prerogatives of the
Pope.   The die was cast.   From this time forward there
should be war between himself and the Papacy—a war like
the wars of ancient times, without truce and without
herald, in which quarter should neither be given nor taken.
It was a terrible decision; and the remorseless speed and
consistency with which it was carried out made it more
terrible still.

Henry's wrath lighted first upon his famous minister.
No greater disaster could have befallen the Church of
England at the close of the Middle Ages than to be placed
under the leadership of Wolsey.   Admirable as a statesman and a diplomatist, he was worse than useless as a
Churchman.   Licentious, luxurious, overbearing, arrogant,
devoted to worldly aims, enslaved to worldly ambitions,
immersed in secular business, he cared as little for the
spiritual duties and the spiritual claims of his priestly
office as Pope Leo the Tenth and the Primate of Germany.
That one of the bitterest satires of the sixteenth century
should have been written against him and widely circulated, is sufficient proof of the light in which his religious
character was regarded.   A weapon forged and sharpened
by his predecessors lay ready to Henry's hand.   The
Statute of Præmunire, one of the most remarkable
testimonies to the independent spirit of English Kings
and English Parliaments, had been directed against the
claims and encroachments of Papacy, and had been
designed to secure the liberties of the English people.
By a glaring distortion of justice Henry declared that
Wolsey had fallen under the penalties of the statute.
The proud spirit of the Cardinal was crushed; he pleaded
guilty, and threw himself upon the King's mercy; and
Henry had the ignoble satisfaction of pillaging the servant
whom he had enriched.   But with this revenge he was
only half satisfied.   Having punished the head, he
determined to punish the members.   The Clergy were

informed that, by acknowledging Wolsey as Papal Legate, they had been guilty of a breach of the same statute, were compelled to gratify the King's greed by paying an enormous fine, and were forced to acknowledge him as Supreme Head of the Church of England.

After he had completely cowed the Clergy by these drastic measures, Henry turned to the Laity. In 1529 he summoned the Parliament, which in a few years wrought a greater revolution and left a deeper impression upon the policy of England, than any of its predecessors or successors. What the temper of the Laity was, and how much disaffection the conduct of the Clergy had excited, was shown by a significant incident. When Parliament met in November, an attack was made upon the grasping covetousness of ecclesiastics. This let loose the floodgates of invective, and the Prelates were so irritated by the strong language used in the Lower House, that Bishop Fisher in the House of Lords described the Commons as no better than a pack of Hussites. The Commons complained to the King, Henry intervened, and Fisher was forced to retract his words. This preliminary skirmish did not augur well for the fortunes of the Clergy in the coming campaign.

The first attack was made upon the extortions of the Roman Curia. At one blow Peter's Pence and Firstfruits were abolished; if the Pope in consequence refused the Bulls for the confirmation of Bishops, they should be consecrated without them, and any excommunications and interdicts should be disregarded. The next attack was directed against the English Clergy. The independent position of Convocation, their power of assembling without leave from the temporal government, their right of passing ecclesiastical laws without the consent of King and Parliament, had long been a grievance to the Laity. In future no Canons might be issued unless they had previously received the Sovereign's consent and confirmation, and all existing Canons were to be submitted to a mixed Commission of Clergy and Laity. By this radical measure Henry effectually plucked the pinions from the wings of the soaring ecclesiastical order.

In February, 1533, the Statute of Appeals was passed. It was complained that Bulls were still obtained from Rome in probate questions, matrimonial questions, and questions of tithes, and that appeals were carried to Rome from English Courts: in future all such questions should be decided by spiritual Courts in England; any one who procured any decision or censure from the Roman Curia, or made or allowed any appeal to Rome, should fall under the terrible Statute of Præmunire. In the following year Convocation decided that, according to Scripture, the Pope had no jurisdiction in England, the Papal Primacy was formally abolished by Parliament in terms of studied insult, and two Italians were ignominiously expelled from their English Bishoprics.

The independence of the Clergy had been effectually broken down by these acts, but Henry was not yet satisfied. The Bishops were the heads of the English Clergy; if they were his creatures, he was secure of the obedience of the whole body. The scheme which he devised reflects the highest credit on his ability as a statesman. In future, when a bishopric fell vacant, the election should devolve on the Dean and Chapter of the Cathedral Church, but it should be carefully reduced to a mere form. The King should nominate the new Bishop, and if the Dean and Chapter, from independence of choice or scruples of conscience, declined to accept him, they should fall under the Statute of Præmunire, and resign their places to more obsequious successors. Thus the highest spiritual offices in the Church of England were placed under the control of the secular government with a completeness which no other Church in Christendom could rival.

Even now, in Henry's opinion, there was something lacking, and he hastened to supply the deficiency. He ordered the Bishop of Rome's name to be erased from all prayers, orisons, missals, and service books, and never to be remembered " except to his contumely and reproach." He required every member of the regular and secular Clergy to take an oath recognizing him as Head of the Church, and acknowledging the marriage with Katharine to be invalid, and the marriage with Anne Boleyn to be valid. Bishop Fisher and Sir Thomas More were sent to the block for refusing to take this oath, and a number of Friars who followed their example were ruthlessly executed. He further commanded all Church dignitaries and beneficed clergymen to preach assiduously that he was under God the true Head of the English Church, and to denounce the usurped authority and grievous tyranny of the Popes. With an apparent ardour which must have moved Henry's admiration, the leaders of the English Church threw themselves into the fray. Gardiner and Bonner inveighed against the Pope with a heartiness which their enemies in after years were careful to remember against them. Tunstall, who held in succession the Bishoprics of London and Durham, and was one of the most respected of Henry's prelates, preached a famous sermon. According to this Bishop, who for years had been the faithful henchman of the Pope, the Pope's pride is like Lucifer's: he is full of pestilent malice, his avarice is insatiable, his purpose is devilish, his instigation is devilish, his enchantments are devilish—in short, he is a child of the Devil. It was plain that Luther did not enjoy a monopoly of strong language.

One great monument and stronghold of the Medieval system still remained in England—the Monasteries. Whether Henry's thoughts were first turned to the advantages of suppressing them by the fierce pamphlet of Fish; whether the idea was suggested by the Papal Bulls which had authorised Wolsey to appropriate the income of a number of them for the endowment of his new Colleges; whether he was moved by the glowing eloquence of Cromwell, who was now his trusted Minister, who had been Wolsey's agent in executing the Papal Bulls, and who drew a vivid picture of the boundless wealth which the King would gain by a more sweeping and wholesale spoliation; whether his hostility to them had been stirred by the open defiance of the Friars, who had condemned the divorce in unsparing terms; or whether all these motives had combined in shaping his resolution—this is one of those questions to which no answer can be given. It is scarcely conceivable that in any case Henry would have left them untouched. The monks, it was well known, were the chief adherents of the Papacy; they were the staunchest supporters of the old order which Henry was rooting up; they had disappeared from all lands where the Reformation had prevailed; and they were formidable in England both from their numbers and their wealth. To pave the way for their destruction a Visitation was ordered; the Commissioners naturally drew up reports which would favour the King's purpose; a Parliament in 1536 empowered him to dissolve all monastic houses whose revenue did not exceed two hundred pounds. But, for the first time, Henry encountered serious resistance. A rebellion, known as the Pilgrimage of Grace, broke out in the North, and was only put down after a bloody contest. The failure of the revolt left Henry stronger than ever. Charges of treason were scattered broadcast. Four great Abbots were executed as traitors; and in 1539 all the remaining houses, which had not succumbed to violence, or threats, or persuasion, were delivered by Parliament into Henry's hands.

The causes which made Henry's dissolution of the Monasteries so simple and easy a task are clear. For many years past the foundation of the monastic system had been silently and surely undermined. In earlier ages the poverty of the monks had been a reality as well as a name, but they had long ago exchanged their poverty for wealth which eclipsed the wealth of great nobles. In earlier ages the Monasteries had been the homes of literature and learning, but their ignorance had long ago passed into a proverb with humourists and satirists. Tyndale alone had done more to promote theological and scriptural knowledge in England than all the English monks of all the monastic Orders during the first thirty-five years of the sixteenth century. In earlier ages their lavish hospitality and care for the poor had been an unmixed blessing; but in the changed economic conditions of the sixteenth century their undiscriminating charity had probably been productive of as much evil as good. In earlier ages the monks had set a noble example of industrious and productive toil, had cleared forests, drained marshes, and reclaimed waste lands; now they were indignantly pointed at by moralists as a set of lazy lubbers, of stalwart beggars, who ought to be tied to a cart's tail and taught to work under the lash.

There is another consideration which must not be left out of sight. A very large portion of the monastic wealth has been obtained from the unquestioning faith of earlier ages. Men had endowed religious houses richly in the firm belief that these endowments would mitigate or annul the Purgatorial sufferings of themselves and their forefathers by providing ceaseless Masses for the dead. But as the faith in Purgatory grew weaker, this use of monastic property appeared to a sceptical generation sheer waste. An incident in the Scottish Reformation illustrates this point. At a public disputation the Romanist spokesman was incautious enough to admit that there was no propitiatory sacrifice in the Mass. The nobles present broke out into loud murmurs: "If there is no propitiatory sacrifice in the Mass, why did our ancestors strip themselves of their possessions to enrich worthless monks?" What the nobles of Scotland said, the nobles of England unquestionably thought.

All these causes had greatly changed the feelings of the laity. One large section of the laity hated them for their blind hostility to the new learning; others eyed them with undisguised dislike for their profession of sham holiness; others regarded them as an absurd anomaly;

others cast covetous glances upon their vast possessions; many viewed them with profound indifference, and would not lift a finger in their defence.

The dissolution of the Monasteries completed the greatest social, financial, political, and ecclesiastical revolution which England had witnessed since the Norman Conquest. The thoroughness with which it had been carried out, and the dramatic incidents which marked its course, enhanced the deep impression which it made. The mightiest force and the stateliest institution of the Middle Ages, which had stood unbroken and unimpaired for ten centuries, had been levelled to the ground in ten years. The devastating waters of the great flood had overspread the whole land, had riveted the gaze of every eye, and had affected every life—from the peer's in his stately castle, to the peasant's in his humble cottage. This was true above all of the destruction of the Monasteries. Popes might rise and pass away; Cardinals might triumph and fall; Bishops might purchase immunity by ignoble submission, or might perish like martyrs for conscience' sake; Acts of Parliament might be passed amid the assenting cheers of an unanimous Senate; and yet the lowly tillers of the soil might rise for their day's work and lay them down to sleep again in profound ignorance of these mighty changes. But when the religious Houses through the length and breadth of the land crashed down like the giant oaks of the forest, all felled together by a single blow, not a hamlet from Carnarvonshire to Norfolk, from the banks of the Dart to the banks of the Tweed, could fail to know the solemn truth. To all alike it was the visible and tangible sign that the old age had run its course, and that the light of the new age for weal or for woe had begun to dawn.

It is most probable that Henry adopted another startling measure from the conviction that it would produce a similar effect upon the popular imagination. Of all the English saints none had cast a more potent spell upon the nation than Thomas à Becket. A pilgrimage to his shrine was an indispensable part of the religious life of every Englishman. The earliest star in the great galaxy of English poets had immortalized the Canterbury Pilgrimage in one of the most famous of English poems. It was generally believed that the most wonderful miracles of the Middle Ages had been worked at his tomb. The Clergy revered him with a boundless enthusiasm as the santliest, the bravest, and the wisest of their Order, who had died a martyr's death amid circumstances of peculiar brutality and horror in defence of the sacred and inalienable rights of the priesthood. The people were taught to believe that so holy and upright a champion of Mother Church flung the blessed shadow of his sanctity over all who approached the spot where his hallowed bones were enshrined. To breathe a doubt that Becket was one of the greatest of Saints, standing within the innermost circle of the Paradise of God, was a blasphemy of which only the accursed Lollards could be guilty. Two days consecrated to his memory were counted amongst the chief festivals of the Church. Every fifty years his Jubilee was celebrated, and lasted for a fortnight; a Papal Indulgence was granted to all who visited his shrine; and in 1420 no fewer than 100,000 pilgrims were said to have earned the Indulgence. The offerings presented by the worshippers swelled to a fabulous amount; in two years they exceeded £20,000 of our present money. The fame of the illustrious Saint had spread far beyond the bounds of the British Isles. Foreign princes and nobles deemed it an honour to enrich his shrine with costly gifts. He was adored even on the distant waters of the Elbe, and a Guild of Hamburg placed itself under the guardianship of the canonized Archbishop. But Becket, in Henry's eyes, had committed the inexpiable sin: he had "defended the enormities of the Clergy"; he had been the champion of the Pope's "usurped authority"; so far from having anything saintly about him, he was a simple rebel and traitor; his doom was sealed; his shrine should be stripped bare of its ill-gotten wealth; his bones should be dug out and publicly desecrated; his festivals might no longer be observed; his images and pictures in all churches and chapels throughout the whole realm should be cast down and shattered; and all services, offices, and antiphons in his honour should be razed out of all service-books. The royal Iconoclast had left all the clumsy image-breakers of the sixteenth century at an immeasurable distance behind him.

It would be incredible, if it were not an unquestionable fact, that during the whole of this revolution the Roman Catholic prelates, with one solitary exception, neither criticised, nor opposed, nor resisted any of Henry's measures. Insult after insult, outrage after outrage, was heaped upon the Pope and the Roman system, yet all was borne by the Heads of the Church without a murmur or an expostulation. The wildest theorist in his most exalted moments never dreamt of a passive obedience such as they consistently practised. Even members of their own Church and creed bitterly pointed the finger of scorn and execration. They signed what they were told to sign, voted as they were bidden to vote, swore what they were ordered to swear, preached what they were commanded to preach. At a few weeks' or a few months' notice they renounced the opinions which they had cherished, and the beliefs which they had professed, for a lifetime. As time went on, they only cringed more humbly before the throne of the despotic monarch, and licked the dust more assiduously beneath the feet of his insolent and arbitrary Vicar-General. While scores of poor Netherlanders and poor Huguenots, without any advantages of birth, wealth, position, or education, were cheerfully and joyfully suffering the most cruel of all deaths; while the English Reformers were facing the fires of the stake with unshaken constancy; magnificent Bishops and stately Abbots bent and swayed with every breath of royal caprice. Had Tyndale, Frith, Ridley, and Latimer been moulded of equally ductile

and pliable metal, the English Reformation would have
been long indeed in coming.   No one can be blamed for
declining to become a martyr.   But men must be made
of sterner stuff than the craven hierarchy of Henry the
Eighth if they would ensure the triumph of a rising or
a falling Church.

Thus far Henry had been as successful as his most
sanguine hopes could have anticipated.   Yet he had no
sooner placed on his brows the duplicate of the Papal
tiara than he was forced to realize the difficulties which
lay before him.   He would, and he would not, "like the
poor cat i' the adage."   He would not recognize the
authority of the Pope, and yet he would retain the system
which the authority of the Pope alone had made possible.
He would place the Bible in the hands of his people and
encourage them to read it, and yet he would not suffer
them to hold the doctrines which the ablest students of
Scripture were drawing from its pages.   Europe was
divided into two Houses, the Romanist and the Protestant;
but Henry thought it possible to erect a fabric of his own,
in which the structure should be Protestant, but the
façade, the storied windows, and the ornamentation should
be Roman.   It is astonishing that a man of his acuteness
did not recognize the anomalous position in which he was
placed.   How could a church exist which did not rest
upon any well-defined logical, theological, or religious
basis; a Church governed by a band of Prelates of whom
one half were unconscious Protestants and the other half
secret Romanists; a Church to which the force of his
character gave a temporary and delusive cohesion, but
which would inevitably fall to pieces as soon as his strong
hand was withdrawn?   And so Henry went on, pulling
down, sweeping away, joining, dovetailing, forbidding
to-day what he had ordered the day before, commanding
this year what he had prohibited last year, without the
least suspicion that one half of Europe was contemplating
his work with derisive laughter and the other half with

indignant contempt. At one time all his subjects might read the Bible, at another the perusal of the sacred writings was confined to the upper classes. In one book Purgatory was eulogized, in another it was condemned. The Sacramental system of the Church of Rome was rejected, but the doctrine of Transubstantiation was retained. The marriage of Priests was forbidden, and yet the Primate of England was a married man. The Clergy were to preach sincerely and purely according to Scripture, but they were to enforce the belief in auricular confession and communicating in one kind. Such were the inconsistencies in which he floundered hopelessly ; and as his reign advanced, the devious and eccentric course in which the ship of the Church was steered revealed more clearly the uncertainty and embarrassment of the pilot.

The evils of the system which Henry introduced and sanctioned are obvious, and produced the gravest results. In no other reformed country had the Sovereign imposed his own creed upon his people. In no other country had the Church oscillated between varying creeds to suit the varying moods of its Head. How was it possible under these circumstances to preserve that inflexible allegiance to the sacred cause of truth which was one of the chief principles of the Reformation ? By what standard could truth be tested, if the erroneous belief of yesterday was proclaimed to be the infallible doctrine of to-day, and if this year's truth were identical with last year's falsehood ? What wonder was it if men eyed with a cynical contempt the truth which, like the chameleon, was ever changing its colour, or if they echoed Pilate's question with mocking derision ? Consistency is a primary element in the religious truth which inspires respect; and the inconsistencies of Henry's creed were too glaring to escape the notice of the simplest peasant. Many years had passed before the wounds which his action had inflicted on the character of Englishmen were completely healed.

No event during the latter half of Henry's reign affected the fortunes of the English Reformation more profoundly than the authorized publication of the English Bible. It is to Tyndale that the English-speaking race throughout the world is indebted for this inestimable gift. Cut off in the midst of his labours by the cruel hand of persecution, which struck down no costlier victim among the many Englishmen who died for their faith, it was natural that the work which he had been forced to carry on in the land of his exile should have been marred by imperfections. But many and great as the improvements have been which the loving hands of friends, disciples, and successors have made in the original translation, he has earned the imperishable glory, which he himself would have valued far above all earthly fame, of being inseparably associated with the noble version of the Scriptures in his mother tongue. This was only fitting. The Bible had been the joy of his life and the light of his path: he loved it with the passionate devotion of the Psalmist, who found it sweeter than honey unto his mouth, dearer than thousands of gold and silver. He had steeped his soul in its sacred truths; he had drawn his inspiration from its divine thoughts; he had acquired a natural elevation of language from the incessant study of its simple and stately diction. The hidden treasure which he had found he longed to share with others, and his wish was fulfilled far beyond his expectations and his hopes. Before the middle of the century the Scriptures had ceased to be an unknown book in England: artisans and peasants could hear them read and explained in their parish churches, and could test by this touchstone the doctrines which they had been taught from their youth.

Tyndale's translation of the New Testament was finished in 1526, and printed abroad. The Bishops were up in arms at once. Tunstall, then Bishop of London, whose diocese was the most widely infected with heresy, and who therefore was more nearly touched than his brethren by the publication of the English version, ordered all copies to be called in, and bought up as many as he could in order to commit them to the flames at Paul's Cross. Tyndale immediately issued a new and revised edition, which met with the same fate. Stokesley, who succeeded Tunstall in the see of London, followed his predecessor's example. The translation of the whole Bible was printed at Hamburg in 1532, and before a second edition could be issued Tyndale suffered martyrdom in Flanders. Fearing that the name of a heretic on the title-page would injure the sale, the printers issued it under the feigned name of Thomas Matthews. Fortunately for their venture, Cromwell had become Henry's trusted Minister, and extended his powerful patronage to their publication. He ordered six copies for his own use, procured the King's licence, and issued it under his Privy Seal. What made the translation peculiarly galling to the Roman Priest-hood was the addition of notes and a concordance of passages bearing upon the disputed question of the Eucharist and the marriage of the Clergy. In 1538 the Bible was for the first time openly sold in England, and a royal injunction ordered a copy to be placed in every parish church. All incumbents were commanded to read a declaration eulogizing the King's gracious goodness in throwing God's Word open to his people, urging the reverent use of it, forbidding unseemly disputations about it, and bidding all men conform their own lives and the lives of their households to its teaching.

From the imperfect accounts which have come down to us, it is evident that this formal authorisation of the English Bible gave a powerful impulse to the Reformation. All who could afford to buy a copy bought and eagerly studied it. Elderly folk and young boys learnt to read for the express purpose of mastering its contents. In households where the tone was still strongly Romanist, the youthful heretics pored over it in the early morning before the other inmates of the house had risen, and late at night when everyone else had retired to rest. During the day the precious volume was hidden in the straw of the bed. In the churches small knots of eager listeners gathered around those who were able to read it aloud, and drank in the strange accents. In the town of Chelmsford several poor men clubbed together to buy the New Testament with their hard-won earnings, and read it on Sundays at the west end of the Church while the incumbent was chanting the Latin service in the choir.

The first edition, consisting of 1,500 copies, was soon exhausted, and the printers resolved to issue another without the notes and prologues which had given offence, but with marks in the margin to draw attention to important texts and passages which they considered fatal to the errors and abuses of the Medieval Church. This edition they were anxious to print in France, where paper was better and cheaper and the workmen more skilful. At Henry's request Francis readily granted permission for the English Bible to be printed in his capital, and Bonner, the ambassador at the French Court, threw himself into the work with extraordinary zeal, frequently visiting the printing-press in order to watch the progress that was made. But before long the keen scent of the French Inquisitors detected the heretical proceedings: in a flaming document they set forth the spiritual dangers which a Bible in the vulgar tongue involved, and ordered the arrest of the printer. The printing establishment was broken up; the printed copies were seized and publicly burnt in Paris; and the work came to a standstill, until the types, presses, paper, and compositors had been smuggled over into England, and the printing of the English Bible was completed on English soil. From this moment the cause for which Tyndale and his assistants, Rogers and Coverdale, had so nobly fought and risked their lives, gained a complete triumph. Bishops might fume and frown; incumbents might neglect to place the Bible in their churches, or might hide it away after they had formally complied with the injunction; indignant vicars might secretly denounce the pestilential study to their parishioners; the King himself might interpose to check or modify the consequences of his own action; but nothing could undo what had been done. The Bible had been placed in the people's hands, and no one could wrest it from them again. The sacred fountains had been unsealed, and no earthly power could check the flow of their fertilizing streams.

With the death of Henry the Eighth a great change came over the English Government and the English Reformation. Edward the Sixth was only a child; the leading statesmen were divided among themselves; the foreign relations of the country needed a master hand to direct them; the national exchequer was at its lowest ebb; and the chief men at Court, in spite of their loud professions of patriotism, were only anxious to enrich themselves. At the same time no one knew what opinions the Bishops and the majority of the clergy held on religious questions. How many had accepted with hearty approval the changes which Henry had introduced? How many were repenting already of the concessions which they had made, of the innovations which they had adopted, and of the oaths which they had taken? How many had gained a clear view of the exact position of the English Church, and were ready with a definite policy for the future? How many were fully conscious of the inconsistencies in which they were involved, and had taken the full measure of the obstacles and difficulties which still lay in their path? One fact alone was evident to the dullest observer. The people and the Church could not long remain as they were: the only choice lay between retracing their steps towards the Medieval system which Henry had abandoned, and pressing on in the course which the Continental reformers and their friends in England had already marked out.

It would have been well for the Reformation of the

Church of England if, under these changed circumstances, the Primate who directed her policy and administered her affairs had possessed the qualities which are imperatively required of the leaders of men during troubled times. Had Cranmer lived among the theological calms of the eighteenth or nineteenth centuries, when his excellent qualities would have had full play and his culpable weaknesses would have lurked in obscurity, he might have taken a very high place among the Primates of the English Church. But on the stormy arena of the sixteenth century, where the stage was filled by spiritual gladiators, who feared nothing and trembled before no man, the weak and timorous Archbishop shrinks into insignificance. Beza justly boasted on a memorable occasion that his Church was an anvil which had worn out many hammers. But Cranmer was an anvil which the lightest blow of any hammer could shiver into fragments. No man who is called to a high place among his fellow men has any right to accept the honours, and enjoy the privileges, of his exalted station, while he shrinks from its duties and evades its responsibilities. Yet this was precisely what Cranmer did. The most convinced and ardent believer in the divine right of Kings, such as Laud or Sancroft, could not have accepted more unreservedly the maxim that whatever the King did was right. When the measures which Henry took were unusually startling or exceptionally high-handed, Cranmer could only heave the deepest sighs, cast up his eyes, lift up his hands, and break out into a wail of despondency and regret. He had all the servility of Bonner and Gardiner with much less excuse than they could plead. If on any point he differed from the King, he instantly lulled the suspicions, and disarmed the jealousy, of his patron by the humblest apology for his transient independence of thought and momentary aberration of judgment. He was naturally rewarded by the amplest measure of Henry's favour and protection. His real piety and goodness gained the

King's esteem, his ability and learning won the King's respect, and his undeviating pliability secured the King's support.   But it may be confidently affirmed that no man with a high sense of rectitude and a keen sense of self-respect could have stooped to play the pitiful part which Cranmer played during the reign of Henry the Eighth. Not even the palest reflection of the spirit and courage which animated his great contemporaries could be discerned in the English Primate.

It was not long before the predominant party in the State declared for the Reformation.   How far this decision was prompted by conscientious motives is more than doubtful. Northumberland, the most prominent among them, confessed on the scaffold that he had passed through the reign of Edward with a lie in his right hand.   Even if his comrades were not such consummate hypocrites as he was, there is nothing in their lives to justify the historian in crediting them with the honour which feels a stain like a wound.   During Henry's reign they had profited by ecclesiastical plunder; the store was not yet completely exhausted; and they probably saw that under a show of religious zeal they would be able to gratify their unsatisfied cupidity.   The Archbishop took no steps to correct their error.   Other voices were raised even in the King's presence to denounce the growing immorality of political and social life, to uphold the rights of the poor, to plead the cause of education, and to assert the claims of neglected parishioners; but the Primate held his peace. Distinguished members of the Council prostituted their influence and power to base and selfish purposes; but no rebuke and no protest passed the Primate's lips.   Commissioners were sent round to purify the churches from images, pictures, and superstitious objects; and Cranmer, who ought to have recognized more clearly than any one how little these violent proceedings, carried out under such auspices, could advance the cause which he had at heart, suffered them to go on their way unchecked.   Even

when a serious rising in the western counties, hardly less
formidable than the Pilgrimage of Grace, showed how
deeply the people were attached to the old faith, and how
vehemently they were opposed to the new doctrines in
districts where the conservative elements of the nation
were strongest, Cranmer lacked the power or the will to
recognize the real significance of these events. They
might have shown him that the method of his deceased
master had been radically wrong; that a people's faith
must be determined by the people themselves, not by
authoritative declarations of insincere rulers; that a real
Reformation could only be carried out by convincing the
reason and touching the heart, not by overbearing the
will; that ten earnest, able, and self-denying Preachers,
who spoke out of the abundance of a full heart, would
supply the little leaven to leaven the whole lump more
effectively than five hundred lukewarm or hypocritical
Vicars, who droned out beautiful services and masterly
homilies at the bidding of the State; and that an Act of
Uniformity, if it were supported by the strongest and
healthiest elements in the country, might work marvels,
but if it were resisted by the avowed or secret antagonism
of a vast and reluctant majority, would assuredly end in
disaster, and leave the last state of the nation worse than
the first.

The Injunctions issued to the Clergy in 1547 give a
vivid picture of the methods which commended themselves
to the King's vicegerents, and the ideals at which they
aimed. The chief duty of every beneficed clergyman was
to lavish all the treasury of his eloquence and learning
four times a year in the task of inveighing against the
Bishop of Rome's usurped authority. It was a duty of
less importance to preach "once every quarter at the
least" in person or by proxy on the works of faith, mercy,
and charity. What zeal could be inspired, what instruction
could be conveyed, or what impression could be produced
on hostile, indifferent, ignorant, or earnest parishioners by

this quarterly sermon, the authors of the Injunctions did not explain. But this command did not exhaust the Preacher's material; for he was also bound to set forth the iniquity of pilgrimages, candles, tapers, images, relics, praying upon beads, "and like superstition." On Sundays, when no sermon was preached, the Incumbent should repeat from the pulpit the Lord's Prayer, the Creed, and the Ten Commandments in English, that the people might learn them by heart. In every church a Bible should be placed, and an English version of Erasmus' Paraphrase of the Gospels, and each Minister should exhort his flock to read them. The Clergy should refrain from haunting taverns and alehouses, from drinking and riot, from wasting their time, from cards and dice. "But at all times (as they shall have leisure) they shall hear and read somewhat of Holy Scripture." Every Lent all who came to confession should be examined in the Creed, the Lord's Prayer, and the Ten Commandments, and should be admonished "not to presume to come to God's Board without a perfect knowledge" of them. If any of the Clergy had previously extolled pilgrimages, relics, images, or kissing and decking of images and kneeling before them, they should openly recant and reprove their previous teaching, and show that they had no Scriptural grounds for it. All hinderers of God's Word, and favourers of the Pope's pretended power, should be reported to the Council. Every non-resident Incumbent was bound to spend upon the poor of the parish a tithe of the yearly revenue which he drew from it, "lest he be worthily noted of ingratitude." If he receive from his "benefices and other promotions in the Church" £100 a year, he shall give out of it an exhibition to some scholar, and for every additional £100 another exhibition, either at Oxford or Cambridge or at some German University. Every Minister of the Gospel should possess in Latin and English the New Testament and the Paraphrase of Erasmus, should diligently study them, and should be examined in them by the Bishops at their Synods and Visitations. As the sick and dying often sink into despair, the Clergy " shall learn and have always in readiness such comfortable places and sentences of Scripture as do set forth the mercy, benefits, and goodness of Almighty God towards all penitent and believing persons." The abuses which had crept into the observance of holy days, and which led the people to imagine that the hearing of Mass or of some other service justified them in giving up the rest of the day to idleness, pride, drunkenness, brawling, and quarrelling, were sternly blamed. It was ordered that in future they should spend the day according to God's holy will and pleasure in hearing the Word, in communicating, in prayers, in works of charity, and in godly employments. But the Clergy should instruct their parishioners that they might in time of harvest labour without scruple of conscience even upon holy days and festivals. The higher dignitaries of the Church were not bound to preach more than twice in the year; they should instruct those committed to their charge of the great danger of superstitious ceremonies, such as throwing holy water upon their bed, bearing about them holy bread, ringing holy bells, and blessing with holy candles. A Poor chest shall be kept in every church, and parishioners shall be exhorted to give to it what they have previously bestowed upon pilgrimages, trentals, decking of images, offering of candles, gifts to Friars, " and other like blind devotions." The money derived from Fraternities and Guilds, from gifts or bequests for providing torches, lights, tapers, and lamps, shall be added to the same fund. Simony in its various forms was stringently forbidden, whether in the Clergy who obtained benefices, or in the laity who disposed of them, by iniquitous means. Finally, as the people in many parts were sunk in ignorance and blindness, the Clergy were ordered to read one of the homilies every Sunday.

These Injunctions went far beyond any orders of the

same kind which had been issued in Henry's reign, and disaffection soon broke out among the Bishops. Bonner and Gardiner, after some hesitation and shuffling, headed the ecclesiastical insurrection against the new system ; others followed their example; and this enabled the Council to deprive them of their Bishoprics and to place sounder Protestants in their Sees. Another insurrection in an opposite quarter embarrassed the Archbishop and the Council much more. Hooper, one of the most zealous and able of the Evangelical Preachers, was appointed to the Bishopric of Gloucester, but refused on conscientious grounds to wear the episcopal robes, an ominous symptom of a prejudice which soon pervaded the Evangelical ranks far more widely. At length he gave way, not however till he had spent some days in the Fleet prison.

The party to which Hooper belonged had been largely reinforced by allies from without. The news of the change which had come over the English Church since Henry's death spread to the Continent ; and many exiles who had been driven from their own countries by persecution sought refuge in England. The active intercourse which they kept up with the English Protestants, and the influence which their noble surrender, for conscience' sake, of worldly advantages and earthly ties deservedly gave them, undoubtedly added not a little to the strength of the Reformation in London and the eastern counties. Cranmer's hospitality to these exiles, and the constant efforts which he made to utilize their learning and ability for the service of his own Church, are among the most pleasing features of his episcopate. A Divinity Professorship at Cambridge was given to Bucer, and at Oxford to Peter Martyr. Fagius, one of the best Oriental scholars in Europe, was appointed to a Professorship of Hebrew. Foreign Churches were formed in London, and the simplicity of their service and of their system powerfully attracted men who held the opinions of Hooper.

Unquestionably the greatest work which Cranmer

undertook and carried out, a work for which his learning, his ability, and his temperament singularly fitted him, was the completion of the Anglican Book of Common Prayer. Not only has the use of the Prayer Book been one of the most distinctive features of the Anglican Church, the Prayer Book itself is the most important liturgical work which any Reformed Church has produced. As a rule, the breach with the Medieval Church had led the Reformed Churches to reject liturgical forms. They had for the most part, and with unimportant exceptions, adopted the practice of extemporaneous prayer which had prevailed in the Apostolic Church. They shrank from the use of prayers composed and uttered in an unknown tongue, which, through an evil custom of long standing, had degenerated into mechanical forms and vain repetitions scarcely less absurd and less harmful than the praying-wheels of the Buddhists. If the Church of England formed an exception, it is easy to find the explanation. No doubt the conservative instincts of Cranmer and his friends led them to bridge over as far as possible the gulf which yawned between themselves and the Medieval Church. No doubt they desired to make the inclusion within the pale of the Anglican Church as easy as possible for the great multitude of those who were halting between two opinions. But there were other reasons more cogent than these. A large number of Clergy were still so ignorant that they were as incapable of offering up extemporary prayers as of preaching extemporary sermons. For them the Prayer Book was as necessary as the Book of Homilies. A still larger number of the Clergy were in heart members of the Church of Rome, and, if they were allowed to conduct their own services, could not be trusted even for one Sunday to discharge their duties in a manner perfectly satisfactory to the Archbishop and the Council. Who could be sure that, if such secret Romanists were left to their own devices, they would not surreptitiously introduce into the prayers the name of that false usurper, the Bishop of Rome, or of that rebel and traitor, Thomas à Becket? that the worst features of the Canon of Mass would not reappear in the administration of the Eucharist, and that the sacrament of Baptism would not be tainted with the gravest of the Scholastic and Medieval errors? To guard against such real and pressing dangers, it was before all things necessary to draw up full services which should meet all the wants of the Church, and to bind the Clergy absolutely to the use of them by an Act of Uniformity.

Apart from its form, there is nothing in the substance of the Prayer Book as revised by Cranmer and again under Elizabeth to mark any difference of real importance between the Anglican and the other Reformed Churches. On more than one point its doctrine approximates less closely than the doctrine of the Lutheran Church to the teaching of the Church of Rome. Its Eucharistic doctrine, in particular, follows the type of Calvin and not the type of Luther. Knox, indeed, with the one-sided extravagance which was the most fatal flaw in his noble character, declared that the Prayer Book reproduced the worst errors, and countenanced the worst superstitions, of the Church of Rome, and detected in the petition of the Litany against "lightning, tempest, and sudden death," the cloven hoof of the Beast. But it is certain that there is nothing in the Prayer Book to which Luther and Melanchthon would have objected on the score of its Romanism, even if they might have demurred to more than one passage on the ground of its excessive Protestantism. Although the Anglican Church, following the Scandinavian Churches, has retained Episcopacy, and requires Episcopal ordination for all its Ministers, the compilers of the Prayer Book are careful to make it clear that their Church has accepted the Protestant view of the Christian Ministry, and not the Roman view of a sacrificing Priesthood. The omission of the ceremony which held the central place in the Medieval ordination to the Priesthood, the delivery of the Eucharistic vessels, proved with

unmistakable significance how completely the Anglican
Church rejected the Medieval conception of the office.
Equally significant were the questions which the Bishop
asked the candidates and the commission which he delivered
to them. In both they are reminded that the primary duty
of the Christian Minister is to preach the Gospel, and his
secondary duty to administer the Sacraments. It would
be impossible to reassert more completely Saint Paul's
teaching, or to reverse more explicitly the Medieval view.
The Bishop's address in the Ordering of Priests, one of
the noblest passages of religious eloquence for elevation of
thought and beauty of language, might have been delivered
without the change of a single word by Luther in Saxony,
or Calvin in Geneva, or Bugenhagen in Denmark, or Knox
in Scotland. The chief doctrines of the Anglican Church
embodied in the Thirty-nine Articles are in perfect harmony
with the rest of the Prayer Book and the other Reformed
Confessions of Faith. That all Orders of the Ministry are
permitted by God's Word to enter the holy estate of
matrimony; that Episcopacy is not absolutely essential
to the existence of a true Church; that all Christians, no
matter in what particular or national Church they have
been baptized, are made in Baptism members of Christ,
children of God, and inheritors of the Kingdom of Heaven;
that prayers for the temporal Governors must take prece-
dence of the prayers for the Church's spiritual Heads; that
Princes alone have the right to summon General Councils:
these are a few of the notable tenets which prove, if proof
were needed, that the English Church rejected the
distinctive features of the Medieval system.

Even more remarkable was the attitude which the
authors of the Prayer Book took up towards the services
of the Medieval Church. They referred emphatically to
Saint Paul's rule that the service should be read in a
language which the people could understand, and therefore rejected Latin, which the Church of the Middle Ages
had exalted into a sacred language. They reproved the

Medieval practice of mutilating the Bible, according to which three or four chapters of a Book were read in the public worship of the Church and all the rest omitted; they arranged for the reading of the Bible in due order; and to make this possible, they cut out "Anthems, Responds, and Invitations, and such like things as did break the continued course of the reading of Scripture." A great number of rubrics were rejected, the effect of which had been that it was more difficult "to find out what should be read than to read it when it was found out." Many things which were false, doubtful, vain, and superstitious were omitted, and nothing retained but "the pure Word of God, or that which is agreeable to the same."

Still more striking was the manner in which they dealt with ceremonies. The rule which they laid down on the threshold of their work was, that no ceremonies should be retained, except such as served for "a decent order in the Church" or tended to edification. They swept away all that had been turned to vanity and superstition, or introduced into the Church by indiscreet devotion and a zeal without knowledge, or had blinded the people, obscured the glory of God, and darkened, instead of setting forth, the benefits of Christ. They enlarged upon the excessive multitude and the intolerable burden of the Medieval ceremonies, which changed Christ's Gospel into a ceremonial law instead of a religion for serving God "not in bondage of the figure but in freedom of the spirit"; and commented bitterly on the insatiable avarice " of such as sought more their own lucre than the glory of God." In conclusion, they expressly state that in this they, unlike their successors, condemned no other nation, nor proscribed anything except to their own people: "for we think it convenient that every country should use such ceremonies as they shall think best to the setting forth of God's honour and glory, and to the reducing of the people to a most perfect and godly living, without error or superstition; and that they should put

away other things which from time to time they per-
ceive to be most abused, as in men's ordinances it often
chanceth diversely in divers countries."

What the condition of the Church was at the close of
Edward's reign cannot be exactly determined. Thousands
of clergymen, who had complacently exchanged the supremacy of the Pope for the supremacy of Henry, exchanged
the supremacy of Henry with equal complacency for the
supremacy of the Prayer Book. No country in Europe could
present such an unique spectacle of consciences which were
readily sold to the lowest as well as to the highest bidder.
Economic distress and civil war, the moral example of
unprincipled statesmen, and the religious example of
churchmen who strained at gnats and swallowed camels,
assuredly had not tended to foster a deeply religious spirit
among the mass of the population. Now and then for a
moment the curtain is lifted, and we catch glimpses of
churches in which not a single sermon had been preached
for five or six years, of avowed Romanists thrust upon
parishes by simoniacal transactions, of the property of
Grammar Schools sold to grasping landowners, of cattle
given to the poor and forcibly taken from them, of
Episcopal and Cathedral lands which were confiscated on
the pious plea that excessive wealth had in bygone times
demoralized the Clergy, of monstrous exactions practised
upon the laity at time of marriage, or burial, or payment
of tithes, of priests who while conforming outwardly to
the Reformed doctrine claimed the right to hold what
opinions they pleased, of Incumbents with five or six
livings apiece, of patrons who bestowed benefices on their
stewards or huntsmen on condition of receiving half the
income, of services gabbled till they were as unintelligible
as the tongues of Calicut or Tunis, of baptisms slurred
over, of marriages converted into comedies, of the total
absence of all catechizing for the instruction of the
ignorant, of open sinners unrebuked by any public or
private admonitions, of buying, selling, and gaming in

churches and their precincts, of great men appropriating
moneys bequeathed to the Universities, of laymen who
bought livings and left the parishes without Ministers,
of the richest parsonages converted from "shepherds'
houses" into "thievish dens," of parsons' deputies without ability, power, and authority to do anything but
extort ecclesiastical dues, of gentlemen seizing upon
benefices worth £40 or £50 a year and hiring for five or
six pounds curates who never went near them, of noblemen
rewarding their servants with livings in their gifts, of
a thousand pulpits in England covered with dust, of
simple country folk saying of their Curate, "He minisheth
God's sacraments, he slubbereth up His service, and he
cannot read the homilies."   Such were some of the fruits
of five years' Evangelical zeal under the leadership of
Somerset, Northumberland, and Cranmer.

If the conduct of religious affairs during Edward's
reign had not been of a nature to prejudice the people in
favour of the Reformation, still less had the conduct of
political affairs.   The incompetence and unscrupulousness
of the governing Council had undermined the popular
confidence in them; and when it became known that
Northumberland had succeeded in extorting from the
young King on his death-bed an illegal document to set
aside the rightful claim of Mary Tudor and to place the
crown on one of his own family, he met with no sympathy
among the people.   Mary acted with the promptitude
and energy which might have been expected from Henry's
daughter.   The Queen of a day, her foolish husband, and
her unprincipled father-in-law were crushed at once.   A
popular rising on their behalf was put down, and sealed
their doom.   The capital of the nation acknowledged
Mary as their sovereign; and she was seated on her
throne all the more firmly because of the mistakes which
her enemies had made.

It was not long before the Queen made it evident that
she intended to inaugurate another religious revolution.

The events of the last twenty-five years had stirred all
her deepest feelings as a daughter, a woman, a Princess,
and a Romanist. The hated creed which she found at her
accession in the possession of supreme power, had been
the cause of all the sorrow and all the shame of her life.
It had cast out her mother from the throne of England.
It had branded herself with the stigma of illegitimacy.
It had emboldened low-born Councillors to attempt to
bully her, the heir to the throne, into acting against her
conscience and into trampling under foot her dearest
convictions. It had degraded the Holy Father, the Vicar
of Christ, from his rightful place as the Head of the
Church, had loaded him with the most opprobrious
epithets, and had made his name a byword of contumely
and reproach. Her turn had come at last. She would
root out the detested faith and its detested champions;
she would avenge her own wrongs and the wrongs of
Holy Mother Church ; she would bring back the erring
sheep to the one fold ; and the evil years which had passed
since her mother's divorce should only be remembered
hereafter as a bad dream. Her marriage with Philip of
Spain was only the most vivid expression of this sacred
purpose to which she dedicated her life.

The advisers to whom Mary gave her confidence confirmed her in this resolution. Of these, the Spanish
ambassador, Gardiner, Bonner, and Cardinal Pole were
the most influential. In all her troubles the Queen had
received sympathy and support from her Spanish kinsmen, and she admired profoundly the unblemished orthodoxy and crusading fervour of the Spanish nation. The
two Bishops, who had been thrown into the Tower during
Edward's reign, had bitterly repented of their earlier
heresies, and were fully prepared to expiate their sins
in the blood of heretics. Pole, who, Cardinal though
he was, had been talked of as a husband for Mary, was
one of the most ardent Romanists in Europe, all the more
ardent, perhaps, because he was suspected of leaning to

286 THE REFORMATION IN ENGLAND. [CH. VIII.

the Lutheran doctrine of Justification by Faith. When
Henry broke with the See of Rome, Pole had excited
intense indignation among his countrymen by writing a
book in which he apostrophized Henry with a virulence
surpassing Luther's, and summoned all the sovereigns
of Europe to unite for a holy crusade against the apostate
monarch. He had endeared himself still more to the
Roman Curia by another book, written on the eve of the
Council of Trent, in which, with remarkable audacity of
interpretation and ingenuity of argument, he proved from
the fifteenth chapter of the Acts that in a General Council
the Pope was all in all, and that ecclesiastics and laymen
were scarcely more than ciphers assembled to register
his decrees.

With Parliament Mary had no difficulty. As a contemporary ironically observed, they would have voted the
establishment of the Mahometan religion with equal
alacrity and zeal at the bidding of the Queen. Events,
therefore, moved quickly. Acts which had established
the Reformation in the previous reign were summarily
repealed. The Protestant Bishops were deprived of their
Sees, and Romanists installed in their place. The married
Clergy throughout the country were ejected from their
benefices. All strangers who held heretical doctrines
were banished from the country. The Episcopal Courts
were restored. The oath of supremacy was no longer
administered. The new Bishops were ordered to extir-
pate heresy and destroy heretical books, to restore the
Mass, to use the Latin service, to revive the old holy days,
processions, and ceremonies, and to ordain anew the
Clergy who had received ordination from heretics. All
Acts, Articles, and Provisions which had been made in
Henry's reign to the detriment of the See of Rome
were repealed.

It was not long before everything resumed its wonted
aspect as in the golden days of Mary's childhood.
Harpsfield, Chaplain to the Bishop of London, in a sermon

preached before Convocation, graphically described the wolves who had entered into the flock, the countless souls which they had plunged into hell, the pernicious doctrines which they had introduced, the Scriptures which they had corrupted, the slanders which they disseminated against the Catholic clergy, the ceaseless battles which they waged against the truth of the Gospel, and the new Sacraments, new rites, and new manners which they had devised. Feckenham, Abbot of Westminster, preached on Transubstantiation to a great and splendid auditory, who listened to him with the same devout attention with which, not long before, they had listened to Latimer. On Saint Catherine's day the clergy of Saint Paul's went in procession round Saint Paul's steeple, bearing an image of Saint Catherine and carrying five hundred lights. The Universities were purified from heretical and married Heads and Fellows. Walls of churches, which before had been cleansed of pictures, were now cleansed of texts. The Apostles' Mass was resumed at Saint Paul's. In the service books the Pope and Saint Thomas of Canterbury were restored to the place of honour.

At the close of 1554 the great work was crowned by the solemn reconciliation of the kingdom to the Vicar of Christ. Pope Julius the Third appointed Pole as Papal Legate. With a thankful heart, after long years of absence, the illustrious exile set foot once more upon his native soil to fulfil the most blessed of all missions. In presence of the King and Queen, the members of both Houses listened on bended knees to the absolution which the Legate was empowered to pronounce. No legislative assembly in Europe can have needed it more sorely.

But the brightness of these glorious days was darkened by an unexpected cloud. The terrible words " sacrilege " and " confiscation of Church property " were whispered. Instantly all the virtue of the English legislators was on fire. They had gladly changed their religion at the Queen's command, but their consciences forbade them to surrender a single acre which they had received or appropriated. They intimated in the plainest language that there was a definite limit to their obedience, whether to their spiritual or their temporal Head. Even the Convocation of Canterbury supported their claim. Mary and Pole were deeply mortified, but were forced to yield. The Legate not only confirmed all the present owners in their possession of Church lands, but he also secured them in the most express terms against any disturbance through the action of General or Provincial Councils, or through decretal epistles issued by the Pope. Having granted this dispensation with a very bad grace, Pole urged them to do for the sake of their own salvation what the Church would not compel them to do, keeping before their eyes the severity of God's judgment against the sacrilegious Belshazzar. The owners of Church property received this admonition in respectful silence, feeling that they would gladly run the risk of Belshazzar's punishment if they could only get another chance of imitating his example.

Thus far Mary had done no more than the Council had done in Edward's reign. But neither she nor her advisers were content to stop here. Spanish example and Spanish influence suggested the founding of an English Inquisition, which could not indeed emulate the thorough and searching methods of its Spanish pattern, but might be able to intimidate English heretics and to vindicate English Catholicism. In 1555 orders were given to Justices of the Peace to travel on circuit, observing the religious state of the districts in every part of the country, keeping a special watch upon all Preachers, ferreting out all secret meetings and conventicles, and appointing men in every parish to act as eavesdroppers and send in confidential reports of the acts and words of their neighbours. Under such a system there was no fear of heretics escaping. The arrests were numerous; the prisons were rapidly filled; and the government had ample opportunity of selecting its

victims.   An obsequious Parliament, secure in the consciousness of its own consistency and orthodoxy, renewed
Henry the Fourth's and Henry the Fifth's statutes against
which the Parliament of Edward the Sixth had repealed;
heretics and the Catholic persecution had free course.

What excites surprise is that the number of martyrs
was not greater.   The most liberal estimate falls short of
four hundred, fewer than were slain in a single town
of France at the St. Bartholomew, fewer than suffered in
a single month under Alva in the Low Countries.   It is
difficult to assign a reason for this.   The executors of
Mary's decree may have been less zealous for persecution
than the Queen; or as Englishmen they may have
mistrusted the Spanish methods of ensuring orthodoxy;
or they may have half relented when they saw the
constancy of the sufferers; or the consciousness of their
own weakness in days not long gone by may have filled
them with misgivings; or they may have believed from
motives of policy that a partial and intermittent persecution, like the hanging of ringleaders after an insurrection
or a riot, would prove as effectual a deterrent as a wholesale massacre.   Whatever the reason may have been, the
result proved how mistaken a half-hearted and one-sided
justice was, and how little was gained by the arbitrary
selection of a handful of heretics out of a great multitude.

The fiery trial at once separated the sterling gold from
the alloy.   Hooper, whose ceaseless labours moved the
astonishment and admiration even of foreigners, who did
more for the vital interests of his Church in a few years
than Cranmer had done during the whole of his long
Primacy, and who silenced the sneers of his enemies by
showing that he who is faithful to conscience in that
which is least is faithful also in much, died in his Cathedral
city with a humble steadfastness worthy of the cause for
which he suffered.   Not less worthy of admiration was
the conduct of the two noble Prelates, Ridley and Latimer,
of Rogers, the editor of Tyndale's version of the Bible,

and of others like them.   Two Bishops, Barlow and
Scory, recanted; so did Jewell, afterwards Bishop of
Salisbury, and the author of the celebrated defence of the
Church of England. Cranmer's recantation was the most
pusillanimous act of a pusillanimous life. Fortunately for
his fame, his enemies in their malice and vindictiveness
overreached themselves. Determined that he should die
in spite of his recantation, they gave him an opportunity
of which he availed himself; and he met his end with a
calm dignity and contrition which have more than half
redeemed the disgrace of his apostasy. Sir John Cheke,
one of the most distinguished Cambridge scholars of his
day, the tutor and friend of Edward the Sixth, was kid-
napped in the Low Countries, brought over to London,
and forced to save his life by twice pronouncing a public
recantation couched in terms which raise an involuntary
blush on the reader's cheek as he peruses them. Not
satisfied with this degradation of so illustrious a renegade,
his enemies forced him to sit with them on the judgment
seat at the trial of heretics.

But it may be questioned whether the heroism of
distinguished Protestants made as great an impression
upon the popular imagination as the faithfulness unto
death of the many unknown believers, young and old,
men and women. Soon after the beginning of the persecution five men and two women, including a priest, a
gentleman of the Inner Temple, and the daughter of
parents who had been previously burnt, suffered at Smithfield early on a winter's morning. Though a proclamation
had been made throughout London overnight that no
young people should be present at the execution, the
crowds which assembled were greater than on any similar
occasion. Some months later, when eleven men and two
women were burnt at Stratford Bow, an enormous crowd,
computed to number twenty thousand, assembled to
witness the constancy of the sufferers, and to exhort and
comfort them. On another occasion twenty-two more

were sent from Colchester to London. Their journey resembled a triumphal procession. At Stratford Bow they were met by companies of "professors" of the Gospel, who greeted them with words of good cheer; and as they moved on, the sympathizing crowd swelled, till by the time they reached Fulham, where the Bishop was residing, the assembly numbered more than one thousand, to the surprise and indignation of the Prelate, who took care to reprove the Lord Mayor and the Sheriffs for their carelessness and indifference. Later on, nine more heretics were burnt in Colchester on one day, in presence of their nearest relations, their wives and their children, who, instead of urging them to save their lives by subscribing and recanting, earnestly adjured them to stand fast in the truth even unto death. At the close of Mary's reign a still more remarkable scene was witnessed, at which Bentham, afterwards Bishop of Lichfield, was present. Seven men were burnt at Smithfield; and the Romanist authorities, alarmed at the marks of strong sympathy which previous executions had evoked, issued a severe proclamation that no one on pain of death should approach them, touch them, speak to them, or comfort them. Yet in spite of the proclamation, and the threats of the Sheriff and officers who superintended the executions, the spectators took them by the hand and spoke comfortably to them, Bentham himself crying aloud, as the fires were lighted, " We know that they are the people of God, and we cannot choose but wish well to them," adding, " God Almighty, for Christ's sake, strengthen them." The multitudes who were present shouted in response, " Amen, amen," to the astonishment of the executioners. After this manner the inextinguishable fire of a new faith had been kindled in thousands of hearts at the stake of the English martyrs.

Even apart from the effect of the public executions, the seed of the new doctrines was being silently sown throughout the reign of Mary in all parts of the country, and bore fruit more abundantly than in the season of sunshine and prosperity under Edward. The watchfulness and severity of Pole and his coadjutors could not quench the zeal of the Evangelical teachers. Men sent letters from prison, sometimes written in their own blood, full of exhortation and warning for those who were still at liberty; prisoners were visited during their confinement by devoted friends at the risk of their own lives, and were confirmed by the mutual faith both of the bond and the free; others, to refute the calumny of their enemies, who did not scruple to say that every heretic had a different creed, drew up confessions of faith; these, reproduced in numerous transcriptions and copies and scattered broadcast, served the double purpose of testifying to the truth and spreading the knowledge of it abroad. When Priests and Ministers had been arrested or had fled from the country, simple Laymen, wheelwrights, tailors, weavers, or serving-men, took up the mantle which had fallen from the prophet's shoulders, presided over the assemblies of the faithful, read to them the Scriptures, the letters of martyrs and prisoners, and edifying books, prayed with them, and exhorted them to hold fast that which they had that no man might take their crown. Meetings were held sometimes in woods, sometimes in private houses, sometimes even in churches. In Essex godly men travelled from place to place, preaching and exhorting. Persecution often seemed to fan the flame of zeal. The priest of an Essex parish in the patronage of Bonner wrote a letter to the Bishop complaining bitterly that the death of the heretics had not cowed but emboldened the survivors; they refused to attend church, seduced others to absent themselves, and met on Sundays in different houses during the time of service. In Colchester the Parish Priests were openly mocked in the streets and called knaves; the Mass was reviled and blasphemed in every house and tavern; and seditious talk was as rife as though " no lords and commissioners had been sent for the reformation of it." Even under the shadow of Mary's throne, in the heart of London, heresy raised its head more boldly at the close than at the beginning of her reign. For fear of the Cardinal's and Bishop's spies the place of meeting was constantly changed; one congregation, of which Bentham was the Minister, met sometimes at Sir Thomas Cardine's house in Blackfriars, sometimes in Aldgate, now in a clothworker's loft in the great conduit of Cheapside, then in a ship at Billingsgate, again in a ship lying between Ratcliff and Rotherhithe, at other times in Pudden Lane, in Thames Street, in Bow churchyard, in Islington, or in the neighbouring fields. Sometimes the meetings were held in the daytime, often at night; sometimes a hundred, sometimes even more met together, the numbers increasing instead of diminishing towards the end of Mary's reign. At these services collections were made for the Evangelical prisoners, and a sum equal to a hundred pounds of our present money was contributed at one time. Even the activity of the spies was baffled by the restless energy of the "professors." It was sometimes baffled in a more unexpected manner by the conversion of the spy, who fell down before them and confessed that God was among them of a truth. Even in the North of England, which had been least touched by the new doctrines, faithful Preachers were actively labouring—Marsh, who was burnt at Chester; Best, afterwards Bishop of Carlisle, who taught in Yorkshire; and others who moved about from place to place in Lancashire and the adjoining counties, preaching to select companies and administering the Eucharist.

This sketch of the Reformation during Mary's reign would be imperfect without some notice of the exiles for religion's sake. The warm welcome which had been extended in England during Edward's reign to the refugees of the Reformed Churches was amply repaid to the fugitives whom Mary's measures compelled to fly. The proximity of the Eastern counties to the Continent made escape comparatively easy; it was made still easier by the sympathy with the Evangelical doctrines, which was stronger in the Eastern counties than in any other part of the country. The fugitives, including most of those who afterwards took a prominent place in the Church of England under Elizabeth, settled in German and Swiss towns, from Emden and Duisberg in the north to Geneva and Zurich in the south. Everywhere they were received with open arms, except in districts where the civic authorities were under the control of the straitest sect of the Lutheran Church. For the Eucharistic doctrine of the Anglican Prayer Book was too unmistakably modelled upon Calvin's to be tolerated by pure Lutherans. This difference was emphasized in 1555 by a Lutheran publication to prove the ubiquity of the natural Body of Christ, a doctrine which the Prayer Book expressly disavowed. Indirectly the period of their banishment had important results for the exiles. For at that time the literary activity of Germany was to the literary activity of England what England's was to Spain's three centuries later. To come into contact with the literary and learned circles of Frankfort, Strasburg, and Zurich, was in itself a liberal education for Englishmen in the middle of the sixteenth century. The exiles discussed the great questions of the day with distinguished foreigners, pursued their studies with renewed zest amid such favourable surroundings, assisted in the working of famous printing-presses at Emden, Geneva, and Basle, and prepared works of their own to be published in their new home. The Genevan Bible was one monument of their labours, and the great martyrology of Fox, originally written and printed in Latin, was another. In addition to these works, letters and pamphlets, some hortatory and addressed to the persecuted brethren in their native country, others controversial replies to Romanist publications, others dealing with important theological questions of the day, were issued and found their way to England, in spite of the severe censorship which Mary exercised and the ruthless punishments which she threatened.

When Mary died at the close of 1558, after a reign
of five years, her religious policy had definitely failed.
Gardiner had died two years previously, and Pole passed
away within a few hours of the Queen's death. Of the
four able and determined confederates who had united to
replace Romanism on its lost throne, only Bonner was
left. At no time had their attempt been greeted with
enthusiasm, and the methods which they had adopted
did not make their cause more attractive. The Spanish
marriage had been the fatal mistake of Mary's life. Parliament disliked it, the people disliked it ; and when Philip
with his Spaniards came to England, the dislike became
more violent. Wherever the Spaniards had gone, they
had excited the same fierce antipathy, in Germany, in the
Low Countries, and in England. Mary's devotion to her
husband did not soothe the suspicious temper of her
subjects. The prevalent immorality was attributed to
Spanish vice ; the fires of persecution were set down to
Spanish bigotry ; and when the war with France in which
Mary had been entangled by the Spanish alliance led to
the loss of Calais, the prophets of evil naturally triumphed.
The cause of Romanism suffered from its connection
with the hated nation. It suffered also from the want of
intelligent advocacy and support. The restoration which
Mary had carried out was purely external and superficial.
No systematic attempt was made to confront the arguments of the Protestants with arguments as plausible, if
not as cogent. The zeal and enthusiasm of the Protestants
were not encountered by zeal and enthusiasm as deep and
as sincere. The literary achievements of the Romanists
were as insignificant as they had been in the preceding
reigns. One learned Doctor wrote a book in support of
clerical celibacy, as though this were one of the cardinal
doctrines of the Christian faith. Another learned Doctor,
with greater boldness if not with greater wisdom, wrote a
treatise containing more than thirty arguments to prove
the evils which must necessarily follow the publication

of the Bible in an English version. He affirmed that an English Bible was the source of heresies, of spiritual death, and of contempt of all holy mysteries; that the universal Church of Christ had never allowed or approved of the Scriptures in the vulgar tongue; and that the authority of the Church was above the authority of Scripture. Bonner paid the Anglican Church the high honour of imitating the Book of Homilies by a very inferior Romanist imitation. Of able and moving preachers, who could hold the attention, and go to the heart, of large assemblies, composed of all classes, by sermons on the deepest verities of religion, we hear nothing. Still less do we hear of Bishops who supervised their dioceses and laboured among their people with the self-denying devotion of Hooper. And since the new system had been established, there was not a professor at either University who could be deemed worthy to loose the shoe's latchet of Bucer, or Martyr, or Fagius, or Cheke.

That the accession of Elizabeth should have been the cause of another religious revolution in England was only natural. From her earliest years there had been a tacit rivalry between the two sisters, which, as time went on, deepened into unconcealed dislike and mistrust. In character there was a marked difference between them. Mary was as much a religious bigot as any of her contemporaries, probably even more than her husband: Elizabeth had as small a share of bigotry as Maximilian of Austria, or Maurice of Saxony. The former regulated her policy by her religious aims and prejudices; the latter subordinated religion to politics. Mary betrayed the strain of southern blood in her nature by the passionate emotion which on more than one momentous occasion enslaved her, which warped her judgment and dimmed the clearness of her insight. Elizabeth, though she shared to the full the wayward caprices of the weakest of her sex, was too sensible, too completely mistress of herself, to allow her personal feelings to override her sounder judgment, or to endanger the highest interests of her nation and her crown. Mary said what she thought, and carried out what she had resolved, without counting the cost ; Elizabeth weighed every word and every action in the nicest scales, hesitated and paused at every turn of the balance, and became so guarded in what she said and in what she did that she proved herself as complete a mistress of diplomatic prevarication and of political evasion as Francis the First or Charles the Fifth. On one side of their character alone was there a close resemblance between the sisters : both had inherited from their father the masterful temper which overbore all obstacles, and the firm resolve to hold the reins, as well as to wear the crown, of sovereignty.

The caution with which Elizabeth proceeded in religious matters was in perfect harmony with her character. During her sister's reign she had conformed to the established Church, and had attended Mass—a bowing to false Gods with which Knox was not slow to reproach her. Many months after her accession she perplexed and alarmed her ecclesiastical Councillors by her unaccountable aversion to religious changes which seemed to them absolutely necessary. At one time she drove her Bishops half distracted by persistently retaining a crucifix and lighted candles in her chapel when they officiated. At another time, with an obstinacy which seemed to them almost impious, she refused to order the removal of images from churches in spite of their heart-broken remonstrances. Only with great difficulty could she be persuaded to yield to the elaborate arguments of the Reformers, and to allow Communion Tables to be substituted for altars. To the marriage of the Clergy she felt so deep-rooted an aversion that she declined to make it legal, and forced the Primate of the Anglican Church to take the humiliating step of legitimizing his son. Yet at the beginning of her reign she forbade the officiating Bishop to elevate the consecrated elements ; and when

Nowell, Dean of St. Paul's, three years later, placed in her seat as a New Year's gift a prayer-book containing pictures and woodcuts of Saints and Martyrs, she hurried to the vestry, rated him soundly, and accused him of wishing to lead her into "idolatry." These inconsistencies in her religious views made it easy for her to steer a middle course at the beginning of her reign.

Accordingly at first all went on as in the days of Mary. Mass was celebrated in the churches according to the Medieval ritual: the Bishops and Abbots remained in undisturbed possession of their seats in the House of Lords. The only troubles were caused by the riotous conduct of the Protestants at Dover, in Suffolk, and in London, who overthrew images, defaced churches, and damaged vestments and missals; and by the intemperate language of Romanist preachers, who, probably from a presentiment of coming changes, did not scruple to cast doubts upon the Queen's legitimacy. The former were sternly repressed by the Council, and the latter were checked by a proclamation which forbade all preaching for the present. Meanwhile the work of reformation was secretly prepared; the dangers which it involved, and the method by which it might be effectually carried out, were carefully discussed; a cautious beginning was made by allowing the Communion in both kinds. The difficulties which unavoidably attended a change were increased by the presence of a Lutheran party, who advocated the belief in consubstantiation, the retention of crucifixes and images, and the receiving of the consecrated bread with the mouth and not with the hand.

At length, when Parliament met, the Bills which were introduced and carried through both Houses in the early months of 1559 left no doubt what the Queen's intentions were. The Firstfruits and Tithes which Mary had restored to the Church were given back to the Crown, in order to defray the " huge, innumerable, and inestimable charges " of the royal estate ; all the pains and penalties which heretics had suffered in the preceding reigns were annulled; the supremacy in ecclesiastical causes was once more given to the Sovereign; all members of the Clergy as well as of the Laity who held any office were to take an oath that the Queen "is the only Supreme Governor of this realm," and the refusal to take this oath involved the loss of office; finally, an Act of Uniformity made the use of the Common Prayer Book compulsory on and after June 24th. In the divisions on these Bills not more than nine of the Temporal Lords voted in the minority on any occasion: eight or nine of Mary's Bishops were always among the non-contents.

Thus within the space of a few years the English Parliament for the third time formally recanted its religious belief. It is vain to give any creditable reason for this amazing fact. To suppose that in making these changes the hereditary legislators and the representatives of the English people were swayed by spiritual zeal or religious conviction would be the height of absurdity. Even if we give the members of Elizabeth's Parliament full credit for their disgust at a brutal persecution, their hatred of everything Spanish, and their shame at the national disaster which the Spanish alliance had brought upon them, the action of the successive Parliaments still remains inexplicable. The only explanation which bears even a semblance of plausibility is, that the great majority of English laymen in questions of faith had not a spark of sincere conviction, of chivalrous honour, or even of common self-respect; that they regarded all forms of belief as equally indifferent to the legislator and equally serviceable to the egotist; and that they estimated the value of conflicting creeds by the diminution of national taxation and the increase of individual wealth. It is a significant fact that the only Bill on which the Lay Peers in Elizabeth's first Parliament voted with the Government, *nemine contradicente*, was the Bill which enriched the Crown at the expense of the Church. It is a curious commentary on this vote that, as soon as the bishoprics fell vacant by the deprivation of the Marian prelates, Elizabeth hastened, under the fair name of "exchange," to replenish her privy purse and the national exchequer by seizing their richest estates and giving them impoverished rectories and worthless tithes in return.

It was unfortunate for Mary's Bishops that by their conduct they gave their opponents a colourable pretext for deserting their cause. It was resolved that at the end of March picked champions of both the religious parties should hold a public disputation. Three questions were selected for discussion—the use of the vulgar tongue in the services of the Church, the right of every national Church to change its ceremonies and rites, and the propitiatory sacrifice of the Mass. Definite conditions of debate were laid down and accepted by both sides. If we may believe one who was present, the Romanist spokesman opened the discussion with a virulent invective, enunciated the historical fact that Saint Peter and Saint Paul always used the Latin language, and argued that it was inexpedient for the people to understand the public prayers, because ignorance was the mother of true piety. The Protestants replied in a temperate and reasonable tone, and at the conclusion obtained an almost unanimous vote in their favour. At the next meeting, when a great crowd of nobles had assembled, the Romanist Bishops suddenly demanded a change in the proceedings, and when they were held to the terms of their agreement, declined to speak at all. The general opinion naturally was that such a breach of faith was the result of conscious weakness.

The Reformation now made rapid progress. As soon as the proclamation which prohibited preaching was withdrawn, the leaders of the Reformed party were summoned to preach before the Queen and at Saint Paul's. Elizabeth eagerly read the letters written by Bullinger and Peter Martyr, and expressed a desire to recall the latter to England. The Pope made a fruitless attempt to support his adherents by sending a Nuncio to Elizabeth. When the news of his coming reached England, it was resolved to refuse him admittance. Between January and the end of June a fierce controversy raged between the two parties over the Book of Common Prayer. The Romanists denied that the book could be imposed upon Christians, because it had not been authorized by the universal Church of Christ assembled in a General Council, because it had not been approved even by the English Clergy, and because it had been forced upon the Church by the Laity, who had nothing to do with spiritual matters. They added that without the consent of the Clergy in Parliament no law affecting religion could be passed. Feckenham, Abbot of Westminster, to stem the tide of prejudice against the monastic Orders, declared in the House of Lords that the Nazarites, the Prophets, Christ, and the Apostles had been monks. But the current was setting too strongly against the Church of Rome for opposition of this kind to have any effect. The feeling against the Marian Bishops was especially strong; they scarcely dared to venture abroad for fear of being mobbed, and when they appeared in public, many called them " butchers " to their face.

If, as report said, the Bishops trusted in Elizabeth's inability to replace them, and fancied that a show of firmness on their part would induce her to retain them, they were grievously disappointed. They may have interpreted the summons to appear before her, and the appeal which she made to them personally, as a sign of weakness. The Archbishop of York, in the name of the rest, reminded the Queen of her sister's Catholic zeal, and of Mary's promise soon after her coronation to suppress all heresies—a promise which was binding upon herself, her successors, and the whole realm. Elizabeth's answer was prompt and decisive : like Joshua, she and her people would serve the Lord ; no contract made by her sister could bind her ; she followed the example of her

predecessors, who had rejected the usurped authority of the
Bishop of Rome and all foreign jurisdiction; henceforth
she would regard any of her subjects who acknowledged
the power of the Pope or any foreign potentate as enemies
to God and to herself. The oath of supremacy was then
tendered to the Bishops, but all, with the exception of the
Bishop of Llandaff, refused to take it, and were deprived
of their Sees.

In the low ebb to which public morality had sunk in
England the sacrifice which the Romanist Bishops made
to their conscientious convictions must be regarded as
eminently honourable to them; and the treatment which
they received after their deprivation proves that the more
liberal and fair-minded among their opponents looked at
their conduct in this light. The example of the Bishops
was followed by nearly a hundred dignitaries of the
Church, Abbots, Deans, Archdeacons, Prebendaries, and
Heads of Colleges. But of the rest of the Clergy less than
a hundred out of more than nine thousand raised any
objection. It would be too much to expect that the rank
and file of the beneficed incumbents should have felt
scruples, when the vast majority of the Lords and Commons felt none; or should have declined an oath which
Henry's Prelates had found no difficulty in taking. But
this wholesale conversion left a root of bitterness behind
it. It was possible for men to disown the Supremacy of
the Pope without rejecting a single one of the Medieval
doctrines which were so offensive to the Reformers.
Apparently no attempt was made to test the religious
beliefs of those who quietly took the oath and silently
accepted the Book of Common Prayer. Accordingly, only
a few years later men who were brought up before the
ecclesiastical Commissioners for declining to attend their
parish churches, excused themselves on the ground that
their Minister was a Papist in disguise, or that he had
persecuted God's saints in Mary's time, and was now
permitted to hold his living without having made any sort

of recantation. In Lancashire, where avowed Romanist priests were harboured, churches were shut up, the use of the Prayer Book was discontinued, and parishes were only supplied with priests who had already been deprived of their livings, it was thought necessary to establish an ecclesiastical commission, and the Queen publicly reprimanded the Bishop of Chester for his negligence and want of energy. Indeed, it may be questioned whether the vitality and activity of the Romanist party during Elizabeth's reign were not greatly fostered by the easy-going policy which suffered incumbents to enjoy the benefices of the Church of England and to hold the doctrines of the Church of Rome.

On August 1st, 1559, Matthew Parker, formerly Chaplain to Anne Boleyn and Henry the Eighth, afterwards Master of Christ's College, Cambridge, and Dean of Lincoln, was elected Archbishop of Canterbury by the Dean and Chapter. The other vacant Sees were rapidly filled up with leading members of the Reformed party. A Visitation was set on foot at the same time, and the picture which it gives us of the state of the Church is melancholy enough. Sermons were seldom preached; many of the Incumbents and Curates were non-residents, and their duties were discharged by ignorant persons ; many discouraged their parishioners from reading the Bible either in English or Latin, extolled pilgrimages, images, relics, and vain repetition of prayers, frequented alehouses and taverns, and took to drinking, rioting, and gambling ; many had bought their benefices or obtained them by fraud. The Laity often bore as bad a character as the Clergy. In London the effect of the Visitation was seen in the destruction of roods, images of the Virgin Mary, Saint John, and other Saints, vestments, altar cloths, missals, banners, and sepulchres. About the same time Jewell was commissioned to travel through Reading, Gloucester, Bristol, Bath, Wells, Exeter, Cornwall, and Dorsetshire. Everywhere, even in places where he expected to find most opposition, the people were well disposed to the Reformed faith.   But he reported that during Mary's reign a complete wilderness of superstition had sprung up : votive relics of Saints, the nails with which Christ had been fastened to the Cross, and fragments of the true Cross, abounded ; the most obstinate opponents whom he encountered were the Romanist priests, chiefly those who had professed the Evangelical doctrines. In Jewell's opinion congregational singing had produced an extraordinary effect.   The practice originated in a small London Church, had immediately been taken up by the neighbouring Churches, and had eventually spread to distant towns, which vied with one another in maintaining the laudable custom.   He had seen at Paul's Cross great congregations of 6,000 people, old and young, men and women, join in the singing of Psalms and hymns.

But the difficulties which hindered the progress of true religion were acknowledged and deplored by the Laity and Clergy alike.   Lord Keeper Bacon, at the opening of Elizabeth's second Parliament, blamed the Preachers for lack of diligence in their vocation, and the Laity for want of faith and for ungodly living : he complained that, owing to the imperfect discipline of the Church, the due ceremonies were omitted or neglected, few came to Church, and all lived as they listed.   The Speaker of the House of Commons on the same occasion bewailed the decay of Schools : formerly England had maintained 10,000 scholars, but now he knew of great market-towns which were left without Preachers or Schools : at least 100 more schools were required, and for want of these and of efficient teachers, the rising generation were growing up in ignorance.   The Bishops confessed that there was still an immense number of Romanists.   So great was the deficiency of Clergy that Ministers were forced to serve three or four Churches.   In the four Archdeaconries of the Diocese of Norwich, Bishop Parkhurst reported that there were about 430 Parishes without Incumbents, or

only partially served by Curates.   The incomes of many
Vicarages were so reduced, partly owing to the payment
of tithes which had been left unpaid by former Incumbents, partly owing to the pensions with which they had
been unjustly charged at the dissolution of the Monasteries, that they could no longer support a resident Vicar,
and the parishioners were in danger of lapsing into
heathenism.   Out of a hundred Clergymen who administered the Sacraments scarcely one was able and willing
to preach the Gospel.   How greatly a zealous and competent preacher was valued is proved by the interesting
account which Lever gives of his enthusiastic reception
in Coventry.   Sunday was generally disregarded :   it was
the day commonly chosen for holding fairs and markets ;
guests were received at inns and hostelries, and shops
were opened during the time of divine service ; artisans
laboured, and men went about their ordinary business,
as if it were a weekday.   The state of the Universities
was described by an eminent authority as deplorable ;
they had no godliness, no religion, no teacher, no hope
of revival.   The study of divinity in particular was put
aside, because it was seen how ecclesiastical preferments
were seized by laymen, how the revenues of the Church
were curtailed, and how the dependants of great men
received promotion to the detriment of learned scholars
who had no patrons.   " There are many good and zealous
men in England," wrote a distinguished Bishop, " there are
many lukewarm.   But I fear many evils are impending.
For almost all are covetous, all love gifts.   There is no truth,
no liberality, no knowledge of God.   Men have broken out
into cursing, lying, murders, thefts, and adulteries."

In 1559 Injunctions were issued by the Queen.   Though
many of these were practically identical with Edward's, a
considerable number were new, and some of these threw
an interesting light upon several points in Elizabeth's
religious settlement.   No one should talk or argue about
Scripture rashly or contentiously, but should discuss it, if

occasion offered, humbly, reverently, and in the fear of God, for his comfort and better understanding. Every Parson, Vicar, or Curate on each holy-day, for half an hour at least before evening prayers, should instruct his young parishioners in the Ten Commandments, the Creed, and the Lord's Prayer, and should teach them the Catechism, and examine them in it. The Bishops should appoint three or four discreet and godly men in every parish to see that the parishioners attended service on Sundays and holy-days, to admonish all defaulters, and if they saw no amendment, to report them to the Bishop. Since all changes, especially in rites and ceremonies, breed discord and lead to abusive words and railings, the Queen orders all her subjects to abstain from vain and contentious disputes about religion, and to refrain from abusive terms, such as " Papist," " Schismatic," and " Sacramentary." To check the printing of "unfruitful, vain, and infamous" publications, printers were strictly forbidden to issue any book without the Queen's licence; and the same rule applied to pamphlets, plays, and ballads. As the marriage of the Clergy had in many cases given scandal, it was ordered that no Priest or Deacon should in future marry without the advice and approval of the Bishop of the Diocese and of two Justices of the Peace living in the neighbourhood, on pain of losing his office. Even Bishops might not marry without the approval of the Metropolitan of the Province. To ensure the Clergy receiving the honour and reverence due to the special Messengers and Ministers of God, the Queen commanded that all beneficed Clergy and members of the Universities should wear seemly habits, garments, and square caps, "not thereby meaning to attribute any holiness or special worthiness to the said garments."

On one point Elizabeth was inflexibly consistent. She would not listen to any suggestion that she should on any plea relax the severity of the laws. She would listen to arguments before she had finally decided; she would

listen to none afterwards. The question was then transferred from the domain of religion to the domain of
politics ; and she would not suffer anyone to trench upon
her rights or to impugn her policy as a Sovereign. The
welfare of the body politic demanded that there should be
one Head and one Law: and all must without demur obey
the one Head and bow to the one Law. On two occasions
in the early part of her reign the Emperor Ferdinand
interceded on behalf of her Romanist subjects. Ferdinand,
who had superintended the religious compromise of the
Diet of Augsburg, apparently came to the conclusion that
Elizabeth could without difficulty make a similar arrangement in England. He begged, therefore, that she would
not treat the Romanists as traitors, if they could not with
a clear conscience take the oath of supremacy ; that she
would grant them toleration instead of oppressing and
banishing them ; and that in all cities and large towns she
would assign them churches where they could worship
undisturbed. The answers which Elizabeth sent him were
characteristic. She had shown favour to her Catholic
subjects by remitting their punishments, though they had
endangered the welfare of the Commonwealth by openly
resisting the laws : to grant them churches in which to
hold their own services was impossible ; such a concession
would defeat the laws which her Parliament had made,
and would imperil the safety of her kingdom.

But there was another class of her subjects who were
even more important than the Romanists, and to whom
she meted out the same strict measure. These were the
zealous Protestants, who during the Marian persecution
had fled abroad, had been warmly and hospitably received
by the Reformed Churches of the Continent, and had,
like the Scottish Reformers, conceived a strong admiration
for the more stringent discipline and the simpler forms of
worship of which they had for many months been the eye-
witnesses. They had already during the time of their
exile given proof of the strength of their scruples and the

tenacity of their purpose. In the English Church at
Frankfort there had been serious dissensions: Knox had
sided strongly with the more rigid party; the congregation
had been broken up; bitter speeches had been bandied to
and fro; and each party had accused the other of unfair
dealing. When the exiles returned to England after
Mary's death, it became evident at once that the smoul-
dering fires were ready to break out afresh. The sterner
spirits observed with deep regret that no discipline
deserving the name was established in the Church; that
the Ministers were unworthily burdened with secular obli-
gations, such as the payment of Firstfruits and Tithes; and
that Bishops, in defiance of the law and practice of the
Early Church, were appointed without the consent of the
clergy or laity. Their hatred of the Church of Rome had
been increased tenfold by the sufferings of their persecuted
brethren under the ecclesiastical government of Mary and
Pole, and they regarded with an intense bitterness anything
which savoured of the ceremonies or the system of Rome.
How far the principles, afterwards known under the general
name of Puritanism, had spread among the Clergy as a
whole, was shown by two remarkable facts. Some of the
earliest Bishops appointed by Elizabeth, including Grindal
and Jewell, prayed the Queen that she would be pleased to
dispense with the use of the " Popish garments," against
which Hooper, the Bishop of Gloucester, had so strongly
protested in Edward's reign. But all Elizabeth's con-
servatism rose up in arms against the petitioners; she
remained immovable; Parliament sided with her, and
the Bishops wisely waived their objections. Again, in the
first Convocation after her accession, a proposal was made
in the Lower House that all Saints' days should be
abolished, that the use of the Cross in Baptism should
be discontinued, that kneeling at the celebration of the
Eucharist should be left to the discretion of the Ordinary,
and that organs should be removed. After a hot debate
this motion was only rejected by a bare majority.

It was, however, Elizabeth's Injunction about clerical dress which brought the dispute between the two parties to a climax, and verified the truth of Aristotle's profound maxim.* The Puritans declared that their conscience would not suffer them to conform to this Injunction: these garments had been worn and were still worn by the Mass-priests; they held them in the same abhorrence as the Roman soldier in Tertullian's famous story held the wreath, because it was polluted by the taint of idolatry; when the populace saw the Clergy "retaining the outward garb and the inward sentiments of Popery," could they fail to draw the conclusion that the Roman doctrine had been revived, or would be revived without delay? The moderate party retorted that the most unexceptionable reason for the clerical dress had been expressly given in the Injunction; that the Fathers of the English Reformation, who had sealed their faith with their blood, raised no objection to it; that it had been sanctioned by the distinguished foreign Reformers, Bucer and Peter Martyr; and that in indifferent matters the plain duty was to obey the sovereign as the supreme authority in Church and State. When these arguments proved fruitless, they resolved to appeal to arbitration. Among the Continental Reformers none was more widely and justly respected in England for his learning, his sound judgment, and his wise moderation than Bullinger, the disciple and the friend of Zwingli, and the Head of the Church of Zurich. No one could impeach his fidelity to the cause of the Reformation; no one could accuse him of the faintest partiality to anything Roman; his verdict, therefore, would surely be accepted as decisive. Bullinger without hesitation advised the Puritans to comply with the Injunction, adding the weighty argument that, if able and earnest friends of the Reformation left their posts at such a critical time, they ran the gravest risk of seeing them

* γίνονται μὲν ̑ουν αἱ στάσεις ̑ου περὶ μικρῶν, ἀλλ᾽ ἐκ μικρῶν.
—Arist. Politics, 157.

filled by lukewarm adherents or secret enemies of Evangelical truth. His letters produced as little effect as the remonstrances of the Bishops. The Puritans replied that by wearing the prescribed garments they would destroy and not edify the Church, that the Queen's wisdom and policy passed the wisdom of God, that they could not consent to see the Christian religion depend upon the caprice of Princes, and that, fearing to lose their own souls as well as to jeopardize the souls of others, they would leave the Church at whatever earthly cost. Elizabeth on her part was equally determined; these men were treading upon forbidden ground; they were laying down principles which it was not lawful for them to hold; they were attempting to set bounds to the power of the Queen and Parliament, and to draw subtle and dangerous distinctions between the obedience which was, and the obedience which was not, due to them : she would tolerate none such. Indignantly she called upon the Bishops to perform their duty; and the Bishops with unfeigned reluctance obeyed her commands.

Absurd as the arguments of the Puritans will appear to men of the twentieth century, and exaggerated as their scruples may seem, it is impossible to pass over their action in silence. For it resulted in giving the Reformation in England a character of its own. In no other country were two distinct parties formed, which agreed in all the chief doctrines of the Reformation, but differed irreconcilably on questions of subordinate importance. Yet, however much Puritanism weakened the national Church, it cannot be proved that it weakened the cause of the Reformation. For the impartial student of history will acknowledge that the representatives of it were the leaders in a movement which, for its moral, political, and religious effects, may justly rank with the greatest movements of modern times.

CHAPTER IX.

THE REFORMATION IN SCOTLAND.

THE Scottish Reformation in its origin, its progress, and its final results differed widely from the English. This difference may in great measure be explained by the difference in the position, the constitution, the historical antecedents, and the international relations of the Scottish and the English people. The Kings of Scotland at the close of the fifteenth and the beginning of the sixteenth century, partly owing to defects of character and partly in consequence of long minorities, enjoyed far less power and independence than their Tudor contemporaries. The Scottish nobility, as proud and as turbulent as in the early part of the Middle Ages, had not been broken and exterminated like the English by prolonged civil wars, and were able, as of old, to threaten their monarchs and to dictate to them their policy. The Scottish commonalty for the same reason were enabled to assert their claims and to enforce their opinions with a sturdy boldness to which the English burghers were strangers. The greater distance of Scotland from the mainland of Europe had restricted its commercial activity, and had made it less accessible than England to Continental influences and the spread of Continental opinions. Indeed, the Kingdom of France was the only Continental Power with which Scotland came into close contact : the influence of France and the alliance with France were of vital importance in modifying the fortunes of the Scottish people ; and the hatred of the English and the friendship with the French were for centuries the two pivots on which the foreign policy of Scotland turned.

It is a significant and suggestive fact that the beginning of the religious movement in Scotland dates from the martyrdom of Patrick Hamilton in 1528. Hamilton was a young man of unblemished character and remarkable intellectual powers, who had travelled on the Continent, had formed a friendship with Luther and Melanchthon, and had written a short treatise which proved how fully, how clearly, and how consistently he had embraced the Reformed doctrines. Hamilton's ability and reputation, and the pathetic circumstances of his tragic end, aroused general interest, and awakened a spirit of inquiry which soon bore fruit.

It is again a significant and suggestive fact that in Scotland the early opponents of the old system came from the bosom of the Medieval Church, from the two Orders which had been the most faithful and devoted supporters of the Papal power. One Friar, first at Dundee and afterwards at St. Andrews, publicly denounced the profligacy of the Bishops, and inveighed against the abuses connected with ecclesiastical miracles and the practice of excommunication. Another Friar, the confessor of James the Fifth, preached against the ignorance, the ambition, and the avarice of the Prelates, and declared that, if the Scottish Bishops were tested by the marks of a Bishop in St. Paul's Pastoral Epistles, there was not a single true Bishop in the whole realm. Three other Friars were put to death for their outspoken advocacy of the Reformed doctrines; and no one displayed more energy in persecuting than the King. But nothing could check the rising tide. Men eagerly read the new books; they discussed religious questions at private meetings; and merchants and sailors returning from foreign parts spread the news of the great changes which were in progress on the Continent, and the boldness with which they had heard the claims and the opinions of the Pope and Clergy canvassed.

The death of James the Fifth, the appointment of the Earl of Arran as Regent, and his unmistakable leaning to the Reformed doctrines, wrought a further change in favour of the Evangelical party. When the Scottish Parliament met in the Spring of 1543, a bold attack was made upon the Act which forbade the reading of any part of Scripture, and of any treatise or exposition to elucidate Scripture, in the vulgar tongue. Nothing revealed more clearly the strength of the new party and the weakness of their adversaries than the debate which followed. The Prelates asserted that the Church had forbidden the Bible to be read in any language except Hebrew, Greek, and Latin; but when taken to task they could neither give the reason for the prohibition, nor the time when it was published. Then they alleged the errors of the vernacular version; but on being pressed to point out the errors, they could only reply that "charity" was mistranslated by "love," which drew down upon them the ironical question, what they imagined the difference between the two words to be, and if they had any idea of the real meaning of the Greek "agape"? The result was that the clerical party were outvoted, and by the new Act everyone was at liberty to read the Bible in English, until (it was sarcastically added) the Prelates had revised and corrected the current version. Large numbers availed themselves of this concession. The Bible was everywhere seen in private houses. It became the fashion to carry New Testaments about. English commentaries were introduced into Scotland, and books on religious subjects were issued from the Scottish press.

This defeat made the Clergy redouble their efforts to suppress the Reformation. Arran's character was weak and vacillating, and an attempt to intimidate him proved completely successful. A terrible picture was drawn of the dangers which would attend a weakening of the Church and a change in the country's faith, of the enmity of Scotland's faithful ally, the Most Christian King, and of the doubt which would be thrown upon his own legitimacy, if the authority of the Pope, who had sanctioned his father's divorce from his first wife, were called in question. These arguments, and the threat that he would be deposed for disobedience to Holy Mother Church, determined the inconstant Regent; and the Scottish Reformers heard with mingled shame and indignation that Arran had slunk away to Stirling, had made his humble submission to Cardinal Beaton, had recanted his impious and heretical errors, and had received solemn absolution from his triumphant rival.

But the Cardinal's triumph was short-lived. His vaulting ambition overreached itself. He was surrounded and watched by remorseless enemies. The martyrdom of George Wishart, one of the purest and most persuasive of the Scottish Reformers, who had preached with great success in Montrose, Dundee, and Haddington, and who by an intrigue of the Queen Dowager had fallen into Beaton's power, filled up the cup of hatred against him. A conspiracy was formed, and he was suddenly cut off in the fulness of his power and fame.

It was at this time that a more powerful actor than any who had yet appeared in Scotland came forward on the troubled stage of religious and political life : a more persuasive advocate than any who had pleaded for the Reformed doctrines on Scottish soil lifted up his voice for the first time in a public assembly of his countrymen, and gave an irresistible impulse to the Scottish Reformation. In truth, it is scarcely too much to say that the victorious career of the new movement was due to John Knox, and that the Reformed Church of Scotland was his creation.

The work which Knox accomplished, and the influence which he exercised during his lifetime ; the leading position which he acquired and maintained among the distinguished and able men by whom he was surrounded ; the extraordinary admiration and reverence with which he inspired them and their successors ; the unity of doctrine

and discipline which he stamped upon the Church of
Scotland, and which even after the lapse of more than
three centuries remained unbroken and unimpaired ; the
revolution which he wrought in the current beliefs and
the popular prejudices of his countrymen; the masterly
skill with which he called out and brought into play the
best and greatest qualities of the Scottish character ; the
deep religious enthusiasm, unaided by any attractions of
poetry or art, with which he filled the Scottish people ; the
mighty and fruitful principle of political liberty which by
his precept and example he successfully impressed upon
his own and succeeding generations—these unique achievements mark him as the greatest Scotsman who has
devoted himself to the conduct of practical life, and give
him a place of exceptional distinction and importance
even among the foremost teachers and statesmen of his
age. This result is the more remarkable because some of
the striking features which adorned his most eminent
contemporaries were conspicuously lacking in Knox. In
boldness of conception and originality of genius he cannot
be compared with Luther and Calvin. In learning, in
sobriety, in critical power, in lucidity of exposition he
was far inferior to Zwingli, Bucer, and Peter Martyr. In
breadth of mind and comprehensiveness of judgment he
must, even on the most partial estimate, be placed
immeasurably below William of Orange and Gaspard de
Coligny, St. Aldegonde and Melanchthon. When he had
made up his mind on any question, he was incapable of
seeing that the slightest shred of reason or of argument
could be adduced in support of the contrary opinion.
When he passed sentence upon momentous political acts,
such as the murder of Rizzio or the misconduct of Mary
Stuart, he breathed the spirit, and spoke in the tone, of
an Old Testament prophet and not of a Christian apostle.
But these indisputable defects were far more than com-
pensated and redeemed by merits no less indisputable.
He resembled one of the impetuous mountain torrents of

his native land, which, forced to roll its waters between the narrow banks of a rock-bound channel, gains in speed and strength what it loses in breadth and volume. His glowing eloquence, his dialectical power, his shrewdness of wit, his complete mastery of the resources of his mother tongue, his strength of will, his force of mind, his indomitable resolution, his incisive dogmatism in religious and political questions, his rigid and unbending morality, his absolute unselfishness, his unswerving singleness of purpose, his transparent sincerity of character, above all, his unquenchable faith, gave him a supremacy over the hearts of his countrymen more powerful than any which had swayed them since the dawn of their history. Even in the darkest hour of his life, when he was toiling like a slave, chained to the oar of a French galley, when physical weakness had prostrated his body, and the hope deferred which maketh the heart sick had clouded his soul, he refused to abate one jot of his trust in the ordering of God's Providence, and foretold with something of prophetic insight his restoration to his native shores and the ultimate triumph of his cause.

Knox was born in 1505, being a few years younger than Melanchthon and a little older than his master, Calvin. Like so many of the leading Reformers, he had taken Orders before his adoption of the Reformed doctrines, and had taught the scholastic philosophy in the University of Glasgow, where he had received his education, and where George Buchanan, the celebrated scholar, political philosopher and historian, was his contemporary. Little is known of the mental and spiritual changes through which Knox passed, and which permanently shook his faith in the teaching of the Medieval Church. But the boldness with which he gave utterance to his altered opinions excited so deeply the alarm and hatred of the Scottish clergy that a plan was formed to assassinate him. Escaping from the toils, he became a constant attendant and ardent admirer of George Wishart, the martyr, and

after his death undertook the education of the sons of two
Lowland gentlemen.   He was still, however, in constant
danger, and, unable to find an asylum in England,
seriously thought of escaping to the Continent, when he
was persuaded by his kind patrons, whose esteem and
affection he had gained, to take refuge with them in the
Castle of St. Andrews, and to continue the education
of their children.   Here, by catechizing his pupils and
expounding the Scriptures in the parish church and the
castle chapel, he made so profound an impression on his
hearers that he received a public and unanimous call to
become their Minister.   With unfeigned reluctance and
many tears Knox accepted the office which he held himself
unworthy to fill.   But his ministry was of short duration.
St. Andrews was besieged by a combined force of Scottish
and French which had been mustered to avenge Beaton's
murder.   Knox sternly predicted that the corrupt life of
the defenders could not escape God's punishment, that
they were blind to the vision of the future which he clearly
saw, that the walls of whose strength and thickness they
boasted would prove no stronger than egg-shells, that
their reliance on English help was a broken reed, and
that they would be carried away into a strange land.
The result of the siege verified his forebodings : the
garrison was forced to surrender after a stubborn resistance, and Knox, with other prisoners, was carried to
France in the summer of 1547.

But before this disaster befell him, Knox had been able
to show his friends and his foes of what metal he was
made.   The Dean of St. Andrews had laid down the
sweeping proposition that the Church's authority was
absolute and supreme, that she had damned all Lutherans
and heretics, and that nothing more, therefore, was needed
to settle the controversy between the Romanists and the
Reformers.   Knox at once replied that, before the Church's
verdict could be accepted, it must be proved that she
possessed the marks by which God's Word described the

true Church. He was prepared to prove that, so far from
this being the case, the corrupt Church of Rome was the
synagogue of Satan, and that her Head was the Man of
Sin. His proposal was hailed with acclamation by his
delighted audience; they could not all read what he wrote,
but they could all hear what he preached; let him give
them in his next sermon the proof of what he asserted.
The following Sunday demonstrated for the first time the
extraordinary power of the Reformer's preaching. When
he had finished, loud cries were raised: "Others had
lopped at the branches of Popery, but he had struck at
the root: Wishart had never spoken so plainly. If the
Doctors and Masters of theology could not refute Knox,
their cause was lost; men saw now with other eyes than
in the days of old." The decisive victory which Knox
gained was a presage of his final triumph. Not only the
inmates of the castle but a large number of the townsmen
embraced the Reformed doctrines; and for the first
time in Scottish history the Eucharist was administered
according to the Reformed rite in one of the chief towns
of Scotland.

After Knox had obtained his release from his French
captivity, he gained a wide and varied experience as a
Minister of the Gospel in England, in Germany, in
Switzerland, and in France. Everywhere he displayed
the same fervent zeal, the same power as a preacher,
the same unbending temper, the same uncompromising
consistency. He refused without hesitation an English
Bishopric; he gained widespread notoriety by his denunciation of Charles the Fifth as a second Nero, and of
Mary Tudor as a second Jezebel. During his stay at
Geneva he conceived an unbounded admiration for Calvin
and his system. During his stay in France he saw with
his own eyes how the religious enthusiasm of the Huguenots
had infected all ranks of French society, and had produced an effect unparalleled in France since the mighty
wave of patriotism, a century before, had swept out the

English invader. With the keen scrutiny of a politician as well as of a theologian, he everywhere took the measure of the rival forces which were contending for the mastery in Western Europe. It was not till after the lapse of eight years that he once more set foot on his native soil in 1555.

Great were the changes which Scotland had witnessed during his absence. The injudicious policy of English statesmen had greatly increased the influence of the Queen Dowager. The Regent was deposed; his vanity was gratified by the title of Duke of Chatellerault, and his greed of gain by an increase of his fortune; and Mary of Guise took his place. But though these changes were unfavourable to the Scottish Reformers, the death of Edward the Sixth and the accession of Mary had swelled their ranks by the arrival of English exiles who had fled across the border from the flames of persecution. Harlow and Willock had prepared the ground for Knox by gathering small knots of the faithful around them and confirming them in faith and godliness by their earnest exhortations.

It was characteristic of the Reformer's consistency that his first act on arriving in Scotland was to denounce all compliance with the forms of the Medieval Church by attendance at Mass. The service of the Mass he declared to be idolatry, and to have any part or lot in countenancing idolatry was fraught with peril to the soul's salvation. The vehemence with which he overbore the arguments of those who were for facing both ways deepened the impression which he had made before. He was invited from house to house. One nobleman after another fell under his influence, and the names of his first converts included some of those who in future years shaped their country's destinies. Moving about with restless energy, he preached in Edinburgh, Ayr, Calder, Dun, and Mearns, and administered the Eucharist in both kinds to large numbers.

The success of Knox was increased by his opponents' mistakes.   In the middle of May, 1556, he was summoned by the ecclesiastical authorities to appear before them in the Black Friars' Church at Edinburgh.   Knox arrived in the capital to answer the summons, but found that it had been withdrawn, and had the pleasure of preaching to a larger congregation than he had ever addressed before in that city.   Among his auditors was the Earl Marischal, who was so delighted with the preacher's force and eloquence that he persuaded him to write a letter to the Queen Regent.   It is reported that Mary of Guise, with the natural arrogance of her House, after she had read the letter, tossed it with a scornful exclamation to the Bishop of Glasgow.   She little guessed what were the power and the resources of the new antagonist who had entered the lists against her.

Suddenly, in the midst of his labours, Knox received an urgent call to minister to the English Church in Geneva. As he had been their Pastor at Frankfort before his return to Scotland, he felt himself in duty bound to obey the summons, notwithstanding the pathetic remonstrances of his Scottish friends.   He could only assure them that, if " God blessed their small beginnings," and they summoned him to return, they should find him ready to comply with their request.   Scarcely had he sailed for France when the Scottish Bishops crowned their first mistake by a second still more serious: they again summoned him to appear, and publicly burnt him in effigy at the Cross of Edinburgh as a punishment for his contumacy.   This foolish act only recoiled upon their own heads.   Knox wrote and published a letter, addressed to the Nobility and Commons of Scotland, appealing against the unjust sentence, and his written defence proved as effective as his living speech.

The cause of the Reformation suffered little by the Reformer's absence.   The Evangelical doctrines were preached far and wide by Ministers who rivalled Knox in

zeal if not in ability and eloquence. Images of saints
were surreptitiously removed in different parts of the
country. The festival of St. Giles, the Patron Saint of
Edinburgh, evoked an unexpected outburst of opposition
to the Medieval ceremonies. The image was first drowned
and then burnt by an indignant crowd; the Queen Regent
was so overawed by the numbers and the determined
spirit of the mob that she declined to interfere; the Town
Council openly took the side of the rioters; and when the
angry Bishop threatened to excommunicate them, they
formally appealed to the Pope against his sentence. It
was not surprising that the Evangelical party before the
close of 1557 felt themselves strong enough to summon
Knox to return, and drew up a solemn Covenant pledging
themselves to renounce the Church of Rome and to stake
their substance and their lives in the defence and the
furtherance of the Gospel. It was unanimously agreed
that the Bible should be publicly read in the Parish
Churches, and that meetings for preaching and exposition
should be held in private houses, till the public preaching
of faithful and true Ministers was formally sanctioned.
Graver questions were mooted and decided: questions
about the attendance at Mass, about the administration
of Baptism according to the rites of the Medieval Church,
about the duty of Judges, Magistrates, and Nobles in
presence of the persecution of their weaker brethren and
the suppression of Christ's truth.

Encouraged by the success which attended these
measures, the Reformers pressed on with increasing boldness. In every town fixed days were appointed on which
members of the new Church should meet for common
prayers, for reading the Bible, and for mutual exhortation.
It was resolved to elect Elders for the maintenance of
discipline and for the punishment of open vice without
respect of persons; and the whole congregation took a
solemn vow of obedience to these representative officers
of the Church. In Angus and Fife sermons were openly

delivered by a bold Minister: in Dundee a Reformed
Church was constituted with public preaching and
administration of the Sacraments according to the
Reformed rites. In Edinburgh Willock's influence was
so powerful that it was resolved to set on foot a general
reformation; and with this object two leading adherents
of the Evangelical doctrines were deputed to present a
supplication to the Regent, requesting her favour and
support for the work which they had taken in hand.

The petition contained four clauses. The petitioners
begged that they might be allowed to meet, either publicly
or privately, for common prayers in the vulgar tongue;
that all who possessed the requisite knowledge might be
at liberty to expound Scripture in their assemblies; that
Baptism might be administered in the vulgar tongue for
the instruction of the godparents and the edification of
the whole Church; and that the Lord's Supper might not
only be administered in the vulgar tongue but also in both
kinds, according to the plain institution of Christ. These
clauses were followed by a request that the Regent would
take steps to reform the wicked and detestable life of the
Bishops and Clergy, which of long time had caused the
people to despise their Ministry and preaching; that the
New Testament, the writings of the ancient Fathers, and
the approved laws of Justinian might be taken to decide
the controversy between the two religious parties; and
that if the Clergy were convicted of errors and misdemeanours by these authorities, they should either be
compelled to resign their posts, or to discharge their
office as befitted the true Ministers of Christ.

The daring terms in which this petition was couched
seem to have startled the Clergy and the Queen. The
Clergy betrayed their weakness by parleying with their
opponents, and proposing terms which were indignantly
scouted: the Regent went so far as to grant the petitioners' requests, provided that no public meetings were
held under the shadow of her sceptre in Edinburgh and

Leith. But the martyrdom of an aged Priest, Walter Mill, who was burnt by the Bishop of St. Andrews as an obstinate heretic in 1558, moved the Protestants to a declaration of open war against the persecuting hierarchy. In a storm of fiery words they imperatively demanded that, until a General Council, lawfully assembled, had decided the religious controversies, all the Acts which enabled Romanist ecclesiastics to punish heretics should be suspended ; that all Prelates and their officers should be deposed from the judgment seat, and only suffered to appear as accusers of heretics before temporal judges, with whom the absolute decision in such cases should rest ; that the accused should be allowed all lawful means of defence ; that full liberty should be granted them to explain their opinions and utterances; that this confession should be recorded in legal documents, and should outweigh all depositions of hostile witnesses ; and that no man should be condemned for heresy unless he were convicted of that crime by the plain words of the oracles of God.

To these demands they added a declaration no less significant. As they could not obtain a just reformation of religion, they intended to act in religious matters as their conscience bade them, until such time as their opponents proved themselves to be true Ministers of Christ's Church, and cleared themselves of the crimes laid to their charge. Neither they nor any true believers would submit to any pains or penalties for refusing to obey the ecclesiastical laws and canons. They warned the Regent that, if the diversity of religious creeds led to tumult and uproar, or to the violent reform of abuses, the responsibility rested not with them but with the blind opponents of all reformation. In conclusion, they emphatically asserted that their action had no ulterior object, and that they appealed with confidence to the sacred authority ordained by God for the protection of faithful and obedient subjects.

Unfortunately this appeal to Cæsar completely failed in

its effect. The Queen Dowager was in no mood for the soft answer that turneth away wrath. So far from conceding that the Reformed Ministers should be suffered to preach without molestation, she replied that they should be banished from the realm, even if they preached as truly as Saint Paul; and when two of the leading Reformers attended upon her as a deputation to press for the fulfilment of her promises, she returned the disdainful answer that it was unseemly for subjects to remind their rulers of promises which they had no mind to keep. These hasty and injudicious words were not forgotten by those to whom they were addressed, and from that hour they no longer looked upon Mary as their fair and equitable Governor but as their prejudiced and unjust foe.

That the Regent should have been regarded with ineradicable suspicion by the Reformers was not unnatural. She was the widow of a King who had persecuted the Protestants. She was the member of a House notorious even in that unscrupulous age for shameless lying, open breach of faith, and flagrant perjury—a House whose intrigues had brought the Protestant party in France to the very brink of ruin. Her only child had married into a royal family which had practised persecution with more devout fervour than any Sovereigns in Europe. What wonder if she eyed the Protestant rabble in Scotland with the same hatred and scorn with which her brothers looked down on the Huguenot rabble in France? What wonder if she leant exclusively for guidance and support on the Romanist Prelates, who in Scotland, as elsewhere, were the advocates of despotic and arbitrary power in Church and State? What wonder if Knox, who had seen and heard and read what his brethren in the faith had suffered in France, could not bring himself to believe that the Regent would disavow the infamous maxim, that no faith need be kept with heretics? Under such circumstances the most scrupulous caution, the most ingenuous candour, and the most even-handed impartiality might have been misinterpreted; and

Mary of Guise was certainly not remarkable for caution, or candour, or impartiality. She was convinced that religion had been made a cloak to cover rebellion; she shut her eyes to the signs of the time which he who ran might read; she took no trouble to study the force of the currents that were eddying round her; she gave fair words while secretly resorting to violent measures; she broke in the spirit, if not in the letter, engagements into which she had entered; she committed the fatal error of looking to France for advice and guidance in her Scottish policy; and she consummated her career of political misgovernment by importing French soldiers to repress forcibly the free expression of Scottish opinion.

It was not long before the course of events led to an open breach between Mary and the Reformers. The important city of Perth adopted the Reformed faith; and when Mary appealed to the Provost to suppress it, he bluntly refused. At the Easter of 1559 several towns, in spite of her express command, would not enforce attendance at the Mass. Irritated by this resistance, she summoned the Preachers to appear before her at Stirling. They obeyed the summons, but were attended by such a host of their followers that, while they were still lingering at Perth, Mary, alarmed and exasperated, put them under the ban as outlaws in the harshest terms. This high-handed proceeding was an act of political folly, and led to consequences of which she had been fully forewarned, which she might have foreseen, and for which she and her advisers may justly be held responsible. Enraged at the injustice meted out to their beloved Ministers, the populace broke into a fury of destruction, and within the space of two days devastated the Monasteries of the Black Friars, Grey Friars, and Carthusians so completely that nothing but the walls were left standing. The contagion of this evil example spread like wildfire. Far and wide buildings and treasures hallowed by the reverence of ages were laid waste within the space of a few weeks. To assert, as the enemies of Knox have persistently asserted, that he was responsible for these acts of vandalism is unfair. The assertion is confuted by the explicit denial of Knox; it is equally confuted by the principles which were definitely laid down by Calvin, and unreservedly accepted by all his eminent followers.

From this time it was instinctively felt by both parties that nothing was left but an appeal to the arbitrament of arms. The Evangelical party sent a circular letter to the Scottish Nobles, denouncing the moral and spiritual vices of the Clergy. They sent another to the Clergy, threatening them with a war such as God's people waged against the Canaanites. When the Regent sent her herald to order all to return home on pain of treason, not a single man obeyed. Negotiations proved fruitless. The French soldiers, in violation of the Queen's agreement, oppressed the inhabitants of Perth, and increased the bitterness of the Protestants. But what was more important than all else, some of the leading nobles, including Lord James Stuart, the natural son of James the Fifth, definitely deserted the Regent, and threw in their lot with the Reformers.

This accession of strength induced the Protestant leaders to take Knox in triumph to St. Andrews to carry out the Reformation in that city. The Bishop, undaunted by their display of force, threatened to have the Reformer shot if he mounted the pulpit. The lords hesitated: were they justified in exposing their champion to such a risk? But Knox removed their scruples by a speech eminently characteristic of the man: "More than one have heard me say, when the body was far absent from Scotland, that my assured hope was, in open audience to preach in St. Andrews before I departed this life. And as for the fear of danger that may come to me, let no man be solicitous; for my life is in the custody of Him Whose glory I seek, and therefore I cannot so fear their boast or tyranny that I will cease from doing

my duty when of His mercy He offereth the occasion."
The sermon which he delivered on the ejection of the
buyers and sellers from the Temple was a direct challenge
to the Romanist Bishop and Clergy, and swept away the
provost, bailies, magistrates, and townspeople with the
resistless flood of its eloquence.

This was on June 11th, and before the end of the
month the Regent had been definitely worsted. The
Reformers became bolder in their language and their
demands. But in August and September the reinforcements from France, for which Mary had looked so
impatiently, arrived. They were accompanied by two
Commissioners, who announced verbally and in writing
that they had come to exterminate utterly all who would
not conform to the Roman religion in all points. Reports
were spread of language and conduct even more arrogant
and insulting than this. The French invaders, it was said,
had portioned out the fairest domains and had assumed the
stateliest titles of Scotland; they called each other by the
time-honoured names of Argyle and Ruthven, and discussed
the values of properties and the rent rolls of estates as
though the whole land were in their power.

The Reformers were quick to discern the fatal error
into which the Regent had been betrayed, and to make
profit out of it for the furtherance of their cause. Like
the Romish Prelates in Denmark, like Philip the Second
in the Netherlands, like Charles the Fifth in Germany,
Mary had marshalled in the ranks against her the fervid
patriotism as well as the religious passions of the Scottish
people. A proclamation was drawn up, in which the
graphic and picturesque pen of Knox may be clearly
traced, and which set forth in vivid colours the crimes
and misdemeanours of the Queen Dowager's government.
No one can read it without acknowledging that the
Evangelical party had on their side as large a measure
of political capacity as of religious zeal. They had been
charged with sedition; and the charge was justified, if it

was sedition to lament and bewail to God with heart-
felt tears and sobs the oppression from which their
brethren and their country suffered. Some had been
driven from their houses, some spoiled of their substance,
some cruelly murdered by the Queen's inhuman soldiery;
all lived in such constant fear that they might seem to be
prisoners in an enemy's country, and not citizens in their
own land. The whole realm had been reduced to beggary,
and all traffic with other countries stopped by wanton
debasing of the coinage, that she might provide for the
maintenance of strangers.   Not content with this, in
plain contempt of the Commonwealth and to gratify her
French soldiers, she had ordered that the clipped and
worn French coins, which it was illegal to circulate in
France, should pass current in Scotland. In a time of
profound peace she had deluged the country with thousands
of idle bellies, which battened upon the substance of the
Scottish Commons, hardly gained in the painful sweat of
their brow. And what had been her final object? To
reduce the realm to perpetual servitude, to bring in a
horde of foreigners not as a temporary garrison but as
permanent colonists, to deliver over to them the principal
port and emporium of the Kingdom, and to trample after
this fashion on the ancient laws and liberties of the nation
not only without the consent of the Nobility and Council
but in direct defiance of their wishes.

Such an impeachment of the Queen could only lead
to one issue. On October 21st, 1559, the Nobility,
Barons, and Boroughs were summoned to meet in the
Tolbooth of Edinburgh, and the question was put,
"Whether a Ruler, who was nothing more than a Regent,
should be allowed to govern like a tyrant?" Knox and
Willock were consulted by the Assembly, and the answers
which they gave possess a peculiar interest. They laid
down four propositions. First, the temporal Power was
a divine ordinance, but it was definitely limited by God's
Word; secondly, if subjects were commanded by God to

render obedience to their Magistrates, Magistrates were as clearly commanded to do their duty to their subjects; thirdly, though He appointed Rulers as His Vicegerents, and gave them His own title of "Gods," yet He never established them so absolutely that they might not for just reasons be deprived of their power; fourthly, a direct intervention of God's power was not required for the deposition of unworthy Governors: He often employed human instruments. From these premises they drew the conclusion: the Regent did not administer impartial justice to her subjects; she did not preserve them from the invasion of strangers; she did not allow them the free preaching of God's Word; she was an open and obstinate idolatress and supporter of idolatry; she despised the counsel and requests of the Nobility: for all these reasons the born Councillors, Nobility, and Barons of the realm might lawfully depose her. After listening to these opinions the Assembly, individually and collectively, voted for the Queen's deposition; and a public statement of the reasons which had moved them to take this grave step was issued in the name of the whole party.

It was an easy matter to resolve on Mary's deposition, but when the Reformers attempted to carry it into effect they were confronted by insuperable difficulties. The Queen Dowager had an ample share of the merits as well as of the defects of her family. She was a skilful diplomatist; she had an engaging address; she was an adept in concealing the weak points of a bad cause; and her courage rose higher in the hour of peril. The whole weight of conservative opinion in Scotland was on her side. She was assured of the individual support of the Romanist Prelates, who saw more clearly than ever that her cause was bound up with their own. The possession of Leith, the principal port of Scotland, secured her communication with France, and gave the French fleet as well as the French army access to the heart of the Kingdom. The French army was composed of trained

and veteran soldiers, superior in every respect to the raw
and inexperienced militia of the Protestant army. She
was sufficiently supplied with money, while the Protestant
leaders were unable to provide for their most pressing
wants, and the Protestant soldiers broke out into mutiny
because they could not get their pay. In the Protestant
camp there was a large number of lukewarm and half-
hearted adherents, whose enthusiasm was only skin-deep,
who were zealous for the cause while fortune smiled upon
it, but who were not prepared to make any sacrifices for
it. During the operations before Leith the party of the
Reformers suffered two serious reverses, which depressed
and discouraged them so greatly that their army broke
up, and they were compelled to fall back with their
diminished forces upon the fortress of Stirling.

But the success of the Regent proved as disastrous to
herself and her daughter as the most decisive defeat.
There was one man in the Protestant host whose confidence no failure could shake, and whose spirit no danger
could cow. Knox lifted up his voice in rebuke, in warning,
and in exhortation, and his eloquence once more electrified
his audience. The great preacher once more asserted his
unquestioned supremacy over the men who looked up to
him as their spiritual father. The result was surprising
indeed. It was resolved to seek the help and alliance of
England,— England which for centuries had been the
hereditary foe of Scotland, whose armies within living
memory had again and again wasted the fair Lowlands
with fire and sword, had entered her chief towns in
triumph, had trampled upon her people with all a victor's
arrogance and scorn, had slain the flower of her Nobles
on more than one field of battle, and had inflicted deeper
and deadlier wounds upon the Scottish people than at any
period since the battle of Bannockburn. But all prejudices
melted away as if by magic before the mighty solvent of
the Reformer's influence.

Elizabeth and Cecil did not hesitate long before

accepting the offer of the Scottish alliance.   It is true that
the outspoken language of Knox on the subject of female
government had excited Elizabeth's vehement antipathy,
and, considering her ability, strong likes and dislikes
always had unusual weight with her.   Nor was it probable
that the political liberalism of Knox could ever be congenial to a sovereign who possessed to the full the
autocratic temper of the Tudors.   It is certain that for
the same reason she never regarded with complacency
any rising of subjects against the constituted authorities
of their country.   But she was far too great a Queen to
suffer her policy to be permanently affected by personal
motives like these.   She could not be blind to the advantages which she would gain by the substitution of a
friendly for a hostile Scotland, and by the decided check
which she would in this way be able to give to the
aggressive policy of France.   As a Protestant Sovereign
ruling over a people only half estranged from the Church
of Rome, she saw clearly how her religious position would
be strengthened if she had a Protestant instead of a
Romanist power on her borders.   Knox had written in the
strongest terms to Cecil, assuring him that the alliance
with England was no sudden idea suggested by the
exigencies of the passing hour, but an union which he
had long desired as the supreme safeguard and blessing
of both nations; and it would not escape the Queen's
penetration that Knox had the instincts of a statesman as
well as of a preacher, and that, influential as he was with
his fellow-countrymen, his friendship for England would
be no slight guarantee of the durability of the alliance.
At the end of February, 1560, the Commissioners from
both sides met at Berwick and drew up the terms of the
agreement.   The actions and intentions of the Queen
Dowager, her French Ministers, and her French soldiers,
were set forth in the darkest colours; the evils of the
enmity between the two realms and the incontestable
advantages of their lasting peace and concord were

emphasized. As soon as the power and wealth of England were thrown into the scale, the end of the contest could not be doubtful. On June 10th Mary of Guise died, and six days later a treaty of peace was made between France, England, and Scotland. It was agreed that the French troops should be withdrawn, that twenty-four Councillors should govern the kingdom during the absence of the Queen of Scots and her consort, that the chief offices should be filled by Scotsmen, that an Act of Oblivion should be passed, and that there should be a general peace and reconciliation among all the Lords and subjects of the realm.

This diplomatic and military victory of the Reformed party was followed by a religious and political triumph. When Parliament met a petition was presented setting forth the erroneous doctrines of the Medieval Church, and the evil lives of the Clergy. The petition went on to declare that, owing to the Pope's usurpation of ecclesiastical sovereignty, godly learning had been neglected, schools left unprovided, and the poor defrauded of their due portion and tyrannously oppressed; that, judged by God's Word, the practice of the Apostles, and the ancient laws of the Church, there was not one Roman ecclesiastic in the whole of Scotland who had been lawfully appointed; and that all the Roman Clergy were rebels and traitors to the lawful authority of Emperors, Kings, and Princes, and therefore ought not to be tolerated in any Reformed Commonwealth. At the same time, in obedience to the command of Parliament, the Ministers and Laymen of the Evangelical party drew up and presented a Confession of their faith. This contained several points deserving of notice. It was emphatically denied that antiquity, usurped titles, lineal descent, and sheer weight of numbers were marks of the true Church. To the two primary marks of the Church a third was added, the right administration of ecclesiastical discipline " as God's Word prescribed, whereby vice was repressed and virtue

nourished." All religious controversy about the meaning
of Scripture was not to be decided by what men in former
ages had said or done, but by the words of the Bible; for
the Spirit of God was the Spirit of unity, "in nothing
contrarious unto Himself." To allege that the authority
of Scripture depended upon the authority of the Church
was "blasphemous against God and injurious to the true
Kirk." The value of General Councils was not denied;
but some of them had manifestly erred, even in matters of
great weight and importance; and the chief reason of such
Councils as deserved the name was to confute heresies,
and to give public confession of their faith to posterity.
Sentence of condemnation was pronounced against those
who affirmed that the Sacraments were only naked and
bare signs. In the Article on the Civil Magistrate the
divine power and authority of temporal Rulers were
extolled in the most glowing terms; it was added that
they were not only appointed for civil policy but for the
maintenance of the true religion in the suppression of
idolatry; to resist them in their discharge of this duty,
or even to refuse them counsel, aid, and support, was an
open sin.

The Confession of Faith was read before the assembled
Parliament in 1560. A public challenge was given to all
who had any objections to raise, or any arguments to bring
forward; but the adherents of the old Church held their
peace. A handful of the temporal Lords professed their
intention of believing as their fathers believed; the Bishops
did not say even as much as this. The Earl Marischal commented with grave irony upon their silence: he had for a
long time past had a leaning towards the truth and a suspicion of Rome: but now when the Bishops, with all their
learning and all their zeal, dared not utter a word against
the Reformed Confession, his doubts were fully dispelled;
and if any ecclesiastics opposed it hereafter, he demanded
that no credit should be given them, seeing that, after full
knowledge of their opponents' doctrine, not one of them

ventured, "in a lawful, free, and quiet Parliament," to
oppose a single article of the Reformed Faith. This
speech was followed by an almost unanimous vote of the
Three Estates in favour of the new Church.

Nothing is more extraordinary than the policy of the
Roman Churchmen during the thirteen years which
preceded this momentous vote: nothing seemed to justify
more fully the worst imputations of their enemies. On
the most moderate computation the Clergy, regular and
secular, outnumbered the Evangelical Preachers twenty-
fold. Yet while Knox was so engrossed in ceaseless
labours that, as he complained to a correspondent, he had
not more than an hour a week to himself; while his
brother Ministers were engaged in constant travelling
and constant preaching; the Bishops, Abbots, Priests, and
Monks, whose very existence was at stake, appeared to be
incapable of anything except acts and threats of violence,
a vain trust in the thunders of excommunication, and a
blind reliance on the swords of foreign mercenaries.
Was not the natural conclusion which thoughtful and
intelligent laymen would draw, that the ecclesiastical
army of Rome from lack of learning could not defend
their cause, or from ingrained slothfulness and want of
faith would not defend it, or from the consciousness of
vice dared not address an open assembly of their
countrymen, where they might run the risk of being
upbraided with their guilt ?

The weapons which they had so long used against the
heretics were now turned against themselves. An Act
was passed in 1560 making it penal to administer the
Sacraments in secret, or in any except the authorized
manner to say Mass, to hear Mass, or to be present at the
celebration of it. The penalty for the first offence was confiscation of property, for the second offence banishment
from the realm, and for the third offence death. Another
Act abolished the jurisdiction of the Pope in the most
summary terms: this jurisdiction and authority had

been insulting to God, harmful and prejudicial to the
sovereign's authority and to the common weal of the
realm : any one who made a suit to the Pope should be
punished by proscription and banishment, and should
never enjoy honour, dignity, or office within the realm :
nor should any Bishop or Prelate use any jurisdiction
hereafter by the Pope's authority.

The Confession of Faith was followed by another document still more characteristic of the Church of Scotland,
which separated it by a far broader and deeper line of
demarcation from the sister Church of England. This
was the "Book of Discipline." After demanding the
abolition of all idolatry, idolatrous monuments and places,
and doctrines imposed upon men's consciences by laws,
councils, and constitutions without the express commandment of God's Word, the Book went on to speak of
Ministers and their lawful election. The calling of
Ministers consists of election, examination, and admission.
Each congregation is responsible for the election of its
own Pastor ; and this liberty must be carefully preserved
for every Church, "to have their votes and suffrages in
the election of their Ministers," nor must any one be
violently intruded upon any congregation. Every Minister
must be examined "by men of soundest judgment" in
the principal town of his district. Here he must begin
by expounding some portion of Scripture ; then he shall
be fully examined upon all controverted points of doctrine ;
if he satisfies the examiners that he is able to persuade by
wholesome doctrine, to convince the gainsayers, and to
instruct the simple, he shall be deemed fit for the government of the Church, unless any fault can be found in his
life. The admission consisted in a sermon delivered in
the Parish to which the Minister was appointed, setting
forth the duties of the Minister and the congregation to
each other : although the Apostles used the imposition of
hands, yet, as the miraculous effects of it had ceased, the
ceremony was judged to be unnecessary. If it was urged

that so severe an examination would make it impossible to supply half the churches with Ministers, it was answered that the lack of able men could not in God's sight excuse the ordination of incompetent Pastors: nay, an incompetent Pastor was worse than none, for he would delude the congregation with the vain idea that they were spiritually supplied, while in reality they had a mere shadow, who could not break the bread of life to hungry and fainting souls. Two suggestions were made for supplying the deficiency of Ministers: the rulers were called upon to compel men who had the requisite gifts, but preferred to remain idle, to undertake the cure of souls; others, of honest conversation and ability to read the common prayers and Scripture, should be appointed to serve the churches as Readers, until, having grown to greater perfection and become competent to persuade by wholesome doctrine, they might be admitted to administer the Sacraments.

In view of the inadequate supply of Pastors, and to ensure the preaching of Christ Jesus throughout the whole realm, it was decided to divide the country into some ten Provinces, over each of which a Superintendent should be placed. The Superintendent should be a man endowed with singular graces, on whom should devolve the duty of travelling and preaching throughout his Province, and bringing the knowledge of the Gospel to the simple, the ignorant, and the superstitious, of establishing new churches, and of appointing Ministers. In contrast with the " idle Bishops " of the Church of Rome, they were not to stay more than twenty or thirty days in one place, until they had passed through their whole Province; they were bound to preach three times at least every week ; they might remain three or four months at most in their chief town, resuming their visitation at the end of that time ; the visitation should include the examination of the manner of life, the behaviour, and the diligence of the Ministers, the order of their churches, and the manners of their people; it was also the duty of the Superintendent to consider how provision might be made for the relief of the poor and the instruction of the young, to admonish where it was necessary, to redress abuses, and to take note of heinous crimes.

The election of the Superintendent rested with all the Ministers of the Province. Full liberty was given to all the churches of the Province to nominate fit persons for the office, and every one was invited to lodge objections against any candidate. Then on the appointed day the learning, manners, prudence, and capacity for government of all the candidates should be carefully examined, in order to secure the election of the worthiest: and the Minister and Elders of the Province were bound to censure and correct the Superintendent with the same freedom with which he censured and corrected them.

The election of Elders ranks next to the election of Minister and Superintendents in importance. The Elders shall be chosen out of the men most profoundly versed in Scripture, of the most honest conversation, and of the purest life. Their tenure of office shall be for one year only, lest "by long continuance men presume upon the liberty of the Church," but on the expiration of this term they may be re-elected. The duty of the Elders is to assist the Minister in all public affairs of the Church, in judging and deciding cases, in admonishing evil livers, in watching over the manners and conversation of all men under their charge. It is no less their duty to watch over their Minister. If he be light of conversation, negligent in study, careless of the interests of his flock, or unfruitful in doctrine, if he rule not his own household with gravity, if he be guilty of extravagance in his expenditure, or of avarice in hoarding his stipend, they shall admonish and correct him. If he be stubborn or disobedient to their admonitions, the Elders may appeal to the Ministers of the two neighbouring Parishes; and if their remonstrances are ineffectual, he may, with the consent of the Church and the Superintendent, be deposed from his office.

But the Elders in their turn, as well as their wives and households, shall be subject to the same censure as their Ministers; since they are judges of the conversation of others, their own conversation must be irreprehensible; they must be sober, humble, lovers and maintainers of peace and concord, and an example of godliness to all men. If they be otherwise, they shall be corrected by the Minister or their brothers in office. By these comprehensive regulations the Church of Scotland made the laity as well as the clergy responsible for a high standard in the Ministry, and for the harmonious co-operation of all orders in the Church; and gave a most effective answer to the famous question, " Quis custodiet ipsos custodes ? "

As God has ordained that His Church on earth shall be taught by men and not by angels, and as all men are born in ignorance, spiritual as well as intellectual, the " virtuous education and godly upbringing " of the young is a matter of the highest moment. It is necessary, therefore, that each church should have a Schoolmaster, able to teach Grammar and Latin at the least; in country Parishes, where the congregation meets only once in the week, the Minister or Reader shall be responsible for teaching the young their rudiments, especially the Catechism. In every important town a College ought to be established, in which the Arts, especially Rhetoric and Logic, and the learned languages shall be taught, and in which provision shall be made for those who are too poor to attend without pecuniary assistance, especially the students from country districts. Nor is there any respect of persons in this educational scheme. The rich and the powerful shall not suffer their children, as they have hitherto done, to spend their youth in vain idleness, any more than the labouring, the mercantile, and the professional classes. They must be exhorted, and, if need be, compelled by the censure of the Church, to dedicate their sons to the profit of the Church and of the Commonwealth. The children of rich and poor alike, the rich at their own cost and the poor at the expense of the community, must be put to the test; and if they be found apt for letters and learning, neither class shall be allowed to discontinue their studies, "so that the Commonwealth may have some comfort by them." For the attainment of this noble ideal, quarterly examinations shall be held in every school by the Ministers, the Elders, and the most learned men in every town.

In the Church of Scotland, as in all the Churches which looked up to Calvin as their Founder or Legislator, the establishment and maintenance of ecclesiastical discipline in the broadest sense held a foremost place. It is expressly laid down that, as no Commonwealth can flourish or endure unless it enacts and strictly enforces good laws, so no Church can attain to a high moral standard unless it represses by ecclesiastical discipline the faults which the Civil Power disregards or cannot punish. Such are drunkenness, immorality, wanton words, excess in apparel, eating, and drinking, and oppression of the poor by unjust exactions or by deceitful weights and measures in purchase and sale. The chastisement of these offences appertains to the Church, according to the express commandment of God's Word. This is the more needful because under the Pope's sovereignty virtue was not praised aright nor vice severely punished. The Church of God is, therefore, compelled to draw the sword of excommunication, which God has entrusted to her, against such open and manifest offenders, excluding them from all participation in her prayers and sacraments until they have openly repented. In this process of excommunication there are several stages. If the offence is secret, known to few, or only suspected, a private admonition is sufficient. But if the offender slights the admonition, or relapses after promise of amendment, he shall be admonished by the Minister.

If, on the other hand, the offence is public and heinous, he shall be summoned before the Minister, Elders, and Deacons, and the enormity of his sin and the scandal which it has caused shall be set forth. Should he be unfeignedly penitent and desire to be reconciled to the Church, a day shall be fixed on which he shall make public confession in presence of the whole congregation, and the Church, in answer to his prayer, shall receive him as a penitent and admit him again to their fellowship. But if he is stubborn and hard-hearted, and shows no signs of repentance, his crime shall be notified to the Church without mention of his name, and they shall be asked to pray God to move and touch his heart. On the second Sunday, if he continues in his obstinacy, he shall be named to the Church, his relations and friends shall be urged to remonstrate and plead with him, and the congregation shall be asked to continue their prayers on his behalf. On the third Sunday the Minister shall again enquire into his condition : if it be proved that he repents both of his sin and of his obduracy, he shall be received into the society of the Church. But if not, he shall, by the commandment of the congregation and through the mouth of the Minister, be pronounced to be excommunicated from God and the fellowship of His Church. After this sentence no one, except his wife and family, may have any communication or transaction with him, except by command of the Ministry for the purpose of bringing him to repentance; and his sentence shall be proclaimed throughout the whole realm.

In the case of public offenders, who ought to be punished by the civil government, but for whatever cause are suffered to go unpunished, the Church shall forbid them access to her prayers and sacraments, until they humbly beg the Ministers and Elders to pray to God for them, and to intercede with the Church on their behalf. Then the offender shall appear before the congregation, shall confess and condemn his sin with his own lips, and pray to be received into their society. After the Minister has carefully examined him and tested his repentance, and has called upon the Church to receive him, the Elders and chief men, in sign of their consent, shall take the penitent by the hand, " and one or two in the name of the whole shall kiss and embrace him with all reverence and gravity." It is expressly added that all Estates shall submit to this discipline, Princes as well as peasants, nobles as well as burghers, Preachers as well as the poorest in the Church ; nay, the Minister's life and conversation ought to be more carefully scrutinized than any other, for the eye of the Church must be the most single and her mouth the most irreprehensible of all.

Several points in the regulations for divine worship deserve notice. In great towns there should be a sermon or common prayers every day. In considerable towns one day besides Sunday should be set apart for sermon and prayers, and during this time all work should be suspended. Every Sunday should be strictly observed, in the morning by the preaching of the Word and the administration of the Sacraments, in the afternoon by public catechizing. The Eucharist should be administered four times in the year ; and because in the Medieval Church a superstitious importance was attached to the Easter Communion, " as if the time gave virtue to the Sacrament," it was decided that the four days should be the first Sundays in March, June, September, and December, though full liberty was granted to each Church to alter the days for reasonable causes. A strict injunction was laid upon all Ministers to admit none to " that great mystery " who were ignorant of the " use and virtue of it," and never to administer the Lord's Supper without a previous examination of the Communicants. A Bible should be kept in every Church, and there should be frequent reading and interpreting of it, in order to remove the great ignorance which had prevailed in the Medieval Church. Every head of a house should be commanded to see that his children, servants, and family were instructed in the Christian religion; for if they were too ignorant to understand the mystery of the Lord's Supper, they were unworthy to be partakers. Once every year at least the Ministers and Elders were to hold a public examination of all the members of the Church.

It was natural that the Book of Discipline should meet with a very different reception from the Confession of Faith. It is always easier to convince the reason and to touch the conscience than to reform the life. For more than a century the moral standard had been deliberately lowered and violated by the highest ecclesiastics as well as by Princes and nobles. This baneful example had infected all classes of Scottish society, and found bitter expression in more than one sentence of the " Book." Men who had accustomed themselves to the unbridled licence of an immoral Court and an unscrupulous age, to whom deeds of oppression and violence were commonplace incidents of life, who had cherished without remorse schemes of homicide or vengeance, who were unchecked by any rebuke from Bishop or Abbot, shrank from taking upon themselves the yoke of a stringent discipline administered by a man so terribly in earnest as Knox had proved himself to be. The reluctance of many Nobles to sign the Book, and the contempt with which they mocked the Reformer's "devout imaginations," need not excite surprise. It is far more astonishing that the influence of Knox should have induced so many nobles to give in their adhesion to his policy, and to acknowledge unreservedly the obligation of the Christian law which for so long had been almost a dead letter.

Thus far the Reformation in Scotland had run its victorious course with a more complete and unbroken success than in any other country. But with the death of Mary of Guise and the accession of her widowed daughter a change came. Mary's wedded life had been short, her tenure of the French throne shorter still. Soon after the death of Francis the Second she sailed from France for her

hereditary kingdom, which she had not seen since she was
a child, and with whose bleak climate, uncourtly nobles,
sturdy people, constitutional government, and Reformed
Church she had little or no sympathy. In August, 1561,
amid the exultant cheers of the populace, she landed at
Leith and entered Edinburgh, pre-eminently endowed with
every grace and charm of person and of manner, but
unhappily lacking in the solid and enduring qualities of
intellect and heart which alone can ensure the permanent
felicity of monarchs and of nations.

Had Mary been a wise and politic sovereign, had she
adopted a wary and consistent line of conduct, had she
not constantly yielded to the passions and prejudices of
the passing hour, had she rigidly curbed and repressed the
incurable levity and frivolity of her character, and had
she been capable by a dignified bearing and language of
inspiring her foes as well as her friends with respect if not
with affection, the Reformation in Scotland might even
now have received a disastrous check. Instead of this,
she seemed to have combined the worst qualities and the
gravest errors of the House of Guise and the House of
Valois, and committed one blunder after another with a
recklessness and an infatuation which alienated the affections of the majority of her subjects, which turned the swords
of her own kinsmen and councillors against her, which
confirmed the hostility of the Reformed Church, and
which justified the old heathen proverb, "Quem Deus
vult perdere prius dementat."

Mary's arrival alarmed and perplexed Knox and his
friends, and both their alarm and their perplexity were
natural. Mary had been brought up amid the bigoted
and intolerant influences of the French Court : was it
possible to believe, as the more sanguine Protestants
believed, that, when she lived in the full blaze of divine
truth, she would be weaned from her errors ? and, if not,
would her autocratic temper accept the resolutions which
the Scottish Parliament had passed in favour of the

Reformed Church, and allow her to deal fairly with its members ? Again, according to the definition which Knox had laid down and which Parliament had accepted, Mary was an " idolater " who openly avowed and practised idolatry ; and the Three Estates had formally enacted that all idolaters, in obedience to God's law, should die the death. But even the stern spirit of the uncompromising Reformer seems to have shrunk from this extreme application of his principles. Yet what middle course could he recommend without wounding his conscience ? Was not idolatry in a sovereign infinitely more harmful than idolatry in a subject ? Could it be right to condone the example of the former and to punish the offence of the latter ? This inconsistency in the Reformer's position, this secret consciousness that he had proved unfaithful to his sacred commission, explains in great measure the harshness with which he treated Mary Stuart, and the violent terms in which he spoke of her.

Mary had not been long in Scotland before she sent for Knox. Why she took this step can be only conjectured. She may have wished to disarm her formidable antagonist by the fascination whose power she had often proved, or to overawe him by her queenly authority, or to get the better of him with her keen wit. She would certainly have been wiser if she had preserved a dignified silence. When she charged him with raising a rebellion against her mother and herself, Knox denied the charge ; he had only established true religion. When she blamed him for writing against her just authority, he allowed that he disapproved of government by women ; but if the Scottish people were willing that she should rule them, he withdrew his personal objection. When she taxed him with being the cause of sedition and slaughter in England, he had a ready answer ; during all the time he was in England there had been neither battle nor sedition nor rebellion in the part of the country where he was. Completely silenced on these points, Mary was injudicious enough to accuse him of inducing her subjects to adopt a religion which their Princes did not allow. This false step drew from Knox a crushing retort, which mortally offended the Queen's imperious and despotic temper.

Subsequent interviews between Mary and Knox ended in the same way with the Queen's discomfiture. In 1563 the Romanist Clergy, trusting to the Queen's protection, celebrated Mass at Easter, and the laws were put in force against them. Full of indignation, Mary sent for Knox and remonstrated with him. He had a complete answer. The Judges were only acting as their duty bade them : the Act of Parliament was clear and explicit : her subjects were bound to obey the Queen, but she was equally bound to observe the laws : if she failed to do her part, there was every reason to fear that they would fail to do theirs. Again Mary was silenced, and compelled to acknowledge that Knox had reason on his side. The question of Mary's marriage led to another interview. Knox in his sermon had thundered against the Queen's union with an " infidel." This time Mary lost her temper and forgot her dignity : she stooped to threaten Knox with her personal vengeance. As soon as her hysterical sobs had ceased, Knox quietly observed that in the pulpit he was not his own master but God's servant ; it was his vocation to blame evil-doing in plain language, and if the Scottish nobility consented to her marriage with an unbeliever, they would renounce Christ and betray the liberty of the realm. The Queen appealed to her Council whether such outspoken language did not deserve punishment, and to her great chagrin received an answer in the negative. At last the opportunity for which she had been watching seemed to have come. A letter written by Knox came into her hands, and the Council of the Cabinet decided that the language was treasonable. Knox was forthwith summoned before the Queen and Council. Mary took up her own quarrel : Knox had accused her of cruelty ; what apology could he make for his conduct ?

The Reformer retorted that he had not accused the Queen but the Romanist party of cruelty : could the Queen and the Council deny that they longed to exterminate the Protestants ? Mary did not speak a word : the Council sided with Knox. He resumed his speech, defied the Queen to point out any law which he had broken, denounced the Romanists with his usual vehemence, and ended by praying God to purge Mary's heart from Popery and to keep her ear from flatterers. When the question, " Whether Knox had offended against the Queen's Majesty ? " was put to the vote, he was unanimously acquitted by the Nobles present. The interview ended in a deepened and irreconcilable enmity between Mary and her powerful subject.

But any danger to the Reformed Church from the Queen's hostility soon came to an end. The great tragedy of Mary's life developed with bewildering rapidity. The marriage with Darnley, the murder of Rizzio, the murder of Darnley, the marriage with Bothwell, the rising against Mary, the battle of Carberry Hill, the imprison- ment in Lochleven Castle, the deposition of the Queen, her escape from Lochleven, the battle of Langside and her flight into England, followed one another within three years. In only one of these events did the Reformed Church officially take any leading and conspicuous part, the marriage with Bothwell. The incident, remarkable in itself, is still more remarkable because it sets in a clear light the contrast between the Romanist and Protestant ecclesiastics, and explains why the latter by their consis- tency, courage, and firmness permanently retained their influence over the Scottish people which the former had justly forfeited. Though the Romanist Clergy knew the loathsome story of Bothwell's divorce from his wife and the unutterable vileness of his character, though they were fully aware that the marriage would be celebrated in a manner which would invalidate any wedlock, though the marriage of the Catholic Queen with a husband who was a heretic ought to have moved their deepest indignation, they did not utter a single word in public protest or remonstrance against the unhallowed union. The honourable duty of giving utterance to the outraged moral sense of all right-minded Scotsmen was reserved for a Reformed Minister.

When the Queen ordered Craig to publish the banns in the Reformed Church of Edinburgh, he refused pointblank, partly because he had not the Queen's written authority, partly because it was rumoured that Bothwell had obtained possession of her person and imprisoned her by violence. Then Mary sent by the Justice Clerk a paper bearing her signature, in which she fully denied the rumour referred to by Craig. The Minister a second time refused unless he had obtained the consent of the Church. After the matter had been argued by the members of the Church and the Justice Clerk, it was decided that the banns should be published, but that the marriage should not be solemnized nor approved by the Reformed Ministers. Immediately after this, Craig demanded a hearing before Bothwell and the Council; and being admitted into their presence inveighed against Bothwell in such terms as must have made even that brazen-faced criminal wince. The answer which Bothwell made naturally failed to satisfy the honest Minister, and he left the Council Chamber protesting that he would speak his mind openly before the Church. This he did on the following Sunday, calling heaven and earth to witness that he abhorred and detested the marriage as " odious and slanderous to the world "; and that, though the best part of the realm approved it by their flattery or their silence, it was against reason and good conscience. It was impossible for Mary to let such a public impeachment of her conduct pass in silence. Craig was summoned before the Council and charged with passing the bounds of his commission by applying the epithets " odious and slanderous " to the Queen's marriage. The

Reformer made a spirited reply : God's Word, good laws,
and natural reason were the bounds of his commission
and justified his language ; if they considered all the
circumstances of the marriage, their own conscience would
tell them that it was odious and slanderous. This home
truth was too much for his hearers, and he was dismissed
before he had finished his speech.

After Mary had disappeared from the stage of Scottish
history, the position of the Reformed Church was definitely secured. The General Assembly, or Synod, met
with a frequency which proved how rich a tide of life was
flowing through the veins of the young Church, and
watched over her interests with a vigilance which nothing
could escape. During the seven years which elapsed
between the first establishment of the Church in 1560, and
its second establishment in 1567, the General Assembly
held sixteen sessions, and it is impossible to understand
fully the character, power, and influence of the Church
without a brief survey of the proceedings of the Assembly
during that period.

That the Church was no respecter of persons, and that
the regulations of the Book of Discipline were not a dead
letter, was soon demonstrated to the satisfaction of friends
and foes alike. All Ministers, including Bishops, who had
not entered upon their office conformably with the order
of the " Book," were inhibited. One Superintendent was
charged with being slack in visitations and preaching,
given to worldly affairs, rash in excommunicating, and
too sharp in exacting payment of small tithes. Another
Superintendent was charged with admitting Romish
priests as Readers who were unqualified and of vicious
life, with rashly admitting young men to be Ministers
without the careful trial and examination prescribed in
the Book, with making gentlemen of vicious life Elders,
with suffering Ministers to be non-resident, to neglect
the visitation of the sick, and to perform their duties in
a perfunctory manner. Adam, Bishop of Orkney, was

ejected from the Ministry for solemnizing the marriage between Bothwell and Mary in defiance of the law respecting adultery. One Minister was suspended for borrowing money without repaying it, another for seducing his wife before marriage : a third was admonished to observe a decent form and order in teaching : a fourth was forbidden to travel for the purpose of acquiring knowledge without the Assembly's leave. When it was found difficult to provide a sufficient number of Superintendents, the Assembly appointed Commissioners to serve for a year, with delegated powers in establishing Churches, Schools, and Colleges, in suspending, depriving, and transplanting Ministers, in conferring vacant benefices, and in abolishing monuments of idolatry.

A number of important regulations were passed at different times. Parishioners were allowed to appeal to the Superintendent against the sentence of Ministers, Elders, and Deacons, and to the General Assembly against the sentence of the Superintendent. The education of the young was committed to Protestant teachers only. It was ordained that temporal Judges should be appointed to try matrimonial causes, and that the question of the marriage of first cousins should be referred to the decision of Parliament. The difficulties relating to tithes received the special attention of the Assembly : in one session it was decided that poor labourers should have the tithes in exchange for a reasonable composition ; and the Duke, the Earl Marischal, Argyle, Murray, Glencairn, and the other nobles who were present, agreed to this : in another session the labourers complained of the rigorous exaction of tithes, and the Lords who were present promised to accept money or victuals in lieu of them : in a third it was decided that tithes are the patrimony of the Church, and ought to be exclusively devoted to the maintenance of Ministers, the relief of the poor, and the education of the young : in a fourth it was resolved that the Clergy ought to admonish all that perverted them to "vain uses," and that, if the admonition were disregarded, the Church should censure the offenders.

The language of the Assembly on the subject of notorious vice was as energetic as might have been expected from a representative body under the influence of Knox. No Minister should admit to public repentance open sinners who had relapsed for the third time, but should send them to the Superintendent to have their punishment assigned to them. Whensoever terrible crimes were committed, notice should be given to the Superintendent, and he should summon the offender : if he appeared and was sincerely penitent, the severity of the punishment should be mitigated, and he should only be excluded from the Sacraments till his repentance had been tested; but if he was impenitent or did not appear, he should be excommunicated. At Christmas, 1565, the General Assembly complained that sins of licentiousness were regarded as " pastimes of the flesh," that murder was esteemed a small sin to any one who had a friend at Court, that feasting and riotous banqueting prevailed in Court, country, and towns, and that the poor had increased more than ever in Scotland.

When occasion served, the Assembly rose to loftier heights. At one time they presented a petition to the Queen, begging her to put into execution the Acts passed against open vice, to suppress the Mass, to devote ecclesiastical property to the poor and the schools, to punish severely the many horrible crimes which were left unpunished, and to devise some way of easing the poor labourers of their tithes. At another time they laid down the principle that, though the patronage of benefices might belong to the sovereign, " the retaining of them in her own hands is ungodly, contrary to all public order," and brings confusion on " the poor souls of the common people," who are left without instruction in the way of salvation. At the close of the year 1565 a Fast was appointed because the Mass had been set up again, because the Queen, turning a deaf ear to all petitions, had declared her intention of maintaining and defending her religion, because the hearts of many had waxed cold and Christ's truth and His messengers had been reviled. In the summer of 1567 the Assembly raised its voice in solemn warning. The Reformed Churches, it declared, were threatened with the deadliest dangers by the decree of the Council of Trent proclaiming a holy war for the extirpation of heretics : what fruits this decree had borne might be seen in France, in the Low Countries, and in Scotland during the last three years : let all Nobles to whom the Evangelical faith was dear rally round the Assembly to withstand the rage, craft, and violence of their enemies. A few weeks later the General Assembly required all the Nobles and faithful brethren to subscribe a series of articles which it had drawn up, calling upon Parliament to ratify all Acts concerning religion passed in the Parliament of 1560, to put into execution the Act for the maintenance of the Ministry, to test the qualifications of all teachers, to enable the poor labourers to pay their tithes in a reasonable manner, to punish severely all crimes, vices, and offences against God's Law, to enact that all Kings, Princes, and Magistrates, before entering upon their office, should make their "solemn league and promise to maintain, defend, and set forward the true religion of Jesus Christ at present established in this realm." "So the bond and contract is to be mutual and reciprocal in all times coming between the Prince and God, and the Prince and the faithful people."

About the time that these articles were drawn up George Buchanan wrote his celebrated treatise "De jure regni apud Scotos." In this remarkable work he discusses the reciprocal duties of rulers and subjects. He shows how the Medieval Popes and ecclesiastics, by their flagrant and unscrupulous evasion of the Canon Law, have lowered the moral standard, and debased the political tone, of all rulers in Western Christendom. He denies that a King who has no fatherly affection for his people, who tyrannically oppresses them, and who thinks that they are entrusted to him for his own profit and not for their welfare, can be justly regarded as a true King, because he bears the empty title. If the King transgresses the laws which limit his powers, he deserves condign punishment like any other criminal. That this was the principle which animated the Scottish people during the Middle Ages is proved by the fate of cruel and wicked Kings who have been imprisoned for life or punished by exile and death. These punishments were justified by the solemn oath which they took at their inauguration, that they would observe the laws, customs, and statutes of their predecessors. Hence it follows that in a hereditary no less than in an elective monarchy the King's power is limited by the laws and the consent of the people. If it is objected that the teaching of Scripture contradicts this theory, Buchanan finds no difficulty in disposing of this objection. Saint Paul urges Timothy to pray for Kings and Magistrates, " that we may lead a peaceable life in all godliness and honesty," which is a prayer not for the King's safety but for the Church's tranquillity. In the Epistle to the Romans he describes a true and lawful Magistrate, not a tyrant ; nor does he speak of individual rulers, but of sovereignty in the abstract, of the function and office of those who bear rule ; nor does he distinguish between superior and subordinate Magistrates, but includes all in his definition : all alike are commanded to obey God's laws, to be a terror to the evil and not to the good. If Kings may transgress the laws with impunity, why may not Mayors, Provosts, Bailies, and Sheriffs do the same ? Supposing Saint Paul were living in the sixteenth century under a King and among a people professing Christianity, and were to see the King trampling the laws under foot, bidding his subjects revere and obey his nod and beck as a law, dividing the revenues of the Church among villains and rascals, and mocking the sincere worshippers of God, he would certainly refuse such a man the title of sovereign, and would leave him to the people to be punished by the laws. Under the Old Dispensation God appointed the King, and therefore God and not the people punished him : under the New Dispensation the King is appointed by his subjects, and therefore they have the same right to punish him for violation of the laws as he has to punish any one of them for the same cause. Can it be denied that the people are the authors of the laws, that, if it is in their power to make the laws, it is in their power to enforce the laws, that, when a King is summoned for trial before a people, the less is judged by the greater, and that, as there is a mutual compact between King and people, the King who is guilty of a breach of this compact loses all the privileges and rights which the people gave him ? If these facts are indisputable, the people are completely justified in waging war against an unconstitutional monarch as a public enemy of their country.

There can be no question that this masterly dissertation, which was dedicated to the young King in 1575, expressed the political views of the leaders of the Scottish Church. It was written by an intimate friend of Knox : it is in perfect harmony with the opinions of Knox upon the same subject : the Biblical arguments and illustrations of Buchanan and Knox are identical. The conclusions of the scholar are the same as those of the theologian. How deeply it influenced thoughtful Scotsmen, how completely its teaching was assimilated by them, and how widely it differed from the tenets of divine right and passive obedience held by the majority of the Anglican Clergy, was incontestably proved during the disastrous reign of Charles the First by the consistent attitude which the Scottish people maintained, and by the vigorous and successful resistance which they offered to the foolish schemes of Charles and Laud.

INDEX

THE END.

F